£32-00

ONE W

THE ORIGINS OF THE VIGILANT STATE

THE ORIGINS
OF THE
VIGILANT STATE

THE LONDON METROPOLITAN POLICE
SPECIAL BRANCH
BEFORE THE FIRST WORLD WAR

Bernard Porter

THE BOYDELL PRESS

First published 1987
Reissued 1991 by The Boydell Press, Woodbridge

The Boydell Press is an imprint of Boydell & Brewer Ltd
PO Box 9, Woodbridge, Suffolk IP12 3DF
and of Boydell & Brewer Inc.
PO Box 41026, Rochester, NY 14604, USA

ISBN 0 85115 283 X

Photoset by Deltatype, Ellesmere Port
Printed in Great Britain by
Butler & Tanner Ltd, Frome and London

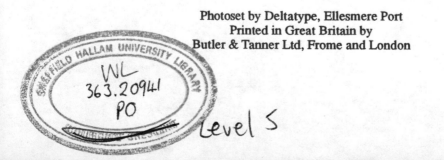

TO THE MEMORY OF TOM THOMAS

Contents

Illustrations

The Board of Trade damaged by a Fenian bomb, from the *Illustrated Police News*, 24 March 1883 (British Library).

A Fenian bomb exploding in the London Underground, from the *Illustrated Police News*, 10 November 1883 (British Library).

The offices of the Special Irish Branch at Old Scotland Yard after being bombed by Fenians, from Margaret Prothero, *The History of the CID*.

'The crocodiles take refuge under England's wings', a cartoon from *Kladderadatsch*, 26 August 1894.

Fictional version of anarchists destroying the Palace of Westminster, from E. Douglas Fawcett, *Hartmann the Anarchist* (1893).

The Walsall bomb (West Midlands Police).

Vivian Majendie, A Spy cartoon from *Vanity Fair*, 23 April 1892.

Interior of the Home Office's bomb defusing hut on Duck Island in St James's Park (Crown copyright. Reproduced with the permission of the Controller of Her Majesty's Stationery Office).

Martial Bourdin blown up by his own bomb in Greenwich Park, from the *Illustrated Police Budget*, 24 February 1894 (British Library).

Melville arresting the French anarchist Meunier, from the *Illustrated Police News*, 14 April 1894 (British Library).

A police raid on the anarchist 'Autonomie' Club, from the *Illustrated Police Budget*, 24 February 1894 (British Library).

A police spy of the 1890s, from *The Idler*, vol. 4 (1893).

A Scotland Yard detective in disguise, from Walter Hambrook, *Hambrook of the Yard* (1937).

The arrest of the Fenian Tynan in Boulogne, from the *Illustrated Police News*, 26 September 1896 (British Library).

Special Branch detectives arresting Mrs Pankhurst, from the *Daily Sketch*, 27 May 1913 (British Library).

Adolphus Williamson, from Margaret Prothero, *op. cit.*

John Littlechild, from *Reynolds's Newspaper*, 17 February 1895 (British Library).

William Melville, from Windsor Magazine, vol. 1.

Patrick Quinn, from Hargrave L. Adam, *The Police Encyclopaedia*, vol. 5.

Patrick McIntyre, from G. Dilnot, *Triumphs of Detection* (1929).

John Sweeney, from his *At Scotland Yard*.

Harold Brust, from his *In Plain Clothes*.

Herbert Fitch, from his *Memoirs of a Royal Detective*.

Preface

One reason why there are so few historical certainties is that so many things in history are done secretly. Some of those secrets are revealed eventually – after thirty years, for example, in the case of most British public records – but many may not be. It is never possible to be sure that the secrets which remain hidden, or which die with their perpetrators, have not had a greater influence on events than the factors that are known about. Every society and age has its secret history as well as its public one. The Metropolitan Police Special Branch has been part of Britain's secret history since 1887, when it was formed out of the remnants of a couple of precursors whose own origins went back another six years.

How important it was in the broader historical scheme of things is difficult to say. If we are to believe the claims made for it by some of its early officers, then no history of modern Britain – or possibly the modern world – is complete without an account of it. The Special Branch was an essential guarantor of stability both in Britain and abroad. It prevented dynamite atrocities, protected royalty, forestalled revolutions, and nipped incipient Great Wars in the bud. Its achievements were clandestine, but none the less effective for that. History would have been very different without it: more volatile, scarier for the propertied classes, and probably a good deal bloodier.

In spite of this, the early Special Branch does not rate even a mention in any general history of modern times that I know of. There are a number of reasons for this. One is the simple fact that until recently very little was known about it. Nothing worthwhile had been written on it, and there were thought to be problems in getting to the documentary evidence. Some of those problems are indeed intractable: Scotland Yard, for example, claims that all *its* Special Branch files were pulped to furnish recycled paper during the last war; but others can be overcome. They were not overcome by Rupert Allason, whose history of the Special Branch published in 1983 is less than satisfactory for reasons I

have spelled out elsewhere.[1] There is nothing else. The Special Branch
may have a history, but it has not had a proper *History* before today.
From the point of view of most of us, therefore, it might just as well not
exist.

In any case it suits most historians to think that it did not *matter*, even
if they are vaguely aware that it was there. Historians as a rule do not
like secret agencies. For an important event to turn on the clandestine
machinations of a handful of folk offends against the order and
rationality they like to discover in things. It is untidy, arbitrary and
unsettling. Besides, it upsets established versions of events, which have
generally been painstakingly built up out of what is *known*. Historians
have already explained why Britain did not undergo a revolution in
modern times; it does not help now to be told that she would have done,
if it had not been for the Special Branch. Even worse would be the
thought that she *might* have experienced a revolution, but that no one
will ever be able to tell, because the whole truth about the Branch will
never be revealed. Historians may be willing to accept some degree of
uncertainty, but not that much.

In this case they may be perfectly justified. There are reasons, as we
shall see, for believing that the most ambitious claims for the efficacy of
the Special Branch were exaggerated. There may also be cause to doubt
the significance of the conspiracy factor in British history more
generally. This really depends on one's broader political point of view.
If you believe that a society can be subverted by individuals, either
from the left or from the right, then you are also likely to believe that
that subversion can be thwarted by a secret political police. If you do
not, then clearly no amount of political policing is going to be seen to
have this kind of effect. It may have other effects: like trampling
liberties and undermining democracy and breeding corruption; but it
will not be the saviour the political policemen think or pretend it is.
This may be another reason for liberal historians' neglect of the Special
Branch. Special Branches are conspiratorial, and conspiracies can
have no significance or lasting impact on the pattern of events.

The mid-Victorians used to feel the same way; which is why they had
no secret political police worth the name until the 1880s, and then only
in a very circumscribed form. The real significance of the emergence of
the Special Branch at that time is what it tells us about a political
society which quite suddenly came to feel that it needed something of
the kind, after twenty or thirty years of relative liberal purity and
innocence. Thereafter the Branch established itself as a permanent
feature of the British executive's armoury, expanding its size and role in

response to new perceived threats, and to a growing feeling of vulnerability in Britain which may have had other roots. There is also a possibility that it engineered its own expansion, by provoking 'outrages' in order to justify its existence. One problem with the Special Branch was always its lack of proper accountability, which could tempt officers into this kind of villainy. By 1914 it had developed into a body which present-day Special Branch personnel would probably recognize as akin to their own. That is where this narrative will stop: partly because one effect of the Great War was to interrupt and distort the 'natural' development of the Branch, and partly because the difficulties of gaining access to the primary evidence become insuperable then.

Before 1914 they are not. The apparent loss of the Special Branch's own archive is sad. One ex-Special Branch hand claimed that 'locked away' in it were 'real-life stories of stark tragedy, high romance and desperate adventure which would make any fiction-writer bite his finger-nails with envy'.[2] We could probably do without those, but other clues in it would have been invaluable. Nevertheless a great deal survives outside the walls of Scotland Yard. My main sources have been Metropolitan Police and Home Office papers in the Public Record Office, and three or four private collections. Many of the Home Office papers do not appear in any official index of documents, and have had to be traced through the daily registers of letters passing in and out of the Home Office. Most relevant documents were destroyed by 'weeders' some time ago, but about a quarter escaped. Of those, a high proportion is in a category of papers, HO144, which is normally 'closed' to public inspection for seventy-five or one hundred years. My own research has been immeasurably aided by the liberality of successive Departmental Record Officers at the Home Office in granting me access to all save six of the scores of 'closed' files I asked their special permission to see. I understand that the general closure on most of those files has been lifted since, which means that my references can be independently checked. I have been granted similar facilities with 'closed' Police documents by the Departmental Record Officer at New Scotland Yard. Other categories of papers have been more immediately accessible. They are listed in the Notes and Bibliography at the end of the book.

I have undoubtedly missed a great deal. The earliest explorers in an entirely virgin territory invariably do. In central Africa in the middle of the nineteenth century some of them put mountains where there should be lakes. I trust that none of my mistakes will be as gross as that; but there are bound to be a few. Some of my conclusions (I try to indicate which) rest on thin evidence. This is why they are stated so tentatively. It is possible, and indeed likely, that better evidence will come to light eventually which will modify them. Some of that evidence will be amongst the bales of dusty Home Office files which still lie in the Public Record Office, unindexed and so untouched since they were sent away from Whitehall, and whose trails, if there are any, I have failed to spot and follow. Better still would be the sudden discovery that the Special Branch's registry was not pulped after all; or of a cache of private papers belonging to one of the Special Branch's early senior officers – Littlechild, perhaps, or Melville, or Quinn – which someone may find in an attic somewhere, and realise the importance of. I have not exhausted even those possibilities that have occurred to me: provincial police records, Scottish judicial records, the papers of civil servants, collections of anarchist materials, Irish state papers, and some newspapers, to name just a few: simply because the task would be too vast for one person to complete. I think I have done enough to restore large parts of a structure which has lain buried and hidden for nearly a century. I shall be happy if others can build further on this, even if some of my bricks are displaced as a result.

The purpose of this book is to explain the origins, development, organisation, methods and contemporary significance of the modern British state's first official and regular secret political police force, with a view to filling out our broader picture of the late Victorian and Edwardian years. It has no didactic aim; if readers want enlightenment from it about the contentious present-day issues of political policing, counter-terrorism or civil liberties, then they are welcome to it, but they will have to draw it out from the narrative for themselves. There will be a great deal of narrative, simply because so few of the basic facts about the early Special Branch are generally known; and also a great deal of background and context, because its history cannot be properly understood anachronistically. The end-product is, I hope, a balanced and rounded analysis of a corner of *fin-de-siècle* Britain's political underlife whose neglect hitherto certainly belies its intrinsic fascination, and may also have obscured its considerable importance at the time.

The book would have been impossible without help from a large number of people. The research for it was financed by means of generous grants from the Wolfson Foundation and the British Academy. My way into particular collections of papers was greatly smoothed by the assistance given by their guardians. Miss White, Mr

Lloyd and Mr Gower-Kerslake of the Home Office merit my particular thanks for their friendly help, which went far beyond the call of duty. Others who have helped greatly are Mrs Valerie Masterman of the Metropolitan Police Office; Mr C. D. Chalmers and Dr Meryl Foster of the Public Record Office; Dr Frances Harris of the British Library; Mr Robin Harcourt Williams, Librarian and Archivist to the Marquess of Salisbury; Sir Robin Mackworth-Young, Mr Oliver Everett and Miss Jane Langton of the Royal Archive, Windsor Castle; Miss Marion Stewart, Archivist of Churchill College, Cambridge; Patricia Methven, Archivist of the Liddell-Hart Centre for Military Archives, King's College, London; Peter Thwaites of the Imperial War Museum; Chief Superintendent Meller of the West Midlands Police; Ronald M. Bulatoff of the Hoover Institution; Mr D. J. H. Smith of the Gloucestershire Record Office; Mr T. W. Baker-Jones, Archivist to W. H. Smith and Son Ltd; Mr Colin Johnston, Registrar of the National Register of Archives (Scotland), and the staffs of the Bodleian Library, Oxford, the University Library, Cambridge, the Scottish Record Office, Edinburgh, the Irish State Paper Office in Dublin Castle, the Colindale Newspaper Library, the Kent Archives Office, the University of Hull Brynmor Jones Library, and the Royal Commission on Historical Manuscripts. Austin Mitchell, MP, kindly offered to intervene at one stage when I was having difficulty gaining access to certain documents; luckily his intercession was not needed in the end.

Others who have given valuable help and advice include Nicholas Hiley, who put me on to most of the sources for the Special Branch's pre-war counter-espionage work; Christopher Andrew, who helped with information and in launching my (short-lived) television career with a BBC *Timewatch* programme based on my research for this book; Commander G. L. V. Ison of the Special Branch; Michael Turner of English Heritage; John Steedman of the Property Services Agency; Stuart Goffee; Colin Holmes; and Nick Adams.

For access to and permission to publish extracts from correspondence under their control, I should like to thank Her Majesty the Queen; Mr D. J. Blackwood of the Home Office; Sir John Colville, chairman of the Chartwell Trust; the Marquess of Salisbury; and the Hon. Mrs Crispin Gascoigne, owner of the rights in the Harcourt papers. Crown Copyright material in the Public Record Office is reproduced by permission of the Controller of Her Majesty's Stationery Office.

I leave to last the especial thanks which are due to my wife and children for putting up with my abstracted moods while I was writing this book, keeping me supplied with coffee and other (stronger) aids to abstraction, turning down their record players, tolerating (or possibly welcoming) my frequent absences, and keeping me sane and balanced after long periods spent in a historical world of terror, suspicion and deceit.

BERNARD PORTER
Cottingham, East Yorkshire
April 1986

CHAPTER 1

Innocence

It is natural for people in power to want to find out about people who threaten their power. When the threat is a covert one, or is thought to be, then it is also natural for them to use covert methods for finding out. The most common of these methods is a secret political police force: a body of detectives charged with keeping a watch on potential subversives, and with preventing or punishing what is ambiguously termed 'political crime'. Every government in the world has employed such an agency at some time or another, and most governments have never in modern times been without one.

This makes Britain's situation in 1880, if not 'unnatural', then at least unusual; for Britain in 1880 did not have a secret political police force of any kind, and had not had one for more than twenty years. The proof of this, as of any negative proposition, is not conclusive. The most successful secret police force would be one which managed to conceal its existence not only from contemporaries but also from historians; and it is always possible that there did exist, somewhere, a mid-Victorian 'Special Branch' which was so successful in this sense as to have left not a single trace behind. But that is unlikely. As well as the lack of traces, there are other reasons for doubting it. One is the very strong feeling that existed against this kind of thing, among nearly every section of British society in the third quarter of the nineteenth century.

That feeling was most clearly displayed when the mid-Victorians looked abroad. The contrast there was startling, and greatly to Britain's credit. It was put nicely in a travel book by Mrs Dinah Craik in 1871, which described how, when a Frenchman was asked about the prospect of a third republic, he 'looked over his shoulder with that instinctive movement of his countrymen when talking politics, as if there were a gendarme behind; and then recognising that we were all Britons, risked an opinion'.[1] Novels set abroad also drew police spies everywhere. 'In all societies' in Austria, claimed the novelist G. J. Whyte Melville in 1858, 'where half-a-dozen people may chance to congregate, *there* will be an agent of police, always in plain clothes, and generally the least conspicuous person in the throng.'[2] The less conspicuous they appeared, the more of them there clearly were. *Household Words* descried them all over southern Italy in 1850. 'They assume no distinctive dress – make no sign; they walk in darkness, and move like the pestilence, yet they are as real existences, and follow as precise a trade, as the vendor of maccaroni.' In Italy they pervaded the whole of society, with demoralising effect. How very different, *Household Words* went on, was the home life of our own dear police:

> We have no political police, no police over opinion. The most rabid demagogue can *say* in this free country what he chooses, provided it does not tend to incite others to *do* what is annoying to the lieges. He speaks not under the terror of an organised spy system. He dreads not to discuss the affairs of the nation at a tavern, lest the waiter should be a policeman in disguise; he can converse familiarly with his guests at his own table without suspecting that the interior of his own liveries consists of a spy; when travelling, he has not the slightest fear of perpetual imprisonment for declaring himself freely on the conduct of the powers that be, because he knows that even if his fellow-passenger be a Sergeant Myth or an Inspector Wield, no harm will come to him.
>
> It is not so across the Channel. There, while the criminal police is very defective, the police of politics is all powerful.[3]

Nearly everyone in Britain regarded this as a matter for national self-congratulation; one proof, among others, of liberal Britain's superiority over all other societies everywhere.

It was more than this, even. To the mid-Victorians the non-political function of their police was a cause as well as an effect of their national good health. Lord Bloomfield, Britain's ambassador in Berlin, explained how this worked to the Prussian foreign minister Baron Manteuffel in August 1851. Manteuffel had commented on the fact that 'the main business of our Police force appeared to be the apprehension of Robbers and Murderers, and the maintenance of the Publick Peace, and that they were not in the habit of pursuing political criminals'. The remark had been meant critically, but Bloomfield defended vigorously:

> I answered that this was for the most part true, and happily the object of the English Police Establishment was what he stated, and that it was the conviction of the people of England that the Police were solely employed in this manner which commanded respect for the establishment throughout the Country, and which ensured the voluntary cooperation of the respectable classes of Her Majesty's subjects whenever circumstances occurred which called for their assistance.[4]

Political police systems had the opposite effect. They bred mistrust, which undermined confidence in government, and consequently made governing more difficult. They were the cause of subversion, not its cure; not merely unnecessary in Britain's case, but counter-productive in every other.

This was a common set of attitudes. It tied in with the mid-Victorian liberal view of political and social stability generally. According to that view, stability grew best in a free soil. Serious threats to it could only be *provoked*. They did not arise in free societies, only in societies which were repressed. It followed that if a country was governed liberally, it would have no trouble from subversives. Lord Palmerston made this point on countless occasions during the 1850s, in response to pressure from foreign and British reactionaries to take stronger measures against the threat which they saw coming from conspiratorial groups. Such groups, he wrote in 1851 to his Minister in St Petersburg, could only be effective in countries which had 'a great mass of political discontent', and it was 'generally within the Power of all Govts so to order the internal affairs of the Countries which they rule, as to remove any just causes of general dissatisfaction' and hence any lever for violent change.[5] Britain's security lay in the fact that her people were contented; the obverse of this was that the Continent's *in*security was its own fault. Of course there would always, even in the most perfect societies, be some malcontents around, but on their own they could do no harm. Successful revolutions needed revolution-fodder, and revolution-fodder was engendered by governing tyrannically. Some mid-Victorians defined tyranny very broadly. Josephine Butler, for example, in a pamphlet about burgeoning police powers she published in 1879, defined it as anything that took out of the individual's hands his responsibility for himself. Too much state interference on the Continent, she claimed, was already sapping people's 'inventiveness, self-protection, and manly self-dependence' there; if it were extended to Britain, then loyalty to governments would be 'changed to hatred', and 'gloom and factious disorder' would 'prevail by turns'.[6] This applied even more to political policing. Laws and agencies created in order to repress subversion had the very opposite effect. They made people aggrieved, and consequently rebellious. They would not be aggrieved – would have nothing to be aggrieved about – if they were left (as the Victorians liked to put it) 'free'. This was the answer to the problem of subversion, which was really not a genuine problem in the mid-Victorians' eyes. Political societies and systems were best defended – paradoxically – by having no defences at all.

3

At the very least, it was important for governments to give the *impression* that they had sufficient trust in the people not to want to police them politically. The best way to disable 'liberation' movements is to persuade people that they are already free; and the much-vaunted absence of a British political police branch went a long way to doing this. It was a legitimate and highly effective means of 'social control'; and by the same token it was one whose abandonment could not be contemplated lightly. This was the more so in view of the depth and strength of feeling against such a course. The *Daily News* in 1858 called political policing 'a system repugnant to every feeling, sentiment, and principle of English life'.[7] The slightest hint of its incursion into Britain was resisted vociferously. 'Political espionage', wrote the adventure story writer Mayne Reid in 1853, 'is cuneiform. Give the vile system but the smallest insertion, and, wedge like, it will help itself, until it has cleft the columns of our glory and sapped the foundations of our dear liberty.'[8] It was a bold government who would dare to challenge imagery like that. These were powerful incentives to keep things as they were. Disarmament was risky, in the battle against subversion; but not half so risky as the image of mistrust and fear of the people that the mobilisation of a political police branch would give.

In any case the British police were not suited to a political role. A political police needed to be, essentially, a *detective* police, one which discovered – in this case – conspiracies, or the perpetrators of them. The British tradition of policing had always been very different. For many years the creation of a police force of any kind had been obstructed by strong prejudices from all classes against what were taken to be the necessary implications of a detective system, for which the chief model was the French. This prejudice survived even the worst crimes, like the Ratcliffe murders of 1811. 'They have an admirable police in Paris,' wrote the future earl of Dudley in that year;

> but they pay for it dear enough. I had rather a dozen people's throats should be cut in Ratcliffe Highway every three or four years than be subject to domiciliary visits, spies, and all the rest of Fouché's contrivances.[9]

A parliamentary committee of 1818 echoed the same feeling: that though an effective detective police was theoretically possible, 'yet in a free country . . . such a system would of necessity be odious and repulsive, and one which no government could be able to carry into execution'.[10] The result of this was that when the new London Metropolitan Police Force was set up in 1829 its *General Instructions* took pains to emphasize that its object was not the detection but the prevention of crime; which was why it was entirely, from its Chief Commissioners down to the most junior constable, uniformed. 'The English jealousy of any police force at all', reported a Home Office inquiry in 1868, 'would not hear of anything approaching to what was called the "spy system"':[11] until 1842, when the first cautious steps were taken along that path.

In that year a plain-clothes detective branch was set up at Scotland Yard, but with only two inspectors and six sergeants. Twenty-five years later it had expanded to sixteen in the 'Central Office', though in the outlying divisions of the Metropolitan Police district men could be temporarily taken out of uniform for specific plain-clothes tasks. In 1869 the position in the divisions was formalised, with regular detective sections under the authority of the Divisional Superintendents; at the beginning of 1878 these came all told to 217 men, in addition to the twenty-seven who now constituted the Detective Branch at Scotland Yard.[12] By then some of the feeling against that Branch had clearly crumbled, helped in part perhaps by an admiring account of its sagacity by Dickens in *Household Words*.[13] Even his toleration of it, however, had its limits; as did that of the police's own hierarchy. In 1845 a police constable was reprimanded for having disguised himself as a cobbler in order to observe and arrest a counterfeiter, with the approval of the Home Secretary, who ordered that in future 'Police Constables must on no account be allowed to use artifices of this description'.[14] Six years later another constable was similarly censured for hiding behind a tree to watch an indecent offence.[15] It happened again, but only very occasionally, and with the police and Home Office always taking trouble to prevent knowledge of it getting out.[16] Among respectable people devices like this were abhorrent. The respectable hero of Wilkie Collins's *The Woman in White*, for example, refused to seek the safety of a disguise in the pursuit of quite unscrupulous villains because the idea seemed to him 'repellent' and mean.[17] In that case it did him no harm. In other, real ones it must have acted as a considerable restraint on those who were professionally engaged in combating crime. It was a restraint, however, whose disadvantages people seemed willing to accept, in preference to the evils of the alternative.

The prejudice against that alternative was very strong. 'Espionage' was widely frowned on at this time, even in connection with military intelligence, which was mainly gleaned from foreign newspapers and maps, and not at all from spies.[18] The case against it was even stronger with regard to crime. For a start, wrote Josephine Butler, again, 'It is a question whether in free countries a secret police is allowable at all; its place ought to be supplied by public opinion, and the liberty of the press.'[19] It was, in other words, unnecessary; where there was a free press, then newspapers were far more likely to pick up hints of wrongdoing than detectives and spies. As well as this, detectives could not be trusted. 'Men whose business it is to detect hidden and secret things', commented Trollope in 1869, 'are very apt to detect things which have never been done. What excuse can a detective make even to himself for his own existence if he can detect nothing?'[20] Twelve years later a more knowledgeable authority on the subject wrote that 'It may be accepted as a truism that the man who spends his life in deceiving those with whom he comes in contact will have little compunction in deceiving his employers – the Government – if it be his interest to do so.'[21] This seemed likely. It was exemplified quite dramatically in 1877, when three out of the Metropolitan Detective Branch's four Inspectors were convicted and sentenced to two years' hard labour for their involvement in a turf fraud they were supposed to be investigating.[22] This was a blow to a department whose reputation was low anyway, and to a method of policing which had been greatly distrusted for years.

The 1877 scandal provoked a rigorous internal Home Office inquiry into the Detective Force, which showed why the distrust was there. Part of the trouble was that pay and promotion prospects in the Detective Branch were not sufficient to attract good men. Good men who did find themselves there did not stay long, but took the first opportunities they could to get back into uniform, 'so as to advance themselves'. The method of selection, usually on the recommendation of Divisional Inspectors and Superintendents, was also fallible, and resulted in 'the choice of favourites or of good stupid men who have never got into trouble, rather than in that of men' (bad clever ones?) 'specially fitted for the purpose'. Sometimes Superintendents were also 'influenced by the desire of getting rid of some man they dislike'. There were other difficulties too: like the lack of co-operation between police in the divisions and Central Office detectives sent to lend them a hand. 'Everyone admitted that when the Chief Commissioner sends an officer from Scotland Yard to assist in a case, the divisional detectives look upon that officer as an interloper, and that they often keep back information which might lead to an arrest, rather than . . . allow him to carry off the prize.' The result of all this was that the system had 'utterly failed in leading to a proper detection of crime'. The main solutions mooted by the inquiry were higher pay and ranks for detectives, and that all of them, at Scotland Yard and in the Divisions, be amal-

6

gamated into one force answerable not to Divisional Superintendents but to officers of their own.[23]

The outcome of all this was a new 'Criminal Investigation Department' (or CID) of the Metropolitan Police, which started work on 8 April 1878.[24] Its size was about the same as before – 240 men all told; but they were paid more, given higher ranks (there was a mass promotion of constables to sergeants and sergeants to inspectors to man it in the first place),[25] and controlled separately from the Uniform branch. But this did not entirely disperse the cloud which had always loomed over it. Even its senior officers were not happy with it. Superintendent Adolphus Williamson, who had charge of the branch both before and after the change, was fully aware of the 'odium' that remained attached to it in 1880, and which he admitted was deserved. The problem, he wrote, was that despite its higher rate of pay, which was now a source of resentment among the uniformed branch, the CID still failed to attract the best and brightest men in the force. The main reason for this was

> . . . the uncertainty and irregularity of the duties, which are also no doubt in many cases very distasteful and repugnant to the better class of men in the service, as their duties constantly bring them into contact with the worst classes, frequently cause unnecessary drinking, and compel them at times to resort to trickey [sic] practices which they dislike.[26]

This same point was taken up by Williamson's chief, Assistant Commissioner Howard Vincent. The problem for him was mainly one of control.

> I do not think that there is any possible system of exercising continuous & effective disciplinary supervision over upwards of 250 detective officers, operating over a wide area, who must necessarily by the nature of their duties, be allowed wide individual freedom.
>
> I am also of opinion that it is impossible for the majority of men to be in contact for any length of time with all the worst features of human nature, in its most repulsive aspects, without incurring enormous danger of moral contagion. Proofs of this are not, unfortunately, wanting.[27]

These dangers were endemic in detective work. It attracted corruptible men into paths of temptation. This was another reason for keeping it clear of politics.

Of course it could not be kept out of politics altogether. When the CID was founded one of its duties was defined as 'investigations for the government', which were clearly likely to have a political stamp.[28] The old detective department also dabbled in political matters from time to time. Between 1851 and 1859 a few of its officers were organised into a special 'foreign' branch, reporting directly to the Commissioner, to keep a watch on alien refugees.[29] One of those officers was 'Dolly' Williamson, who was a bit of a linguist, and perhaps for that reason was entrusted with most of the serious political cases which came up from then until his death in 1889. These cases were generally of two kinds: inquiries into the activities of foreign revolutionaries in Britain at the request of continental governments, and the prevention of terrorist acts in the United Kingdom itself.

The second kind was very rare. The only significant example between 1850 and 1880 was during the first Irish bombing campaign of 1867–8, when the police did not acquit themselves with any great distinction. Their most abject failure was to miss the Fenian bomb which exploded aginst the walls of Clerkenwell prison killing twelve people in December 1867, even though warning of it was received in good time from Dublin. The reason for that, apparently, was that the warning had specified that the prison was to be 'blown *up*', and not 'down' or 'across', so leading the Police Commissioner to restrict his men's search to *underneath* the prison.[30] Even before this fiasco the Metropolitan force came under attack for its incompetence in the face of this kind of crime. 'They know as little how to discharge duty in connection with Fenianism as I do about translating Hebrew', commented a member of the Dublin police force, which of course was far better equipped. In September 1867 the Irish viceroy, Lord Mayo, suggested that Williamson should be put at the head of a special Fenian department of the police.[31] Instead the government decided to form a separate secret branch outside. An army intelligence colonel called Feilding was brought over from Ireland to head it.[32] Under him was a young Anglo-Irish barrister called Robert Anderson, who remained loosely attached to the Home Office, as its 'adviser relating to political crime', after the immediate crisis blew over and Feilding left.

Thereafter the detective department of Scotland Yard returned to its usual activities, no doubt with some relief. If it got involved in politics otherwise, it was always on some other country's account, and not on Britain's. In the 1850s, when it was most active politically, the motive was to defuse tension between Britain and foreign governments who resented the asylum she granted to revolutionary refugees. To that end it set what appears to have been an effective systematic watch on them, from which it sent reports on their activities, generally underplaying them, to the Home Office and thence to the Foreign Office for transmission – sometimes – abroad. When that no longer seemed to be having the desired effect the 'foreign' branch was instrumental in bringing one of the refugees to trial for conspiracy (with Orsini) to murder Louis Napoleon in Paris in January 1858. That prosecution, however, failed (mainly due to popular resentment at the French pressure that had instigated it); and it was after this that the regular surveillance of foreign politicos seems to have come to an end.[33] Thereafter they were left pretty well alone, except occasionally in response to a specific inquiry from abroad. If they were bothered it was never because they were thought to pose a threat to British society; and there is no evidence that the detective branch took any interest in *British* subversives and revolutionaries (apart from Irish) at all.

For this reason revolutionaries of all political and national complexions enjoyed more liberty of action in Britain than they had anywhere else in Europe between 1850 and 1880. Karl Marx for example was allowed to live there from 1849 until his death in 1883, all the time plotting the course of his revolution, yet entirely unmolested by the classes that that revolution was supposed to be destined to overthrow. The events of 1871 – the Paris commune and the exodus of communards to Britain after its suppression – made little difference to this, though it might have been expected to. Continental governments, by and large, thought it should because of the nature of communism: a doctrine which, as the Spanish foreign minister put it in February 1872, 'flies in the face of all the traditions of mankind, and which effaces God from the mind, family and inheritance from life, and nations from the civilized world'.[34] The Conservative MP Alexander Baillie Cochrane agreed, and asked that Britain co-operate with Spain to put the beast down.[35] In the upper house Lord Elcho asked whether 'the authors of what cannot but be regarded by the civilised world as the greatest crime on record' should not be extradited back to France forthwith.[36] Of course they could not be, because Britain's extradition laws expressly excluded political offences; but in any case the government felt less alarmed. In response to foreign demands, again, they set Williamson to find out what he could about the communards. His efforts appear to have been less thorough than his predecessors' had been in the 1850s, and less successful.[37] One surviving report from a detective-sergeant who tried to infiltrate a refugee meeting in an Islington public house in May 1872 tells a sorry tale of his being seized, thrown out and warned that he would have his head broken if he returned. 'I did not return', he reported back ruefully to Williamson, 'in order that no breach of the peace should take place.' When he tried again the next month he was allowed to stay, but everyone else at the meeting left.[38] The police were clearly unused to this kind of thing. At one stage the Home Office decided to short-circuit the whole process by writing direct to Dr Marx: who told them everything they wanted to know.[39] That was the honest, straightforward, British way of finding out things: not by disguises and subterfuge and lying, but by walking boldly up to the front door to ask.

But the government was clearly not over-concerned on its own account anyway. The Home Office's conclusion from the enquiries it undertook among the socialists on behalf of foreign governments was that Britain, at least, had nothing to fear from them. Most of the socialists in Britain were foreigners. Those who were not were on the whole very mild and theoretical sorts of socialist, not at all wedded to destruction and violence. There may have been one or two fierier revolutionaries among them, but they had no broad following: 'We can safely rely on the good sense of the great bulk of our working-classes to check and defeat the wild and impracticable designs of the few.'[40] *The Times* agreed, that English working men were neither fools nor fanatics, so that, as it put it in April 1872, 'until they are both, and something still worse than either, we need have little fear of the International'.[41] This was the pure unadulterated milk of mid-Victorian liberal self-confidence, strong in its belief in its own security, and unaware of the need to take special measures against any danger to it. Any measures it did take were simply to humour others; and after 1874, when others stopped pressing for them, those special measures were allowed to lapse.[42]

It was natural that they should be. This whole question was after all, as the Metropolitan Police Commissioner commented in 1878 on a Russian request for his help in watching nihilists, 'a very difficult one & requires great caution in dealing with it'. In the past, he claimed, such action had only been taken 'when some overt act had been committed and materials were required in a prosecution in this country,' or to protect visiting royalty; and even then it had been apt to arouse 'great animosity against the Government . . . among a large class of the people'. Any general 'system of espionage' was 'worse than useless' because there was no hope of keeping it secret. If news of it did get out, minuted a Home Office under-secretary to his minister, then

> no-one can say how far the present feeling against Russia, and the long-established feeling on the subject of absolute government, right of asylum, & secret police would not carry the public, when inflamed by political and social agitators. All sorts of falsehoods, incapable of refutation, would be invented. It would be impossible to make clear to the public exactly what had been done, and what had not been done, they would always say there were secret orders besides given to the police.

As well as this, the system could get out of hand. Once the government had embarked on political espionage, 'however moderately', it would be 'most difficult for you to stop'.[43] These were compelling reasons for it never to be allowed to begin. It would be hard to control it; the public was against it; and Britain had no need for one on her own account.

For a society as urban and industrial as Britain's was becoming in the 1850s, as riddled with poverty and inequality, and with such recent memories of Chartism, this degree of unconcern about political subversion indicated a quite remarkable faith in her fundamental unsubvertability. But of course there was more to it than that. For a start, mainland Britain was, objectively, highly stable politically in the third quarter of the nineteenth century: far more so than any of her continental neighbours. Consequently she could afford, as they could not, to relax her grip. For more than thirty years after 1848 there was scarcely the slightest sniff of a challenge from anywhere to the political and economic structure of her society. Chartism effectively died shortly after 1848, if not before, to be replaced on the revolutionary left by a vacuum. Individual socialists who survived, or the few who were made in these barren years, had no material to work with; as neither did Marx, despite his recurrent hopes that it might lie around the next historical corner he turned.[44] This is not to say that the British were entirely compliant. There were dozens of riots and disturbances in the 1850s and 1860s, some of them serious. The most serious was probably the Hyde Park riot of 23 July 1866, when in defiance of a Home Office ban a huge crowd agitating for parliamentary reform got so out of hand – pushing down the railings and rampaging through London's clubland – as to need to be put down by troops. As well as this there were periodic riots over hunger, Sunday observance, ritualism, the Irish, industrial disputes and elections throughout this time. Shop-keepers and 'toffs' were terrorised by mobs 100,000 strong or more; pitched battles between English and Irish led to smashed churches, broken bones and some deaths; factory machinery was sabotaged, blacklegs assaulted and their houses firebombed by strikers; and crowds of 'bread rioters' plundered shops for food.[45] Some parts of High Victorian Britain could be exciting places to live in; not nearly so peaceful as the High Victorians liked to pretend.

But peace and stability are not the same thing. The ruling classes of the time could afford to tolerate a certain amount of riot, so long as it was not organised in such a way as to threaten the basis their system rested on. Even the 1866 riots did not really do that: extending the franchise, slowly, was a policy that came well within the bounds of conventional liberal ideology, and only needed to be rioted over because in consensual terms it seemed overdue. When in 1867 a Reform bill was passed, the trouble stopped. The other occasions for disturbances were less worrying. There was no way in which the state, the monarchy or liberal capitalism were ever going to be toppled by undisciplined mobs of the hungry, or strikers, or anti-Catholics egged on by the ranter Patrick Murphy. If anything these helped the state, by distracting critical attention and violent energies away from it. Most of them could be dismissed as pure hooliganism, as they may have been; middle-class observers generally agreed that the participants were the dregs of society, 'youths of the very lowest and dirtiest class, and dirty women and girls', as the *Annual Register* described the Sunday observance rioters of 1855, with merely 'a sprinkling of respectable persons who partook the views of the populace'.[46] This was no matter for complacency; indeed it provided a salutary warning to some of the Victorian middle classes that there might in the future be incendiary fuel for any revolutionary engine that came along. But there was no imminent danger of this. If all these riotous disturbances and outrages and the rest *were* manifestations of social and political discontent, then they were wild, blind, fragmented ones, with no wiser leaders to guide them than Patrick Murphy, and no revolutionary programme beyond blacking the eyes of a few 'toffs'. To the mid-Victorians it was not a political but a criminal problem, whose potential political sting would be drawn when poverty was eradicated by growing prosperity, and by a few discriminating measures of social reform.

The prosperity would come automatically, as a result of the natural dynamism of Britain's free market economy, whose benefits eventually would filter down to everyone who worked. This was another article of faith for most mid-Victorians, and an important buttress to their confidence. Their system was a progressive one, and progress had the effect of diminishing discontent. The proof of that pudding was contained in the figures: for national income per head, for example, which rose from £23 to £34 between 1855 and 1875, and for average wages, which increased by 35 per cent in real terms.[47] Freed from the last of the old artificial contraints on its growth, capitalism was bringing home the bacon, just as the political economists had predicted; with the poor getting their forks in as well as the rich. This was how it appeared during British capitalism's sunniest boom years; an appearance which may have obscured some flaws in the general pattern, and some trouble for the future, but which at the time seemed justified by most of the facts. Things were improving, prosperity and hence contentment increasing for everyone: which meant that the danger of revolution must recede as time and the mechanism of the market ticked by. In the meantime, the state had adequate defences against criminal riot, in its laws and the ordinary, open and above-board methods of the police.

For to say that the mid-Victorians had no political police is not to say that their criminal police did not have a political function. That was implicit in the formation of nearly all the new police forces which sprang up in Britain after 1829, mainly with the object of maintaining public order, which at that time was usually under threat from groups with political aims. The public order function of the police always had at least as high a priority as the prevention of private crime, and it may have been a vitally important function at those times – like the 1830s and early 1840s – when the emerging capitalist system looked most vulnerable to attack. The police were not always successful against riots; but they were generally less provocative than the alternative, which before 1829 had been to call out the army or the yeomanry with their guns. The Metropolitan Force in particular became experts in crowd control, armed only with truncheons (apart from 1848, when they were issued with cutlasses), and consequently needing to fall back on the gentler weapons of discipline and 'science'.[48] They and their sister forces in the provinces met with a great deal of opposition and resentment in some working-class communities,[49] which undoubtedly saw them as agents of government; but not invariably, and not as much as the militia. Consequently they were found to be ideal guardians of political and social order when the threats to that order were – as in the nineteenth century they generally were – overt. So long as unrest manifested itself in *dis*order they were the best counters to it, and their general effectiveness was a vindication of the kid-glove approach.

That approach took other forms too. The real guarantee of stability for any governmental and economic system is the widespread acceptance of its values, and the mid-Victorian middle classes were adept at propagating theirs. By the time of the Great Exhibition of 1851 their battles against rival ideologies, which had been fierce in the 1830s and 1840s, were all well won. The most important of those battles had been over the education of the poor, most of which was now firmly in the hands of middle-class boards of managers, who exercised a close control over syllabuses and staff. That control was used quite openly to ensure that 'right' ideas about the 'real' world and the place of the poor in it were inculcated into the very young, by teachers who themselves questioned neither the rightness nor the reality.[50] A little later similar efforts were made with the public schools, to make them less resistant than some of them seemed to be to the dominant ideology: again with a success which was only partial, but was enough for middle-class purposes at that time.[51] These victories were further secured by a constant propaganda during the 1860s and 1870s, and, on the negative side, by forms of censorship which may have been more insidious than Victorian liberals knew. These included an overt, and highly constraining, official censorship of the theatre, which was partly designed to prevent serious political and social questions being raised on the stage;[52] and the effective if patchy control which was exercised over the people's reading habits by W. H. Smith's railway bookstall monopoly and by the circulating libraries.[53] All these devices limited access to dissident ideas, and consequently freedom. Nevertheless they were not responsible for liberal capitalism's ideological dominance in mid-Victorian times. The main reason for that was its intrinsic attraction, at a time when everything seemed to be going for it materially, and when it was associated with a range of political freedoms in which everyone seemed to share.

So it happened that the ideas and values of the liberal capitalist middle class spread out from their narrow class base, and permeated enough of the classes above and below them to make them invulnerable: a broad national consensus, with dissidence isolated on its edges. Among the working class the greatest success of this strategy was in prising 'respectable' artisans away from their old quasi-revolutionary base: persuading them to leave off trying to overturn the system, and to work it to their advantage instead. Some did this by accepting the middle-class ethos wholesale, channelling their ambitions not into raising their class, but into rising out of it. Others did it by embracing a separate working-class ethos which was nevertheless consonant with the middle class's: an ethos of collective self-help and self-improvement which was working-class centred but still mirrored the values of the dominant ideology. Various sections of liberals and liberal-conservatives gave encouragement and help to each of these ventures, sometimes at the expense of strict principle and short-term self-interest, but with an enlightened regard for future stability.[54] In this way the large pre-1850 body of putative revolutionaries was deprived of its leaders, isolated, decontaminated, and pared down to a thoughtless 'mob'. Serious protest was reduced to a form that could be categorised as 'crime', and could consequently, without any violence to notions of political liberty, be left to the ordinary police to control.

The mid-Victorians' innocence, in this matter of political policing, is impressive; and of course it impressed the mid-Victorians themselves. Their pride in this aspect of their liberalism, however, as in so many others, was just a little myopic. The British state in the nineteenth century embraced more than England, Wales and Scotland. Ireland was the exception to most British rules, chiefly because so many of the Irish wanted her to be; and then there were the colonies and India, which at this time were often forgotten, or dismissed as temporary or peripheral, but were in fact crucial to Britain's economic well-being, and hence to her liberalism at home. The colonies were part of a broad pattern of trade and investment in the wider world which serviced Victorian capitalism, by enabling it to expand without relying for that expansion on its domestic market alone. If mid-Victorian liberalism depended on stability, and that stability in turn depended on rising economic expectations, then the colonies played their part.

Neither they, nor Ireland, were run particularly liberally, even in the narrowest economic sense. So far as the colonies were concerned the very fact that they *were* colonies was a sign of the breakdown of all kinds of liberal assumptions: about national self-government, for example, though that was never a central article of British liberal faith before Gladstone; and about administrative *laissez-faire*. Mid-Victorian liberalism was always anti-imperialist at heart. Its ideal international arrangement was of a loose community of independent producers and manufacturers freely exchanging goods and capital amongst themselves, with the minimum of state involvement, as with everything else. Whenever the state needed to get itself involved it marked a failure, even when, as was usually the case, it was only to preserve the freedom of exchange. It meant that someone – a rival or a customer – was resisting the logic of the market; and it inevitably led on, by slow stages, to greater degrees of control. That control encouraged the growth of administrative structures and value systems which were inimical to liberalism in other ways. The British empire, and especially India, came to be run by classes of men who had largely escaped or resisted the prevailing liberal-capitalist ethos in Britain, or were distanced from it by the problems they encountered in 'the field'. The Indian and colonial civil services, and the armed forces at the back of them, had qualities and virtues of their own, including in many cases a genuine paternalistic regard for their wards; but they were not always the same qualities and virtues as those of the liberal middle classes back home. In particular, they did not widely share the common liberal assumptions of the time about political freedom and trust; or if they did, then they found reasons for making exceptions to it of the non-European peoples they administered.

It would have been impossible in any case not to make exceptions of them, in view of the fact that many of them were actively and violently hostile to British rule. The Indian 'Mutiny' was only the most serious of a cluster of colonial rebellions which shook the empire in the 1850s and 1860s, and which could be said – if Ireland is counted as a colony – to have culminated in the Fenian outbreak of 1867. Continual unrest, breaking occasionally into open rebellion, was only to be expected from situations in which the civil authority could in no sense be said to have grown out of a community or even an indigenous class, but was imposed from outside: as was widely acknowledged to be the case even in Ireland. To those kinds of situation, regrettably, different rules applied: concerning personal liberty, civil rights, and the administration of the law. Every day in the colonies and in Ireland those different rules were implemented quietly and continuously, with few people in Britain being aware of the discrepancy between their national principles and their agents' practices abroad. Just occasionally that discrepancy was highlighted by a dramatic event in a colony, like Governor Eyre's heavy-handed repression of a black revolt in Jamaica in 1865, which had the result of throwing Britain into a kind of national delirium as the contradiction bit.[55] In Ireland the contradiction was closer to hand, and consequently more troublesome; and was usually resolved for liberals by the hope that better laws would eventually make Ireland as 'easy' to govern as England.[56] But the inconvenient fact remained that, for the time being at least, Britain's liberalism was not coextensive with her authority: did not reach much further than the drawing-room, and certainly not into the kitchens or the estate outside.

The practical significance of this from a domestic point of view was that it meant that the will and the weapons were there to hand to deal with it, if the situation in the drawing-room ever changed. In India and in Ireland there were men who still lived with daily experience of subversion, and knew of different ways to deal with it from the kid-glove way. The Irish police, for example, were different animals entirely from their English and Scottish brethren: organised nationally, quartered in 'barracks', usually away from their own communities, and armed with Enfield rifles and bayonets.[57] They were not at all averse to spying, with paid agents posing as butchers or servants or labourers all over the island sending back intelligence which could not be elicited any other way.[58] A few were sent over to England to keep tabs on suspected Irish dissidents there.[59] It was in connection with Ireland that the Anglo-Irishman Robert Anderson embarked on his career as spymaster for the Home Office in 1868, with the help of Thomas Beach, known as 'Henri le Caron' in North America, where he had infiltrated his first Fenian lodge a couple of years before.[60] In India the set-up was similar. The police were armed, and deliberately distanced from their communities, amongst whom they had a reputation for corruption and oppression. From early on the collection of 'intelligence affecting the public peace' was seen as an important part of their function, which was extended in 1877 with the formation of a proper central political branch. That branch worked through secret paid agents, much as the Irish police did.[61] At home Britain's way with subversion was to try to kill it with kindness; but away from home she knew other ways of killing it, if kindness failed.

Liberal kindness, of course, remained the preferred option, chiefly because of the spin-off benefit that it impressed the domestic populace. But a switch was always possible. The liberal approach to subversion was backed by a contemporary ethos which was widespread, but not universal. It was partly Britain's overseas and Irish responsibilities that ensured it would not be. There was always a considerable number of men and women in Britain who either did not share the prevalent liberal assumptions, or whose absorption of them was only skin-deep. They included colonial hands, and most of the military: from whose ranks, significantly, chiefs of the Metropolitan Police were nearly always drawn. People like this were likely to have a lower resistance to the adoption of sharp counter-subversive practices than middle-class liberal civilians. If that resistance broke down, then they had the materials for a 'political' police force to hand. They had Vincent's shiny-new CID, for example, greatly expanded from its old pre-scandal days, and under an able superintendent who had had experience of political policing in the past. They had Anderson close by at the Home Office, with *his* experience of running at least one secret agent amongst an Irish subversive group. They also had men with immense experience of political policing to call on in Ireland and the colonies: like Colonel Edward Bradford, who helped suppress Thuggee in India and later ran the India Office's 'Political and Secret Department'; James Monro, who was an Inspector of Police in India; Colonel Henry Brackenbury, who set up the first British police force in Cyprus; and all those officers and men of the Royal Irish Constabulary and the Dublin Metropolitan Police who had been combating political crime for decades. Money might be a problem, because it could only be granted by Parliament, which might not approve of the purpose to which it was put. On the other hand British governments had always had *some* money available for what was vaguely and mysteriously called 'Secret Service' purposes, which did not have to be accounted for, and which could certainly be used. In the 1870s the grant for this purpose came to about £24,000 per annum, though in some years as much as half of it was returned to the Treasury unspent.[62] So, if mainland Britain ever wanted to set up a political police branch, it would not need to be conjured out of nothing. There was spare cash available for it; and the personnel were ready and waiting in the wings.

Before they were allowed on to the metropolitan stage, however, the political climate – the bundle of liberal assumptions and prejudices which formed the main obstacle to a political police force – would have to change. That could happen suddenly, with a crisis, or slowly, with the gradual erosion of an ethos, or by a combination of both. In the 1870s there was no crisis; but it was possible to see signs of erosion. One sign, according to Josephine Butler in 1879, was the slow undermining of liberal and individualist values by governments of both political persuasions over the past few years, in a way which she believed was insidiously accustoming people to having their lives controlled for them, which lowered their resistance to what she called 'government by police'. This danger was especially great in London, which had no proper municipal self-government, and a police force accountable to the Home Office rather than to the community. Because of this the Metropolitan Police was already beginning to ape continental methods: becoming more military, for example; extending its authority into areas previously closed to it; and using espionage 'for other purposes than the detection of crime'. This presaged more ominous developments. 'In London', claimed Mrs Butler, 'we have in fact all the materials existing for the same despotic government' they had in Paris: like an 'irresponsible head of the police', and 'the same vast police machinery which, though it may not hitherto have been so used, stands a powerful engine for political purposes.' It had not quite come to that yet; but it surely would, she thought, 'unless the present tendencies are controlled'.[63] This was where the real threat to the British liberal police tradition lay: from changing values, and the apathy of an over-regulated people in the face of them.

CHAPTER 2

Anxiety

The Metropolitan Police Special Branch was conceived in 1881, grew slowly but strongly over the course of the next six years, and was finally born, almost fully-formed, in January 1887. Like all babies it had two parents. One of them – its mother – was the changing political and social ethos in Britain to which Josephine Butler had drawn attention in 1879. The father (because its contribution was more sudden, temporary and violent) was the American Fenian bombing campaign of 1881–5. It is difficult to assess the relative contribution of each. The Fenian bombing campaign required an official response; the fact that the ethos was changing ensured that that response would have long-term implications. Both parents were vital; and neither could have done the job alone.

The two factors – ethos and outrage – may also have stimulated each other (which is where our metaphor becomes a little over-stretched). Fenian bombs struck blows not only at lives and property in Britain, but also at some of the buttresses which had supported the liberal optimism of the mid-Victorian years; while on the other side it was possible to argue (albeit less convincingly) that there would have been no bombs if that liberal optimism had remained intact. In either case, however, the main contributory cause was only one of a number. The main factor behind the change of ethos, for example, was not the Fenians, but a wider perceived threat of which the Fenians formed only a part.

The feeling of threat was a new one in the 1880s. It arose from developments both at home, and in the world outside. At the root of it may have lain Britain's economic situation: the 'depression' in trade and industry which was widely believed to have taken hold of the country in 1873. That depression may have been exaggerated, or mis-named: certainly it affected far fewer people directly than other depressions, before and after, have done. But its indirect effects were considerable. One was to undermine confidence in the ability of the market to cope on its own with the problems of poverty and social distress. Those problems did not seem to have eased significantly, after thirty-five years of nearly-free enterprise. For some free entrepreneurs this was disturbing. One of the virtues of their system was supposed to be that its benefits filtered down. John Stuart Mill, for one, had believed that if this turned out not to be so, then they would do better to go for what he called 'communism'.[1] Filtering down was the condition on which humane people accepted political economy. Investigations by socially concerned journalists like James Greenwood and Christian ministers like Andrew Mearns, however, suggested that this condition was not being met.[2] This was deeply unsettling for those who had banked on free enterprise to – among other things – weaken the material roots of dissent.

That those roots had not been permanently weakened became clear during the course of the 1880s, when native British socialism revived after its long post-Chartist sleep. The first important stage in this resuscitation was the foundation of the marxist Social Democratic Federation in June 1880. That was followed by the secession of the quasi-anarchist Socialist League in 1884, the formation of the collectivist Fabian Society in the same year, and the creation in 1893 of the first Independent Labour Party. Better organisation led to more effective propaganda, with socialist tracts and pamphlets galore, several new socialist weekly newspapers, and street meetings which by the mid-1880s were beginning to turn riotous. These culminated in bloody disturbances in Trafalgar Square in February 1886 and November 1887, which bore all the signs – rampaging crowds of unemployed hurling paving stones at jeering upper-class clubsters, for example – of that conflict between the classes which the mid-Victorians had thought they had disarmed. The same conflict was also evident in the militancy of what was called the 'new' trade unionism of the time, which rejected the collaborationism of the older union leaders and set in motion a wave of strikes amongst unskilled workers at the end of the 1880s, some of which were successful. A large section, at least, of the working class had clearly broken with that moderate radical consensus which the more enlightened middle classes had regarded as their system's salvation before.

The middle classes' response to this was divided. For some of them the failure of the system both to deal adequately with social problems and to win the long-term allegiance of the working classes indicated that that system was, at least on its edges, at fault. Their solution was to try to repair the fault, by measures of state and municipal intervention which transgressed the strictest canons of economic liberalism but which, in their view, were necessary to protect its core. These mainly comprised legislation against rights of property which another section of the middle class still believed should be sacrosanct. That section reacted to the situation of the time in an entirely different way from the trimmers. Less impressed than they were by the threat on the streets, it marshalled its forces instead against this other more subtle socialist threat it saw creeping in under the doors of Parliament itself, in the guise of liberal interventionism. The result was an unholy ideological row within the Liberal party which went on for years, pushing cohorts of disaffected champions of property out into the embrace of the Tories in waves.

This rift had two important effects. One was to weaken the Liberal party grievously, to the advantage of the Conservatives, who (with their Liberal Unionist allies) held power for all but three and a half of the twenty years from 1886. The other was to begin the long process whereby economic liberalism ('political economy') became slowly prised apart from the political liberalism it had been so closely associated and even identified with before. In the middle of the nineteenth century it had been possible, and indeed was usual, to embrace both philosophies. They buttressed each other: free market-ism created the conditions in which political freedoms flourished best, and political freedom provided a moral justification for free marketism. It was this symbiosis which to a great extent explained mid-Victorian liberalism's attraction and success. But it depended on the free market's *working*, in such a way as to disarm resistance to it which otherwise might need to be put down illiberally. As soon as enough people came to object to the system, perhaps because it did not seem to be benefiting them, a choice would need to be made between the two sorts of liberalism. Economic liberals would no longer be able to rely on acquiescence to uphold their system without compulsion. Of course there might be semantic ways around the problem: like the tautology (which was common) that free enterprise and liberty were simply the same. It might also be possible to defuse it, by means of persuasion, or by distracting people away from their economic ills. This did not alter the fact, however, that political and economic liberalism were beginning to rub up against each other just a little bit. In the future it might be necessary to chip away at one of them, or both, in order to make them match.

The problem was exacerbated by the march of democracy. Democracy had not been an issue in mid-Victorian times, partly because Palmerston would not allow it to be. The most advanced liberals then had only espoused it as a very distant ambition, to be achieved in slow stages, and after the working classes had proved they could be trusted with it from a liberal point of view. Two years after Palmerston's death there was thought to be enough evidence of the working classes' rise to respectability to merit the extension of the parliamentary franchise to some of them; but even then there were many, like Walter Bagehot, who worried that these new voters might not prove as deferential to their betters as the maintenance of a moderate and wise government required them to be.[3] Bagehot's particular concern, that ministers might truckle to their working-class constituents, seemed to be borne out by the trimming of the late 1870s and 1880s, one manifestation of which was a further parliamentary Reform Act in 1884 which gave the vote for the first time to a clear majority of adult males. The great unwashed, and unpredictable, were getting rather close for comfort. In these circumstances it was scarcely surprising that many middle-class liberals should come to shed some of the easy progressive political optimism which had so lightened the hearts of their radical forebears, and start thinking of erecting barricades.

Events abroad will have confirmed their instinct. Things were going badly for mid-Victorian liberalism there too. Mid-Victorian foreign policy had rested heavily on the assumption, or hope, that other nations would in time come to realise with Britain the futility of conflict, and the universal advantages of free exchange. It was a similar faith to the one that had guided mid-Victorian domestic policy too: that the liberal middle-class way was the natural way, which consequently would not, eventually, need to be forced. Since the unification of Germany in 1870–1 that faith had suffered some set-backs. Continental countries persisted in fighting major wars over issues which, in British eyes, were insubstantial; in burdening themselves with great armies; and in regarding trade as a kind of defensive war. Britain kept out of all this as much as she could; but it affected and even menaced her, in quite fundamental ways. In the first place there was the damage that rising foreign tariffs did to her export trade, which some economists blamed for her 'depression'. Secondly, there was the direct military threat that was posed to her and her empire by the rise of these new heavily-armed powers and alliances, especially after they began taking an interest in colonies, which had been a preserve they had by and large left to Britain before. But it was worse even than this. The obvious response to this kind of threat was for Britain to rearm, or to find allies of her own. In her case, however, that response could prove disastrous. Britain had more to lose than other major countries from war; but she also had far more to lose from preparing for war. In the second-to-last resort, what a nation most wishes to defend from attack is its values, its 'way of life'. Britain's way of life depended on certain freedoms which war preparations were almost certain to undermine. Great standing armies, for example, had long been regarded as incompatible with Englishmen's liberties, as well as with the sort of fiscal regime which economic prosperity throve upon. Alliances carried quite horrific risks, for a country which had no conceivable reason for wanting to provoke a European war but might be dragged into one by an ally whose interests were less pacific.[4] Britain's whole situation in the world around 1880 – her dependence on trade, the wide spread of that trade, her imperial responsibilities, her commercial philosophy – made jungle law, if that was to be the way international relations were to be conducted from now on, an ominous prospect.

The old sort of liberalism was floundering: either in its own internal contradictions, or else in the stupidity of folk. Confidence waned and prospects clouded over, as the last quarter of the nineteenth century saw Britain slipping from the sunny uplands of mid-Victorian liberal capitalism towards the valley of the shadow of socialism and war. That slide was not yet by any means complete. Many liberals still clung on to their old hopes for Britain and the world, sometimes in the teeth of the evidence, but because they needed to. Gladstone, who eventually resigned as prime minister because he disapproved of his own government's capitulation to the trend of the times, did what he could in the 1880s to resist that trend by pretending (for example) that he had not really invaded Egypt when he had, and calling the colonies he was forced to seize elsewhere by other names.[5] The central bastions of liberal capitalism remained secure: like Britain's own free trade policy, which never showed any convincing sign of capitulating to the quite feeble seige mounted against it by the new 'fair trade' protectionists. On another political front socialism, though full of hope and energy, had achieved very little tangible by 1890, with the Social Democrats boasting only 2,000 members and the Fabians fewer still. Britain's free enterprise economy was still growing; and the fact that rival economies were growing faster could be a comfort – because of the boost they gave to every other economy – as well as a cause for concern. It was possible therefore, and quite reasonable, to discount the signs. But very few people could be unaware of them. If they did not spell the end for liberalism, they at least eroded some of that liberalism's old relaxed optimism. It could no longer be so widely assumed as it had been that it would triumph regardless, through its own intrinsic logic and human rationality. Consequently it could also no longer be assumed to be invulnerable. And if that was so, then it pointed the need for vigilance in defence of it: a vigilance which might possibly, if the popular prejudice against *that* could be eroded, or even if not, justify at some time the institution in Britain of a secret political police.

The best justification for a political police, however, was political violence; which came to Britain on the afternoon of 14 January 1881 when an explosion outside the infantry barracks in Salford gravely injured a woman who was passing by and killed a seven-year-old boy. That was Britain's first taste of this kind of thing for many years (since December 1867, to be exact); but it was no novelty for Europe as a whole, which had been plagued by politically-motivated crimes of violence for some time. Most of them were attempts to assassinate crowned heads. The German Kaiser was shot twice in 1878; the king of Spain twice in 1878–9; and the king of Italy attacked with a dagger in 1878, after refusing to be protected by plain-clothes police.[6] Russia however was the hottest bed of political violence, with serious attacks on the Tsar in 1879 and 1880, and a successful one on 13 March 1881. Those attacks were carried out by a group of people called 'The People's Will' (*Narodnaya Volya*) by themselves, and 'nihilists' by outsiders; and the means employed was dynamite.

Dynamite was a new feature of this particular landscape (though it had been first perfected and developed commercially by Alfred Nobel as early as 1867). It made two important differences. One was that it was less discriminate in its impact than knives or pistols, and consequently posed more of a threat to 'innocents'. To the nihilists who assassinated Tsar Alexander II this was a welcome side-effect; later it came to be regarded as the main advantage of dynamite, by those whose aim was to terrorise whole societies. The second important difference arose from its efficiency. Revolutionaries had used bombs before, but generally unsuccessfully. Most of them failed, or exploded prematurely, which at least gave their intended victims a sporting chance. Dynamite packed more explosive power than gunpowder, yet with greater stability between bangs. This seemed to swing the odds the bomber's way: like foxhunters using buckshot. It meant that small groups of men and women, provided they were unscrupulous enough, had a potential for destruction out of all proportion to their numbers; which itself rendered many of the old liberal safeguards against political subversion, which depended on *majorities* remaining unsubverted, inoperable.

This was chilling, for those fainthearts who were liberals too. It conjured up all kinds of appalling nightmares, some of which found their way into literature. Robert Louis Stevenson's *The Dynamiter*, written in a literal fever and published in 1885, projected 'the fall of England' and 'the massacre of thousands' at the hands of dynamitards.[7] Donald Mackay's *The Dynamite Ship*, written the year before but published in 1888, had Irish nationalists bombarding the Palace of Westminster with hundred-pound dynamite shells fired from a twenty-foot-long gun with a range of eight miles. 'Science is dreadful in its teachings', mused its hero, 'when it places such a gun as this in the hands of men swayed by the passions of hate or revenge.'[8] And dynamite was not the worst of it. Stevenson's villains had other schemes prepared, in case ordinary explosives failed. One of them was 'to break up the drainage systems of cities and sweep off whole populations with the devastating typhoid pestilence'.[9] Of course all this was romantic nonsense: but a lot can be learned from the romantic nonsense of an age. In the 1880s it appeared to indicate, for one thing, a shift in attitudes to science, which was now showing its malevolent side. The laws of nature were no longer necessarily on the side of good, but could be harnessed for evil, against even the most beneficent government in the world. The lesson of this for a government like Britain's was that it could no longer rest secure on its beneficence. The fondest of nineteenth-century liberal assumptions, the one which had sustained the mid-Victorians' characteristic confidence, was beginning to dissolve.

The reality was kinder than the nightmare, but still not so reassuring as it had once been thought. The stabbing of President Garfield in Washington in July 1881 put paid to the idea that popular governments were immune to this kind of thing. Eight months later Queen Victoria was fired at while getting into her carriage at Windsor station. Her assailant was a madman, which her Home Secretary found reassuring. It was a mark of the universal love which she inspired, he wrote to her shortly afterwards, that the 'outrages of half insane wretches which have at long intervals disturbed Your Majesty's peaceful reign have happily never partaken of the dangerous fanaticism and wicked malignity which from political motives have threatened the lives of other Sovereigns'.[10] As he wrote those words, however, Harcourt knew that they were hollow. No love could be universal which excluded the Irish. Maclean, the Windsor gunman, was not Irish, but the government would not have been surprised if he had turned out to be. This particular incident came at a time of increasing apprehension about the activities of Irish-American dynamitards on the British mainland, which at one stage had the authorities reportedly running dummy royal trains ahead of the real one in case the lines were booby-trapped.[11] The Queen was vulnerable. Britain was under threat from just the kind of political violence which in the past only tyrannies had been thought to deserve.

Ireland was the main cause of Britain's fall from liberal grace in this matter of counter-subversion. For very many years her people had displayed a propensity for politically-motivated crimes of unusual savagery, either because it was in their character, as many Englishmen claimed,[12] or because they were provoked into them by the nature of their relationship to the British government. That that relationship was different from other British subjects' was recognised by many Liberal politicians in the 1880s, including of course Gladstone, and also Harcourt, who reminded the former in December 1883 how 'we hold Ireland by *force and by force alone* as much today as in the days of Cromwell', and with six times as many soldiers per native as they required to hold India.[13] This accounted both for the violence, and for the special measures taken to combat it in Ireland; neither of which however seemed greatly to bother Englishmen while they were confined there. Clearly however there was always the danger that the violence would spill over into Britain; as it did in the 1880s, bringing the policing hard on its tail. The spill-over came a roundabout way. The centre of the Fenian conspiracy was not Ireland itself, presumably partly because of the effectiveness of the police there, but the Irish community in the United States, whose government was – to say the least – neutral to its cause. Within that community, and generously supported by it financially, were a number of secret organisations bent on waging war against Britain, of which the most important were the Irish Republican, or Fenian, Brotherhood, which went back to 1858, and Clan na Gael, founded in 1867. In 1876 these two societies came together to plot more effectively, with the aid of a 'skirmishing fund' which was so well subscribed as to enable them to spend tens of thousands of dollars building what they hoped would be the world's first navigable submarine (shades of our romantic nonsense) to stalk and sink British ships. That plan came to nothing: two boats were built, but the first one would not float and the second would not steer; and so what remained of the Fund was channelled into more conventional and dependable schemes. The main one, after 1880, was for a series of bomb

26

attacks on targets in Britain, to terrorise her into granting home rule.[14]

'Terrorism' was something entirely new in Britain's political experience, and was unusual at that time even on the Continent. The word originated during the French Revolution, and implies imposing one's will through simple fear. That had not generally been the method favoured by mid-century revolutionaries, who relied more on fomenting popular rebellion and tyrannicide. Of course tyrannicide also had its terrorist aspect, especially in the case of *Narodnaya Volya*, whose programme of assassination was intended to strike fear into the successors of its royal or ministerial victims, as well as to remove them from the scene. The Fenians' brand of terrorism was slightly different, in that its targets were not generally rulers, but British public buildings and nearby civilians.[15] Hence the bomb at Salford barracks, and the others that followed it later in 1881: two which exploded (without injuring anyone) at Chester barracks and Liverpool town hall, and one which was defused by a brave police constable just before it could explode near midnight on 16 March outside the Mansion House in London.

That particular little dynamite campaign did not exactly rock the empire; and by the summer of 1881 Harcourt was beginning to feel that earlier fears he had felt may have been misplaced. 'The business is in the hands of a very few miscreants who have neither the resources nor the courage for great crimes,' he wrote to the Queen's secretary in June; '. . . The clumsiness of their contrivances and the stupidity of their proceedings are childish in the extreme.'[16] The lull that seemed to descend after the Liverpool bomb in that month, however, was soon shattered by the murder of Thomas Burke and Lord Frederick Cavendish in Dublin's Phoenix Park on 6 May 1882, and by what appeared to be a renewal of the mainland campaign when a second bomb was found smouldering against the Mansion House six days later. Another lull followed; and then Harcourt quite suddenly found his words to the Queen's secretary rammed painfully down his throat.

The major Fenian bombing offensive of 1883–5 hit Glasgow first, and London worst. Glasgow's explosions damaged a gasworks, a coaling shed, a canal viaduct and a dozen bystanders in January 1883.[17] In London the IRB's targets were grander. The first ones, on the evening of 15 March, were the offices of *The Times* newspaper, and of the government in Whitehall. The explosions there caused material damage, but no injury.[18] 'There can be no doubt,' wrote Harcourt to Gladstone shortly afterwards, his tune greatly altered, 'that we are in the midst of a large and well organised and fully equipped band who are prepared to commit outrages all over the country on an immense scale.'[19] This, he told the cabinet, marked a 'very serious change . . . in the aspect of the Fenian Conspiracy . . . it is not a spasmodic or occasional outbreak we have to deal [with,] it is an organised & relentless *war* having murder for its weapon'.[20] On 30 October two more bombs were planted, this time on the London underground railway, in tunnels near Praed Street and Westminster Bridge stations. Both exploded, injuring seventy passengers at Praed Street.[21] 'Whatever else may be said,' wrote the Queen to Harcourt on this, 'they exhibit a diabolical spirit, & an utter disregard of human life dreadful to contemplate.'[22] At the end of February the following year a bomb went off – with no injuries – in the left-luggage office at Victoria Station, and others were found and defused at Charing Cross, Paddington and Ludgate Hill.[23] In April some bombs apparently intended to blow up the government were found in the possession of John Daly, arrested in Birkenhead on Good Friday; a few days later Harcourt had one of them exploded for an experiment in a mock-up cabinet room with twelve wooden dummies: 'The bomb only had a drop of 2 feet but there were wounds in every figure, the smallest being 17 and the largest 49.'[24] On 30 May there were three more explosions, one at the back of the Junior Carlton Club in St James's Square, and another demolishing part of Scotland Yard. Altogether ten people were hurt in these blasts. The next day a bomb was safely discovered under Nelson's column.[25] An attempt to blow up London Bridge in December 1884 killed the three men who placed the bomb.[26] On 2 January 1885, another underground train was bombed near Gower Street. And then, on 24 January, came what was intended to be the Fenians' *coup de grâce*. Their final targets were the Palace of Westminster and the Tower of London, no less. One bomb exploded in the Chamber of the House of Commons; another at the top of the stairs leading from the crypt into Westminster Hall; and a third behind a gun carriage in the Banqueting Room of the Tower.[27] Two policemen were injured by these explosions, two women, and two boys; making a total bag since January 1883 of three bombers killed, a hundred innocents injured, and twelve dummies.

If all these explosions were 'genuine' – which is a question we shall come on to later – this was the most serious bout of terrorist violence London had ever known. It was bound to have an impact on general attitudes as well as on policy. That impact can be detected early on in the official and public reaction in Britain to an entirely different affair: the case of the London-based German-language newspaper *Freiheit*, whose editor, the anarchist Johann Most, was tried and convicted for seditious libel in June 1881 after publishing an article applauding the assassination of the Tsar and expressing the hope that it might be copied elsewhere. Most's prosecution was the first of its kind for very many years. It was instituted by the cabinet and the law officers, at the secret instigation of the German government, with some trepidation because it was felt that an English jury might not take kindly to what it could construe, if it was perverse enough, as an attempt to shackle free speech. The example of Palmerston's ignominious fall in February 1858 over a not dissimilar affair (Orsini) was a constant worry.[28] The classes from which London juries were drawn were notoriously resistant to foreign governments' influencing British governments to prosecute dissidents for speaking their minds. In the event, however, ministers need not have fretted. His London jury found Most guilty after only a short deliberation, and he was put away for fifteen months. A year later two more members of *Freiheit*'s staff were convicted on a similar charge, with the jury this time not even bothering to leave the court. The verdict here was no doubt affected by the fact that it was the Phoenix Park murders that the *Freiheit* had on this occasion chosen to extol. Nevertheless times had clearly changed. The protective wall of liberal and xenophobic prejudice which had surrounded foreign sedition in Palmerston's time had crumbled.[29] 'Twenty years ago,' claimed the *Radical* newspaper, 'there would have been a revolution in the country, had the bare suggestion been made of such proceedings as took place' against Most. 'The events of to-day show how lamentably,' it went on, 'the spirit of the British people has fallen off.'[30]

This was a gross exaggeration; but the reaction of other newspapers both to the *Freiheit* case and to Fenianism confirmed that there had been a change. Most of the press felt that Britain had been provoked into it. The view of the Liberal *Daily News* after Most's arrest was typical. 'Englishmen,' it said, 'would once have laughed securely at this style of ferocious pedantry.' That was when it had been thought that the best remedy for it was contempt. But now 'the times have changed. Assassination is not merely talked about.'[31] It made the same point again after the Whitehall bomb. 'Time was when spoken or written threats against public men or public institutions in this country were wisely treated with disdain. That time has, unhappily, gone by.'[32] The reason was obvious. Commenting on the anarchist Kropotkin's views in January 1883 (before the main Fenian campaign), *The Times* meditated on how even the firmest political maxim, 'however fortified by historical examples', could be undermined. 'The notion that the highest wisdom consists simply in standing aside and letting every unregulated impulse and movement have its way, becomes questionable when the movement happens to be one for abolishing things in general by means of dynamite.'[33] *The Times* also remarked, as did nearly every other newspaper, on how indiscriminate this new breed of revolutionaries was. It was not as if they had any clear political target in view: 'the assassination of a Sovereign or a Minister, or even the destruction *en masse* of a legislative body.' That was wicked, but at least, in its way, intelligible. 'The Irish-American "dynamite fiend" chooses, by preference, for the scene of his operations crowds of the labouring classes, of holiday-makers, of ordinary travellers, and sweeps them at random into the meshes of his murderous plot with at least as little concern for their personal merits or demerits as the Thug feels for those of the victims of his deadly cult.' This was worse than 'the blackest barbarism'.[34]

It was indiscriminate in another way too. Mid-nineteenth-century revolutionaries had generally confined their hatred to what Englishmen regarded as real tyrannies. Now that too was changed. 'The doctrine of murder preached by Herr Most,' said the Liberal *Daily Telegraph* in May 1881, 'is so *wholesale* that no parallel can be found for it except in the infamous ejaculations of Marat.'[35] It set itself not only against despotisms and foreign yokes, which were fair game, but against *all* governments, which even the most liberal of Victorians found it much harder to take. It seemed less a political doctrine than a sort of anti-politics; an ideological negativism which in this violent form seemed committed against life itself. There was no justification for it, and apparently no hope in it: for as the *Pall Mall Gazette* observed in 1883, even if Ireland were granted home rule in full there was no guarantee that 'a similar class of criminals would not arise to prosecute a dynamite campaign in the heart of London in revenge for some grievance, real or imaginary, of the few against the many'.[36] It lacked rationality: and consequently could not be abolished by persuasion or concessions. Nearly everyone accepted this: even those Liberals (like the *Pall Mall Gazette*) who still wanted the government to concede.[37]

For some people this justified extraordinary and illiberal measures. The *Morning Advertiser* believed the Fenians should be 'treated as vermin outside the pale of ordinary law'.[38] *The Times* thought that the situation demanded some modification of the Englishman's jealously-guarded liberties. 'Liberty is a most excellent thing, but the kind of liberty which is to be enjoyed on the top of a barrel of gunpowder with a lighted match just on the point of being applied to it is a somewhat insecure and questionable blessing.'[39] That was in connection with a foreign bomb-making factory discovered in Westminster in November 1883, which was at first thought to be part of a socialist plot against the Germany embassy. It later turned out to be something less dangerous;[40] but one result of the Fenian outrages was to make the idea of mutual co-operation with other governments menaced by dynamitism more palatable to some. Again, it was the circumstances that had altered. 'It is no time now,' said *The Times*, 'to indulge in the old talk about foreign tyrants and the right of every desperate conspirator to seek a refuge on these shores. The conspirator now shows himself as the common enemy.' Genuine political offenders, of course, should still be able to rely on shelter and protection in Britain. But 'Murderers and dynamiters, by whatever fine names they may be pleased to describe themselves, and whatever grandiloquent motives they may avow, can look for no such favour from us.'[41] 'It is simply a perversion of language,' agreed the *Morning Post*, 'to term these crimes political.'[42] Even the *Daily News* thought that a modification of Britain's traditional policy to meet this point was a good idea.[43] Others mooted plans for international anti-terrorist police forces.[44] This indicated quite a significant shift of attitude: towards continental approaches which Britons had always felt themselves to be above in the past.

And yet it was not all *that* significant. By and large Britain's liberal values stood up well in the 1880s to the worst the Fenians and anarchists could throw at them. 'Englishmen,' said *The Times* in 1883, 'are proverbially jealous of anything that looks to them like an encroachment on their individual liberties. Rather than permit these to be interfered with, they will put up with a good deal of preventable annoyance and risk.'[45] *The Times* felt this was overdone: but even it did not suggest any concrete ways of remedying it. It was full of fine exhortations to firm and resolute action, but with very little in the way of practical advice. 'What we want,' it declared after the Whitehall bomb, 'is courage on the part of the authorities and the country to look the thing fairly in the face, and to act with the decision which has saved this nation from many more formidable dangers':[46] which was all very well, but hardly helpful. *The Times* clearly had not yet decided what the authorities should be decisive about. The clue it gave on another occasion did not advance matters much further. There was, it declared, 'but one course open at this moment – to unite to put down, by every means known to a civilized community, the policy of outrage, its authors, and its advocates.'[47] 'By every means known to a civilized community' at least implied some limits; and in fact indicated the difficulties of any more coercive approach. People were not ready for it. Certain measures they would accept: stricter regulations for the purchase of dynamite, for example, which Parliament passed in April 1883, and restrictions on the entry of people into the House of Commons – 'even the Ladies' Gallery' – after the 1885 Westminster bomb.[48] But there was no call to go further than this. No one seriously suggested press censorship, for example; or the banning of extremist organisations; or even *searching* people – especially women. ('An apparently enceinte matron could conceal under her apron enough dynamite to wreck the Abbey,' suggested the *Pall Mall Gazette* in 1885; 'How can police vigilance prevent that?')[49] One or two people advocated the expulsion of foreign dynamitards, but only very half-heartedly. No-one would have dared to suggest sending *Russians* back, to a system of justice which even *The Times* regarded as violating every civilised rule.[50] In the political climate of Britain in the 1880s, all this was simply not on.

Most of the bitterest press fulminations against the Fenians were the product of impotent anger: impotent just because of this. The situation created exasperation, which the *Pall Mall Gazette* acknowledged was 'natural'; but it warned that 'the dangers are too grave for exasperation to be a safe adviser'.[51] Very few allowed it to be. *The Times* in its calmer moments counselled that 'the first requisite is that people should not lose their heads or give way to a panic terror': not least because panic was precisely what the terrorists were out to induce.[52] Apparently they did not. Sir Algernon West, at the time of the St James's Square bomb, mused: 'It is very curious how calmly people take these outrages as matters of course!'[53] The press made a great deal of this: of the fact that the British were not the kind of people to be frightened into hasty measures by a few bombs. That was one of the marks of their superiority over the bombers: the dignity with which they went about their ordinary business, 'Unshaken, unseduced, unterrified'.[54]

There was in any case no call for panic in England, for two reasons: the failures of the dynamite campaign, and its lack of native roots. No amount of Fenian fire and smoke could obscure the former. 'In the midst of the long continued series of plots in which we are now living,' said *The Times* in November 1883, 'it is some satisfaction to think of the comparative ill-success with which many of them have met.'[55] The *Standard* in April 1883 found that it could 'hardly repress a smile of contempt'.[56] Even after the Westminster bomb in January 1885, the *Pall Mall Gazette* felt able to crow. 'Never was so vast, so vulnerable, a target' as London, it said, 'exposed to the malice and ingenuity of the soldiers of despair.' Yet after a dozen different attempts in the space of two years, what had they to show? 'Altogether they have not done more damage than £100,000 would easily make good. They have not killed a creature, blocked a railway, destroyed a building, or in any way checked for a moment the even flow of English life.' There was nothing here to frighten even the most timorous of Englishmen. 'A wretched twopenny halfpenny affair it is to be sure.'[57] This put it into perspective. So did the fact, which *The Times* dwelt upon, that so far 'the conspiracy is all connected with one question' – Ireland – and did not affect any other group. 'There is no spirit of general anarchy abroad, as there is in many Continental nations.'[58] This was another cause for calm. The British people were immune from the virus. 'Dissatisfied they might be with much in their lot, trades-unionists they might be, perhaps not always wise and moderate in their demands': but they were not anarchists. 'Their whole history and character, the whole history and character of their race, are dead against such a hypothesis.'[59] So far as Britain was concerned, there was no convincing sign yet of any 'enemy within'.

The Times implied that this was for racial reasons. A more general explanation – a venerable one – was that it was because of the virtues of Britain's institutions. 'We can, in this country,' said the *Saturday Review* in 1881, 'afford to look on the Socialist movement with greater composure than some of our neighbours, for our own institutions, being so free and constitutional, are less pregnable.'[60] The *'less* pregnable' may have marked a slight change in emphasis from the early 1870s, when Britons had generally considered themselves to be *entirely* safe. Nevertheless strong traces of the older doctrine still remained. ' "Infernal machines," ' claimed the radical *Reynolds's Newspaper* in July 1881, 'are the product of bad laws and bad governments, just as disease in the human frame is engendered by bad blood and a bad habit of body. Remove the former causes in both instances, and the effects will disappear.'[61] This sort of diagnosis was clearly behind the jury's recommendation in Most's case to mercy: 'he being a foreigner, and, perhaps, smarting under some wrong.'[62] It cut no ice with the judge, and it did not survive the Fenian campaign of 1883–5 unscathed; but still there remained for many years in liberal circles a presumption that the most hideous political atrocities could be explained as responses to suffering. Even those whose sense of outrage baulked at the sympathy and forgiveness this way of looking at it seemed to entail, were content to discuss dynamitism in terms of mental illness, which implied much the same. *The Times* in a single paragraph of a leading article in January

1883 talked of the dynamitard's 'distempered mind', his 'morbid fancy', his 'moral madness', his 'mania', his blindness to 'reasoning', and his liability to 'sudden outbreaks of frenzy':[63] language which suggested the need for restraint and treatment rather than punishment. It also implied a state of abnormality which seemed to absolve the social system: which was no more threatened by Fenians, therefore, than it was by the lunatic Maclean. Some people called them 'mad dogs'. Mad dogs can be menacing: but not to the fabric of society.

For all these reasons Fenianism provoked far more anger in Britain than fear; and anger was not a powerful enough engine to undermine her liberalism fundamentally. The consequence of this was that pressure from below on governments to do just this was almost non-existent. Even the angriest newspapers and politicians couched their prescriptions, as we have seen, in only the most general and vacuous terms, and adjudged the measures they saw the Liberal government taking against the Fenians – the 1883 Explosives Act and increased police protection of public buildings – entirely adequate. Any anger left over they generally vented on the American government for sheltering Fenians, on Parnell for tacitly encouraging them, or on Gladstone for 'pandering to treason' by wishing to conciliate Ireland.[64] Some people, including Johann Most when he was led down from the dock after sentence, muttered about the possible 'Russification' of Britain in the wake of these events;[65] but that was never remotely likely by any stretch of any imagination less fevered than Most's. Draconian laws against terrorism lay quite outside the bounds of acceptability in Britain in the 1880s. Which was nice for liberals, but created difficulties for their leaders: who had other pressures to face, as we shall see, besides popular ones.

CHAPTER 3

Foundation
1881–4

The pressures on governments in the 1880s to take extraordinary action against political extremists were of three kinds. In the first place there was the pressure that came with office: the burden of knowing that it was ministers who in the last resort were responsible for public safety in Britain, and in particular for the safety of public figures. It was all very well for newspapers and others to adopt attitudes of contemptuous indifference; but if a terrorist bomb ever did injure a minister, for example, or a visiting head of state, or – God forbid – the Queen, then that indifference would very soon, and very rightly, turn to blame of the government. The second source of pressure was the international community, of which Britain was perforce a part, and which ministers were more aware of than most people because it was to them that its demands were directly addressed. Those demands often had the support of the Queen, who in this matter of counter-subversion was far more internationally minded than most of her subjects. The third source of pressure on the government was its security forces, which at the beginning of the 1880s were very thin on the ground in mainland Britain, but were nevertheless ministers' only source of professional advice. Together these three sorts of pressure acted to incline governments of both main political persuasions to the view that more needed to be done to counter subversion than the general public seemed prepared to admit.

The minister directly responsible for these matters in Gladstone's second government was Sir William Vernon Harcourt, who was Home Secretary during the whole course of it, from April 1880 to June 1885. Whatever measures were taken to strengthen Britain's defences against terrorism in this period were Harcourt's doing, and his *enthusiastic* doing, by many accounts. Other members of the government appear to have taken little interest in what he got up to, apart from the Lord Lieutenant of Ireland Earl Spencer, who approved, and the President of the Local Government Board Sir Charles Dilke, who did not. In June 1882 Gladstone for example confessed to being 'absolutely ignorant of the machinery by which Secret Service is worked in either of its branches'.[1] He seems to have preferred it this way. In August the same year he did not cavil when Spencer told him that he purposely 'avoided writing about' such matters because he 'thought it better to let as few people as possible know exactly what we were doing as to detective work';[2] and a little later he was supposed to have deliberately absented himself from a cabinet meeting at which, against Harcourt's wishes, the subject was raised.[3] The subject was in fact raised at very few cabinet meetings, and then merely as a matter for report.[4] The result of this was that state security, so far as it affected the British mainland, was left in Harcourt's hands; and it may be that its development under him was consequently affected more than a little by his particular outlook and personality.

Both were complex. Harcourt was an unusual Liberal, even for this very confusing political time, when it was difficult to say how a usual Liberal should be defined. His antecedents were Whig and Tory, and he claimed Plantagenet blood, but passed himself off as a Radical: partly, some people felt, out of opportunism or cussedness. His Liberal credentials were in fact widely suspected amongst his colleagues: though this may have derived partly from the strong personal antagonism and irritations his abrasive manner provoked. Together with Lord Rosebery, with whom he continually quarrelled, Harcourt was one of the late-Victorian Liberal party's two rogue elephants. It is just possible that this contributed to his attitudes towards political terrorism and policing, which were not altogether wholly characteristic of the liberalism of his time.

They were not characteristic in the first place because of the seriousness with which Harcourt took the terrorist threat. This probably owed much to the special responsibilities of his office: 'If anything occurs,' he wrote to his Head of CID in January 1881, 'there will be a terrible outcry'[5]; and much also to the secret intelligence from America his office was privy to.[6] Sir Charles Dilke believed that much of that intelligence was unreliable, the fabrication of some 'sharp Yankee' out for a reward;[7] but Harcourt took it seriously, and became increasingly alarmed. That alarm subsided a little in the summer of 1881, as we have seen, when the first 'skirmishing' campaign failed; but Harcourt never allowed this to loosen his vigilance thereafter, for as he wrote to the Foreign Secretary in July 1881 'I know there are things which do not bear trifling with . . . & must be *stamped out*.'[8] He was more shocked than his colleagues by the *Freiheit*'s 'gross and shameful breach of public morality', and took the lead in bringing it to trial.[9] He was also shocked – as was everyone – by the Phoenix Park murders, after which one of Gladstone's secretaries described him as 'most frightfully despondent and as far as I can make out, bloodthirsty', to an unstatesmanlike degree.[10]

Harcourt's despondency was deep seated, and was another trait which distanced him from his colleagues. It was naturally aggravated by the main Fenian bombing campaign of 1883–5, which he regarded as rooted in the Irishman's 'unextinguished and inextinguishable hatred' of Britain, which only seemed to increase the more conciliatory the latter became.[11] At an 'informal' cabinet meeting in February 1883 he startled his colleagues with his 'violent views about Ireland', expressed in language which Lord Carlingford characterised as 'that of the lowest Tory'. According to Dilke he shouted out that no more concessions should be granted to Ireland, which henceforth could 'only be governed by the sword'. This outburst may have been, as Dilke noted later, 'only temper';[12] but it was born of a fundamental pessimism which few other ministers admitted to. Gladstone was not present at that meeting; but later on he too expressed his disagreement with Harcourt over this. Its particular focus was the bill being discussed in cabinet during 1882–4 to create a new municipal government for London, to which Gladstone was keen that the running of the Metropolitan Police should be transferred. That would bring the Metropolitan Police into line with all other mainland forces, and with what Gladstone conceived to be the basic liberal principle of local accountability. Harcourt's strong opposition to this police clause, which was eventually to scupper the bill, arose from his conviction that the immutability of the Irish problem made it essential that the state should always have at least one major anti-terrorist arm of its own. To abrogate all its powers to Watch Committees, which might not be entirely sound on the Fenian question, would be 'neither wise nor safe'.[13] Gladstone's resistance to that argument was founded partly on his reluctance to accept Harcourt's gloomy view 'that Fenian plots . . . are a permanent institution of the country'.[14] The contrast between them over this was significant. Gladstone still believed in progress, improvement, perfectibility; Harcourt, in this area, seemed not to any more. His attitude personified the change of ethos which has been mentioned before as one of the main factors behind the growth of Britain's political police. It helps to explain the vigour of his reaction to the Fenian threat; to which it is possible that any of the more traditional

37

liberals in Gladstone's cabinet would have reacted less vigorously.

It was not merely a question of attitude. Sir Charles Dilke's account of Harcourt's response to the London bombings suggests that it may also have been coloured by his emotional make-up. Dilke felt he *over-reacted*. At a cabinet meeting two days after the Whitehall bomb his fulminations provoked one minister to whisper that he seemed to want 'to expel all Americans including his own wife'.[15] At other cabinets he was pictured erupting frequently like an active volcano, and getting his way 'by dint of physical force'.[16] On one occasion when he was crossed over the matter of Secret Service money, he stormed out shouting that he was 'expected to fight Rossa with both arms tied up'.[17] He immersed himself in the task of countering the bombers to an extent which Dilke found faintly risible: 'I noted,' he commented later, 'that Harcourt thought himself a Fouché and wanted to have the whole police work of the country and nothing but police.'[18] From the very beginning of the London bombings he complained endlessly of the burden this work imposed on him.[19] Gladstone suspected at one point that this was merely to get out of other tasks, 'through laziness';[20] but it might also suggest that he found the pressure hard to take. The dejection and the sense of anxiety which pervade Harcourt's own letters as well as Dilke's recollection of his conduct indicate that he may have been acting under strain.

Of course one person's over-reaction is another's resolute response; and it may be that, in view both of the danger that threatened Britain in the early 1880s and of his colleagues' apathy in the face of it, Harcourt's expressions of alarm and frustration were reasonable. One person who certainly thought so was the Queen, who did not generally like Liberals but liked Harcourt at this stage of his career, regarding him, as her private secretary wrote to him in June 1881, as 'the only Minister of the present Government that had any determination'.[21] This however merely underlines the distinctiveness of Harcourt's contribution. It may be that any Liberal Home Secretary confronted with the situation of that time would have reacted similarly: that Harcourt's was the only possible response. Harcourt himself sometimes argued so: that if, as he wrote to Gladstone in March 1883, 'you had only to pass 24 hours of the life I am now leading your judgment on the subject' – of the control of the police – 'would be as fixed and unchangeable as mine'.[22] But it seems unlikely. On that particular issue, and on the question of the Secret Service fund, it is not easy to imagine any other Liberal minister fighting with quite so much *il*liberal conviction as Harcourt did. This may be important. The counter-terrorist measures of the early 1880s were very much the Home Secretary's personal pigeon. No one else in the government, apart from Spencer, was allowed any say at all in the details of them. More than most executive developments of modern British history, this one was the responsibility of a single man. It follows that that man's personal and in this case slightly idiosyncratic approach will probably have left a significant mark.

Harcourt was the sort of man, therefore, who was likely to respond positively to pressure put on him for strong measures against political crimes. That pressure came from a number of directions. One was the crimes themselves: dynamite explosions, political assassinations, and violent articles in Fenian and socialist prints. Another was popular opinion: though we have seen that that opinion was by no means as bloodthirsty in the face of these outrages as might have been expected. A third was the sometimes very *un*popular opinions of the Queen, who took a particular interest not only in Fenianism, but also in the activities of international anarchists in Britain.[23] One of her main complaints against Harcourt's Liberal successor at the Home Office, Hugh Childers, was that he failed to keep her as closely informed of 'the movement of dangerous foreign political intriguers' as Harcourt had used to do.[24] Her concern was probably derived partly from her obvious situation as a target, and partly from her special and highly informed interest in the continental European stage where most of the bloodiest anarchist dramas were acted out. Such influence as she exerted on Harcourt – always in favour of sterner measures[25] – was insignificant on its own. But it assisted in channelling another form of pressure, from abroad, which was almost certainly not.

Foreign pressure on Britain, to be of more help to continental countries in *their* battles against terrorism and subversion, went back at least to the 1850s.[26] It was a running grievance always, but especially at times like the early 1880s, when political violence on the Continent was particularly rife. Though it was kept hidden, it was the main factor behind the *Freiheit* prosecution of 1881. The particular agent of that pressure was Bismarck's minister in London, Count Münster, who requested the prosecution; but more important was the consideration that the case would act as a general palliative. Britain in the 1880s was in an awkward situation with regard to political crime. The targets of that political crime (before 1883) were nearly all foreigners, but many of its perpetrators, and the organisers that were supposed to succour them, were based in England, for obvious reasons. As the Home Under-Secretary put it in 1893: 'Of course if other States possess &

39

exercise the power of expelling Anarchists &c. from their Countries & England alone does not, all the Anarchists are bound to come to England.'[27] To the English themselves these people posed very little direct threat. The continentals' perspective, however, was naturally different. For many years they had been far more vigorous than Britain in their efforts to suppress subversion, and insistent that this could only be done really effectively internationally. Sporadically – generally when there were spates of revolutionary activity abroad – they devised schemes of co-operation between government and police forces to this end, only to be met, in every case, with resistance from Britain, whose participation was obviously vital. After the Tsar's assassination in March 1881 these schemes were renewed, with a Russo-Austro-German proposal for an international conference to discuss measures against nihilism, for example, and talks between Russia and France in June to the same end.[28] Britain's difficulty now, as in the past, was that international co-operation of the kind envisaged by continental governments generally implied altering her laws in ways which were thought to be 'politically impossible'[29] – allowing extradition for political offences, for example; and under a form of pressure – foreign – which would compound their unpopularity. The prosecution of Johann Most had the effect, and probably the object, of deflecting that pressure. 'The most effective way to avert the pressure of Foreign Govmnts to alter our laws,' wrote Harcourt to the Queen in April, 'is to demonstrate that those laws are adequate to give the protection which all Govmnts have the right to demand of their friends and neighbours.'[30] The Queen's secretary confirmed from her own sources of foreign intelligence that Most's conviction, when it came, was considered 'equal to joining the Nihilist Conference'.[31] It had placed Britain, as Harcourt told the Foreign Secretary in July, 'in a sound position both at home & abroad'.[32]

Another advantage of the Most prosecution was that it gave Britain a platform from which to berate the United States for its toleration of the Fenians. This may have been its intention. There can be little doubt that the Fenian outrages which had hit Britain just before the *Freiheit* article – the Salford barracks explosion and the Mansion House bomb – gave the British government a sense of common interest with the victims of continental political crimes which it had not, by and large, felt in the days when Britain had been thought to be immune. She now clearly needed American help against Fenianism as much as Germany or Russia needed her help; yet she could not ask more for herself than she was prepared to give to others. The conviction of *Freiheit* enormously strengthened Britain's case to the American government to prevent similar, and worse, sedition from being published in the New York *United Irishman*. That case was made forcibly in June 1881, and repeatedly thereafter: with Most (who was to become a fly in America's own ointment very shortly afterwards) featuring prominently as proof of Britain's own good record in this field.[33]

It was for this kind of reason that foreign pressure on Britain seemed less resistable in the early 1880s than it had been before. The Irish bombing campaign made the difference. For the first time for very many years it put Britain in the same boat as her continental neighbours, buffeted by the same terrorist waves. She was now, in this sense, part of the European community at last. It only remained for her to accrue to herself some of the other marks of membership: one of which was the institution of a proper political police.

The first move in that direction came very soon after Harcourt's arrival at the Home Office, in response to the Salford barracks bomb of 14 January 1881. Harcourt's reaction to that event was conditioned by the fact that he had been braced for it for some months past by the alarming prognostications of much worse outrages coming to him from the USA. These predisposed him to regard the Salford explosion – rightly, as it turned out – not as an isolated event but as part of a more general and ominous conspiracy, which consequently required general measures to be taken against it. The first of those measures was an order he gave on 23 January to his Head of CID, Howard Vincent, to put aside all his other work and 'to devote himself *exclusively* for the next month to Irish and Anglo-Irish business'.[34] What he particularly had in mind was intelligence, being, as he told Vincent, 'much disturbed at the absolute want of information in which we seem to be with regard to Fenian organisation in London'.[35] For this purpose, what was called a 'Fenian Office' was set up at Scotland Yard.[36] That office was to co-operate closely with Anderson, the Home Office's Fenian adviser and American spy-master; with Colonel Vivian Majendie, the Home Office explosives expert; with British provincial police forces; and with an Irish police inspector brought over specially.[37] 'A spiders web of Police Communication has thus been woven throughout the United Kingdom,' Harcourt reported to the Queen, 'the centre of which is in my office.'[38] In order to pay for an expansion of anti-Fenian undercover work – presumably rewarding informants – Harcourt in February asked for and got an increase in the Home Office Secret Service allocation, which for years had stood at £500 per annum, of another £300.[39] The idea behind the new arrangement, he wrote at the time, was to centralise the anti-Fenian effort, so that 'concentrated action may be taken if necessary with the least possible delay'.[40]

Shortly after this came the *Freiheit* affair, one of whose incidental effects was to extend the political activities of the police further still. Before it, the police had taken very little notice of foreign revolutionary exiles in Britain. Because of this, when the case first came up the police had no direct knowledge of their own about it. This was mildly inconvenient for the government, whose first intimation of the offending issue of *Freiheit* consequently came from the radical press and a foreign ambassador. The lack of police surveillance created a bigger problem in connection with a socialist meeting held on 23 March 1881, where Most was said to have repeated his original libel, but which the authorities could not proceed against because they had 'no authentic record' of it.[41] It was immediately after being informed of this meeting, by the Queen's secretary who had read about it in the *Daily Telegraph*, that Harcourt decided that from then on a regular watch should be kept on events like it. 'These meetings', he minuted to his under-secretary on the 26th, 'should be looked after for the future. Tell the Police to look after them.'[42] The instruction, though brief and casual in the only form it has come down to us, evidently envisaged a regular surveillance of at least some socialist organisations, whether or not any of them was suspected of contemplating crimes. This was new.

Clearly not too much should be made of these two developments; but they did mean that by March 1881 the Criminal Investigation Department of the Metropolitan Police had an embryo political arm. It did not involve any fundamental changes of practice or of principle. The detective branch had never shrunk, as we have seen, from investigating politically motivated crimes *ad hoc*, or from making enquiries into foreign politicos at other governments' request. Howard Vincent, the founder and Head of the CID, took the new duties easily in his stride. One of the qualifications he had brought to the job in 1878 was the close study he had made of the French police system, which had always had a political role; and he had clearly had tasks like this partly in mind when he had instituted his reforms.[43] He had men in the Central Office of the CID at Scotland Yard who had had experience of political work in the past, especially Adolphus Williamson, who a little later was described as having 'For a long series of years . . . been charged with matters of the greatest importance to the governments & of the most confidential character';[44] and two newly-promoted detective-inspectors, Hagen and von Turnow, who could understand

and interpret what the German socialists said.[45] Their efforts appear to have been diligent. In the summer of 1881 Harcourt confirmed to Granville that the 'Communists and their meetings' were being 'carefully watched';[46] and by October 1882 Vincent told him that 'early information upon the doings of the socialists' was flowing in.[47] In their case the surveillance exercised over them was probably sufficient: but only because there was little real danger from them. In the case of the Fenians, however, it may have been different. That the measures Harcourt took in 1881 against the Irish-American conspiracy were not altogether satisfactory is indicated by the fact that it was not long before they needed to be improved. The need for improvement was demonstrated by two more dramatic events: the Phoenix Park murders in Dublin in May 1882; and the beginning of the main London bombing campaign in March 1883.

The Phoenix Park outrage showed up the Irish police more than it did the English; but still it had repercussions on both. Its immediate effect was to highlight the inadequacies of the two Irish forces, the Royal Irish Constabulary and the Dublin Metropolitan Police, which Lord Spencer, for one, had no confidence in. To Gladstone two days after the murders he wrote that the 'case' he had against them was 'overwhelming'; every day, he claimed, brought 'fresh evidence of incapacity'.[48] The RIC, especially, had 'got out of hand of late years'; it all came, he said, 'of having only second rate men at their head'.[49] Others blamed the system, or the fact that the police were recruited from the peasantry;[50] but no one in the wake of Phoenix Park gave them (with the single possible exception of Inspector John Mallon of the DMP) high marks for detective skill. Consequently something drastic needed to be done. To Spencer there were a number of particular problems – leadership, for example, and lack of co-operation between the two forces; but the main one, as in London, was want of intelligence. It was, he emphasised to Gladstone more than once, essential to 'ferret out the Secret Societies'.[51] The trouble was that 'At present we know little more than that they exist.'[52] Occasionally well-founded rumours came to them of great plots coming to the boil, but never anything specific; 'We live therefore in anticipation of some disasters, but cannot prepare against them by previous information.'[53] It was with this in mind that Spencer on 7 May asked Gladstone if he could have 'some distinguished and experienced officer' sent over from England to 'help the heads of the Police' in this kind of work; someone, he suggested, like Colonel Henry Brackenbury, whom Sir Garnet Wolseley had recommended to him.[54]

Brackenbury was a protégé of Wolseley's, whose other qualification for this task was his apparent success in organising a military police force in Cyprus in 1878.[55] He was not at all keen on the Irish job offered to him on 9 May, itching, as he explained to the War minister, for 'active service'; but accepted on being told that Britain was effectively at 'war in Ireland', and that he could not very well refuse.[56] He did not stick at it for long, resigning only two months later with the intention of joining Wolseley in Egypt, to the great annoyance of the government, who accepted his resignation but stopped him going to Egypt out of spite.[57] Nevertheless while he was in the post, of 'Assistant Under-Secretary for Police and Crime', he achieved a great deal. Like Spencer, he despaired of the existing Irish police forces as effective agencies against political conspiracies and crime. Rather than trying to work through their existing structures, he believed that the responsibility for counter-Fenian work should be taken out of their hands. His idea was for a separate and highly secret organisation to be set up under him, which could call on the RIC and the DMP for assistance, but should also employ, as Spencer explained to Gladstone in June, 'men and methods' of his own. For this purpose he demanded an increase of £20,000 over and above the £4,600 customarily expended on secret service work in Ireland; 'The sum asked for is large,' Spencer admitted to Gladstone, 'but the forces to which we are opposed are very powerful and supplied with large sums of money as it is generally supposed.'[58] Gladstone and even Harcourt cavilled at this a little, but the money was pledged, for fear that Brackenbury might resign if it were not.[59] With it he embarked on the creation of an intelligence network aimed to destroy Fenianism at all its various sources, in America and mainland Britain as well as Ireland. That work, however, can hardly have got off the ground when Brackenbury's eventual resignation, according to Spencer, 'checked' it seriously, leaving his successor still with a daunting task.[60]

That successor was Spencer's own private secretary, Edward Jenkinson, who had been an Indian civil servant until ill-health had forced him home. This made him an object of intense suspicion to Irish Nationalists,[61] and Spencer admitted that 'Like many Indians he has not sufficient political instinct or regard for Parliamentary opinion'; but he also claimed that he was 'an excellent Liberal', 'very strong on the Land question';[62] and some of Jenkinson's letters reveal that he was indeed very far from being a straightforward 'rule them by the sword' sort of man. At bottom he believed that Fenian outrages grew out of genuine grievances, which could only ever be cured by means of Home

Rule; a policy he consequently urged strongly both on Spencer and on his Conservative successor, Lord Carnarvon.[63] In the meantime, however, outrages needed to be prevented some other way. That way, essentially, was Brackenbury's, which Jenkinson took over and extended thereafter, to the satisfaction of Spencer, Harcourt, Gladstone and the Queen.[64]

By March 1883 the Irish bastion of Britain's counter-Fenian fortress was built. 'During the past year,' announced Jenkinson in a memorandum, 'a system for watching the movements of the Fenians, and the operations of Secret Societies, has been established in Ireland, and a staff of specially selected Policemen, and of informants has been organised.' He was also in receipt of regular information from America.[65] The efficiency of this network was demonstrated by some impressive discoveries of explosives in Liverpool and Cork made at the end of March by the police acting on intelligence gleaned from Jenkinson,[66] and by a waning of political crime in Ireland generally. The weak link now was Britain, as the Glasgow and London bombs of early 1883 proved. The Fenian conspiracy, wrote Jenkinson, was as deeply implanted there as in Ireland itself. Yet apart from occasional reports from the sixteen RIC men stationed in Britain (four each in London and Liverpool, and two each in Birmingham, Manchester, Holyhead and Glasgow), and from Anderson at the Home Office, 'nothing is known of what is going on in England'.[67] Harcourt's perception of the problem was slightly different. For him the trouble lay partly with Anderson and his 'stray Irish constables', who found out 'mighty little', and neglected to pass *that* information on to the Metropolitan Police. 'When these two forces hunt the same game,' Harcourt wrote to Spencer, 'they spoil all sport.' He needed, therefore, 'a clear understanding with Jenkinson on this point'.[68] It was with a view to such an understanding that soon after the first London bombs he asked Spencer for the loan of Jenkinson for a while; as a result of which Jenkinson became involved in political police work on the mainland for the first time.

Jenkinson's recall was one of a number of moves made in response to the London bombing campaign. Another was the formation of a new 'Irish Bureau' within the Metropolitan Police CID around 17 March. That Bureau was headed by Chief Superintendent Williamson, who was instructed 'to be relieved of the greater portion of his regular duty & to devote his time entirely to Fenianism'. Under him was placed a staff of twelve, 'selected from the officers most conversant with Irish affairs'. There was also to be clerical and financial help. Williamson was to keep in daily touch with Vincent, Anderson, and the RIC men in London, and to report important facts directly to the Home Secretary.[69] The new body came together for the first time at 10 a.m. on the 20th:[70] it is generally taken to be the origin of what later became known as the 'Special Branch'.

Jenkinson, when he arrived in London, thought little of it. He had found, he wrote back to Spencer, 'not a man in Scotland Yard worth anything', with the possible exception of Williamson, who was 'steady' and 'trustworthy' but without 'a trace of brilliancy or dash'. He also had a low opinion of Anderson.[71] What *he* felt was needed was a new Home Office department over and above the new Scotland Yard branch, and over and above the provincial detective forces too, with Williamson and everyone else involved responsible to its head. That head in his turn would be responsible to the Secretary of State alone, who would give him wide discretion, much as Jenkinson himself was given in Ireland: what Jenkinson was proposing, in fact, was an almost exact replica of his office there. As well as being able to call on Williamson's services, the new official would employ agents of his own, to send to provincial towns with the object of setting up networks of informants, who would be given 'ostensible occupations' to avoid suspicion, and kept in ignorance of each other to preserve secrecy. Jenkinson was adamant that the new arrangement should be permanent. It was, he wrote,

> not a work to be taken up in troublous times, and then to be abandoned. It must be carried on persistently, patiently & methodically, and with a liberal expenditure of money, through quiet & uneventful times without any interruption, just in the same way as the Fenians carry on the work of their organisation.

If this were done he believed a great deal could be achieved: not immediately, for 'It would be up hill work at first and it would be some time before any important result would follow', but 'by degrees'.[72]

Harcourt took all these points. But he also foresaw difficulties. One was the fact that the new organisation would undermine local police autonomy, and so create friction. One solution to that was to keep it secret from provincial Chief Constables.[73] Another problem was 'to find *the man*'. Harcourt knew of no one suitable in England. 'What we want is a second Jenkinson. But where is he? J. was a happy accident. Can we hope to reproduce him? An incompetent man would do more harm than good.' They toyed with one or two names, including Charles Warren's,[74] before Jenkinson suggested Major Nicholas Gosselin, whom he knew as a Resident Magistrate in Ireland. Two of the qualities which recommended Gosselin to Jenkinson were his 'tact', which would help him with the Chief Constables;[75] and the fact that 'He understands these Irish scoundrels, and can *talk* to them'.[76] Another was that he was small enough to be sent back 'if the experiment did not succeed'.[77] But Jenkinson was confident that it would. Gosselin, he wrote, 'seems keen about the work and will I think do well'.[78] So he was given the job, in May.

Gosselin's task was to oversee Fenian intelligence-gathering 'in Glasgow and the Northern towns of England where large Irish populations congregate', under the direct command of the Home Secretary.[79] Jenkinson started him off with information and contacts,[80] to which he soon added his own. He also employed boys, *à la* Baker Street, for 'shadowing'.[81] By August he had recruited three brand-new (and presumably grown-up) informers, in Birmingham, Manchester and Liverpool.[82] Through one of these he told Harcourt that he hoped to provide him soon with 'a Paper giving the address of every [Fenian] Centre in Great Britain, and all the higher officers too'.[83] In January 1884 he reported triumphantly that 'I know every Fenian Leader of importance from the Tweed to Birmingham and could put my hand on them tomorrow.'[84] This was progress indeed. Jenkinson was highly pleased; for 'when he was appointed,' as he wrote to Harcourt in September 1883, 'I never hoped that his work would bear fruit so soon'.[85] Gosselin was also getting on well with those provincial police chiefs he needed to let into his secret because he lacked local resources of his own, like Chief Constable Farndale of Birmingham. His approach here was to assure them that his position was temporary, that he wished only to co-operate with them, and that they would get all the credit for anything they did together.[86] This mollified them, and contributed to the apparent success of the new spy system in its first eight or nine months.

It certainly seemed to be more successful than that of Anderson, whom Gosselin in effect displaced. In May Anderson was deprived of his right to receive intelligence from Williamson and the RIC, which made him 'a little sore';[87] but he was kept on at the Home Office on the understanding that he would extend his own 'staff of informants' in northern England and America.[88] By September, however, Jenkinson reported that he had still not 'found a single agent'.[89] His main value was the line of intelligence he had with Le Caron, who would report to no one else, and who on 30 April had signed a new contract (worth $1200 a year plus expenses) to inform on the activities of the Fenians in

Chicago.[90] It is likely that Le Caron was Anderson's *only* reliable spy. Harcourt gave the latter a dressing down at the beginning of 1884, which would have provoked most men into resigning, but not Anderson, who claimed he could not do without the money.[91] A way was found round this with a gift of £2,000 'as compensation'. In 1884 he was finally relieved 'entirely for the present of all my responsibilities & duties relative to Fenianism in London': apart, presumably, from his function as Le Caron's postman.[92]

This left Britain and Ireland with three new and distinct anti-Fenian agencies in the summer of 1883. Jenkinson had control of operations in Ireland, America and on the Continent; Williamson was in charge in London; and Gosselin had the rest of Britain. In addition there were the government's new Explosives Act, rushed through parliament in just an hour and a half on 9 April 1883;[93] scores of new police put on to guarding public buildings in London;[94] and the provincial city police forces, each of which took its own precautions against terrorism, some of them in co-operation with Gosselin and some in entire ignorance of him. This constituted Britain's defences against the Fenians. On the basis of it Harcourt told the Queen in June 1883 that he thought the 'mischief' was now 'well in hand', and that they had 'the enemy by the throat'.[95] A number of important arrests, including those of the bombers Gallagher and Whitehead in April by the Birmingham police with help from Williamson's men, seemed to justify this optimism.[96] But it did not last long.

Doubts started creeping in even before the end of 1883. From November 1883 Jenkinson's information about Irish-American plots started drying up.[97] 'I hear very little of what is going on,' he told Harcourt at the beginning of March the next year, 'so I cannot give much help.'[98] He was also, thought Harcourt, looking ill.[99] More serious, in view of the hopes he must have raised, was the fact that Gosselin's tide was also beginning to turn. 'I regret to say,' he wrote sadly to Harcourt in January, 'I have nothing but bad news to tell, all my plans have failed so far.' The man he had sent to infiltrate the Fenian leadership had been 'received very coldly', and there had been other set-backs too.[100] This was dispiriting, in view of the extensive new Fenian conspiracy which Gosselin himself had got wind of recently,[101] and which manifested itself in the London railway termini and Scotland Yard bombs of February and May 1884. Once again the dynamitards had proved more than a match for Harcourt, who had clearly not got things right yet.

So there was a new flurry of activity. The guard on public buildings, for example, was reinforced.[102] A urinal was closed at Windsor castle, on Majendie's advice, doubtless with the Scotland Yard bomb, which had been placed in a public lavatory situated directly underneath the Special Irish Branch, very much in mind.[103] (A little later on the Home Office became concerned when it was reported that the entire plumbing of the Palace of Westminster was being overhauled by a firm of Irish workmen.)[104] Another focus of attention was the ports, where it was decided in March 1884 – after several horses had bolted – to organise 'a more complete system of search . . . for dynamite and dynamiters'. It was partly to this end that Harcourt again in March 1884 asked Spencer to lend him Jenkinson; this time for a more extended stay.[105]

This bears all the signs of a measure of desperation. To a great extent it arose out of Gosselin's failure. The need for a more effective organisation of counter-Fenian work in Britain had been felt for some months before the new bombing outbreak, and Jenkinson's name considered in connection with it, but then rejected on the grounds that he was needed in Ireland more.[106] The railway bombs, however, rapidly shifted the government's priorities. Harcourt now had to have him. '*Pray don't refuse*', he urged Spencer; 'it is of most *vital consequence*' – the last two words double underlined.[107] A double underlining from Harcourt was difficult to refuse. Spencer kept him in suspense for one night, and then decided that he could do without Jenkinson for a while. 'He is very anxious about the undertaking', Spencer wrote to Harcourt; 'He fears that you will be disappointed with the results he will obtain.'[108] These apprehensions were not altogether groundless. But Jenkinson overcame them, and agreed to go; with important consequences for his own career, and for mainland Britain's counter-subversive police.

CHAPTER 4

The Irish Connection
1884–7

Jenkinson sailed from Dublin on 7 March 1884, and immediately set about posting police from the Royal Irish and London Metropolitan forces at ports all around Britain and on the Continent. Fifty-four Metropolitan men were involved altogether, including five sent to Rotterdam, Antwerp, Hamburg and Paris; and about thirty RIC.[1] Their role was to assist local customs officers in searching baggage for explosives, and to look out for suspected conspirators. In eighteen months they appear to have uncovered not a single stick of dynamite nor a solitary Fenian; but this by no means negated their value, as Jenkinson pointed out in December 1885, 'as a deterrent'.[2] In any case this was not the most important effect of Jenkinson's tranfer.

Its purpose was stated clearly in a memorandum he drew up for Harcourt the day before he left. 'If the work of uprooting the Secret Fenian Organisations, and of defeating the plans of the Dynamite Conspirators, is to be well and thoroughly done,' he wrote, then 'Great Britain & Ireland must be treated as one.' To this end he suggested that he combine his position as Assistant Under-Secretary for Police and Crime in Dublin with a similar one in Whitehall. From there he could supervise all the domestic secret service work – British, Irish and American – of the government. He should have final authority over his own agents, the Divisional Magistrates in Ireland, the Dublin Metropolitan Police, the Royal Irish Constabulary, Gosselin, and the relevant branches of all the different police forces in Britain. He should also be given a 'recognized position in the Home Office', which would confer this authority formally. The advantages of the system would be co-ordination among the different police authorities, which still tripped each other up sometimes, and continuity over successive administrations. The vital importance of the work demanded this.[3] Spencer, in a separate letter, agreed.[4]

Jenkinson did not get all his own way. One major stumbling-block was his demand for an official position in London, though he could never see why that should be. The problem here was that such a position would need to be sanctioned by Parliament, which might prove difficult – especially its Irish and Radical members – over something so illiberal and unconstitutional. This eventually was to be Jenkinson's undoing. For the time being, however, Harcourt agreed to all the rest. On 8 March he wrote to his under-secretary that he had told everyone concerned 'that my instructions are that Mr. Jenkinson's wishes shall be carried out'. Jenkinson was to be empowered, though not officially, 'to grapple with these conspiracies as a whole'.[5] He was given room 56 on the first floor of the Home Office, access to the Secretary of State, and a direct telephone line to Williamson's office at Scotland Yard.[6] From then until his resignation in January 1887 he remained based in London, though still on the Irish payroll, and in charge of all anti-Fenian intelligence world-wide.

It was in fact a miserable time for him. More than once he wrote back to Spencer to tell him of how 'dreadfully discouraged & down hearted' he was in London, and how much he would have liked to give the work up 'if it were not that I should feel it were cowardly'.[7] One reason for this was the inherent difficulty of his task. 'It is impossible in a secret warfare of this sort,' he wrote, 'that the enemy should not have a success sometimes.' Jenkinson could not hope to be 'omniscient'.[8] The Fenian conspirators were few in numbers, 'But at the same time they represent the feeling of a large class of Irishmen.'[9] That was the rub. 'The feeling against us, and the determination to work actively against us are much stronger than they were, and these we shall *never* conquer.' The only way to abolish dynamitism altogether was to adopt 'measures which will remove the hostile feeling'. By that he meant Home Rule. The only effective alternative to that was the other extreme: 'a system like they have in Russia', which even there was not a complete success.[10] The sort of middle way Britain was following was even less likely to succeed. That was Jenkinson's main problem; but it was one he could have lived with, he claimed, if those around him had helped him more.

Jenkinson's difficulties with nearly everyone around him in London bedevilled most of his three years there. It started with the Metropolitan Police's Irish branch, which he had never much respected, and which seemed to him to deserve his respect less the more he came to know of it. It had two main faults. The first was indiscretion. In April 1884 he wrote to Spencer complaining at an article which had appeared about him in a newspaper, which he said could do 'great harm', and which was the fault of the Scotland Yard people: 'They *cannot* hold their tongues.'[11] That may just have been simple folly. On other occasions it arose from a desire to boast. The result was the same: whenever the police got a clue in a case, for example, 'such publicity is given to it that it is impossible to follow it up'.[12] Majendie, the Home Office's explosives expert, was guilty of the same thing. 'I think he enjoys making his discoveries public,' wrote Jenkinson to Spencer in May 1884, 'but it is very mischievous.'[13] It alerted Fenians to what the authorities were up to, which was the last thing Jenkinson wanted. 'The first requisite in a Detective', he wrote, 'is silence and secrecy, and the Scotland Yard men want to be taught that lesson badly.'[14] Besides this, he regarded the Metropolitan Police's anti-Fenian branch as hopelessly inefficient. 'There is not a man there with a head on his shoulders,' he wrote after the Scotland Yard bomb explosion in May 1884; 'They have no information and if anything happens they all lose their heads, and everything is confusion.'[15] For this sort of work they were 'worse than useless'. What was needed was 'a really good man in Vincent's place', to reorganise the whole CID from the top down.[16]

That new man came in the middle of June 1884; but immediately proceeded to make things worse. Vincent's replacement was James Monro, whose previous job had been as chief of police in Bengal, where as Harcourt told the Queen 'they had to deal largely with secret societies';[17] and it may be that this experience persuaded him that he could cope on his own with Britain's secret societies, without Jenkinson's aid. For his part Jenkinson regarded Monro as 'a very good man in his way', but with little 'energy or originality', and too content to leave things to Williamson, 'who is very slow and old fashioned'. 'I was hoping', he wrote to Spencer, that Monro 'would carry out some reforms in the office and in the system of working, but he does not seem inclined to move, and is rapidly becoming a real old Scotland Yardite.'[18] In December 1884 he found he 'could not possibly hold my tongue any longer', and gave Monro and Williamson 'a bit of my mind', which left them both feeling 'very much hurt',[19] and cannot have helped relations between them thereafter. In January 1885 he told Spencer, as an illustration of Scotland Yard's incapacity, how they had failed altogether to trace a suspect whom *he* had then managed to ferret out 'with a little trouble in an hour. And this is the kind of thing which is happening constantly.'[20] Later that month he blamed them for not acting more effectively on information he passed to them in December 1884 about a plot to blow up the House of Commons: 'What is the good of getting good information,' he asked Spencer the day after the Westminster explosions, 'if this is all that comes of it'?[21] He claimed that they made 'no attempt whatever . . . to obtain information' of their own: 'In the whole of London they have not got a single informant, & they do not know in the least what is going on.'[22] His impatience with the Scotland Yard people increased, to such an extent that by July 1885 he was accusing them of wholesale corruption: 'There is hardly a man among them who does not take money.'[23] But the main quarrel between them was over intelligence, which each complained the other kept jealously to himself, to the obvious detriment of the national effort against the Fenian threat.

The main offender in this regard was clearly Jenkinson,[24] though to his own mind he had a perfectly good reason for it. That reason was Scotland Yard's ineptitude, which made it dangerous to entrust almost any information to it until it was necessary in Jenkinson's judgement for it to act. 'It is always a long time before information becomes ripe for action,' he wrote to Spencer in June 1885; if he was made to 'hand over information from day to day *piecemeal* to the Metropolitan Police', there was no saying what blunders they might commit.[25] The chief danger was that they might move in too soon. This could easily 'throw suspicion on my informants & endanger their lives', as nearly happened on a couple of occasions;[26] or else warn the major conspirators away before a case could be made out against them. The same result would follow if the police's surveillance was too clumsy. If the Fenians suspected that they were being watched, Jenkinson wrote to Harcourt in March 1883, then 'they will be off and the whole game will be up'.[27] In January 1884 he asked the Birmingham Chief Constable to call off his surveillance of the dynamiters Daly and Egan for just this reason. 'I do not want Daly to be driven away from Birmingham because I do not know where he would go,' and because – he added ingratiatingly – he could not trust a police officer in any other town 'to deal with such a delicate matter so well as yourself'.[28] Gosselin suspected that policemen warned Fenians off their patches on purpose; that, as he put it to Harcourt, 'Chief Constables in Great Britain, as a rule, act in these matters with a view to merely keep their own Districts free, and let other look out for themselves'.[29] This was another way in which Britain's lack of a national police force, which Jenkinson and Gosselin both deplored, hampered her efforts against crime. Consequently it seemed only prudent for them to keep their hands hidden. Monro greatly objected to this; and also to the fact that Jenkinson's secret (RIC) police in London were entirely outside Monro's control. (Jenkinson claimed that Monro, ludicrously, 'encouraged his men to follow the R.I.C. about & to report about them'.)[30] This was seen as an insufferable incursion on his legal authority, not only by Monro, but also by the Home Secretary, who had always insisted – whatever Jenkinson's understanding had been – that 'I must have everthing done through the *Met. Police* and the *Met. Police alone*'.[31]

It was Harcourt's siding with Monro over these matters which hurt Jenkinson most. He felt that his new chief had lost faith in him as early as the summer of 1884. Harcourt seemed more impressed by dramatic police *coups* than by quiet prevention behind the scenes, and Jenkinson had none of the former to show after the arrest of Daly and Egan at Easter 1884. That impressed Harcourt immensely, and possibly gave him false hopes, *via* Gosselin who had intimated beforehand that it 'wd about finish them'.[32] It did not, however, but was followed by a spate of new outrages, which no one managed to prevent. 'I daresay Sir W. Harcourt blames me,' Jenkinson wrote to Spencer in June 1884, 'and thinks I am doing nothing and know nothing.'[33] In December he apparently told him so: that 'I have told you Jenkinson that your system of secret working is useless. It comes to nothing.' Jenkinson naturally found this 'really very disheartening'.[34] He insisted that they prevented more crimes than they missed. But he admitted that 'we have not got the better of these Dynamitards. They still go on plotting outrages, and when they do commit an outrage our police are not successful in finding them out.' One reason for this was the inherent difficulty of the task. 'I never expected to be always successful. In a war such as this there must be some reverses and some failures.' It was becoming harder all the time, because the Fenians themselves were getting cleverer. 'Experience has taught these dynamiters the necessity of working secretly and of using only picked and trusted men. A plot is confined to three or four men, and not one of them can be got at.' He was not to blame, therefore, for the inadequacy of his intelligence, which was inevitable.

Less inevitable, in his view, was the continued inefficiency of the police, on whom Jenkinson tried to shift most of the blame. 'As regards action & turning information to account', he wrote, 'I was much more successful in Ireland than I can ever possibly be in England.' The reason for this was that he had had 'good materials ready to hand' there, 'and the Force being an Imperial one, I was able to establish a system which could be worked by one Head'. In England, by contrast, there was 'the greatest jealousy of me & my Irish staff'; the detectives were 'utterly useless'; and it was 'quite impossible to establish any system because there is no central authority over the Police, and each Force whether in County or Town is separate from & independent of the other'. All that Jenkinson could do was to give advice, which was often disregarded, or 'rendered valueless by the clumsiness or the stupidity of some so-called detective'. The 'real fact', he finished up, was that 'nothing short of an Imperial Staff of Police specially selected or organized for this particular purpose', and under a single Head, would give them 'real hope of success, or rather comparative success' in this field. In the meantime they could only struggle with what they had.[35]

If this was supposed to make his political master think better of Jenkinson, it appears not to have worked. Harcourt only became more convinced of his impotence. 'Our enemies are making rapid progress in the art of attack', he wrote to Spencer shortly afterwards; '– we none in those of defence. O'Donovan Rossa and Ford send their men over just when they like and do just what they please. We get little information and what we do get is useless to us and our informers are always found out'.[36] (He had just been told that one of them, Thomas Phelan, had been murdered in New York.)[37] In January he wondered whether he was getting any value at all for his department's by now considerable secret service bill.[38] Jenkinson continued to try to divert his fire towards Monro, especially over the matter of the Westminster bombs,[39] but to no avail. On 21 May 1885 the row blew up. In an effort perhaps to persuade Harcourt that his system did work, Jenkinson saw him and began to retail to him some of the intelligence his agents had gathered recently. He was not allowed to get far.

> He stopped me abruptly & said 'Does Monro know of this.' I replied 'No – no action is contemplated at present. When the time comes I shall tell him. Secrecy is very important and if the Scotland Yard men get on to these men, my sources of information will be endangered.' He then said 'It is monstrous that the London Detectives should not know of these things. For two years you have been flying in my face, spending money on getting information and doing nothing. I shall this evening write a minute ordering you to tell everything to Mr. Monro, & if you like you can take the responsibility of disobeying my orders. It is all jealousy, nothing but jealousy, you like to get information & keep it to yourself. You are like a dog with [a] bone who goes into a corner and growls at any one who comes near him.[40]

The next day Harcourt apologised; but it did nothing to heal the rift. Four weeks later he summoned Jenkinson and Monro to his room at the Home Office to sort the quarrel between them out. He had clearly made up his mind against Jenkinson.

> He would not listen to anything I had to say about the necessity of protecting my informants. He insisted that I should give all my information

at once to Scotland Yard, and once even went so far as to say that I should place my informants at Mr. Monro's disposal. And he also desired me to withdraw all the R.I.C. men who are getting information for me from London.

In Jenkinson's view this amounted to a betrayal of the assurances made to him (in writing) in March 1884. The result, he wrote to his patron afterwards, was that Harcourt 'has thrown me over altogether'.[41]

This row between Jenkinson, Monro and Harcourt had a number of different aspects. The least important was probably the personal. All three participants were men whose temperaments were liable to clash. Monro's seems on the surface to have been the least abrasive, but that may be because fewer letters expressing his feelings survive. It may be significant that his quarrel with Jenkinson was followed shortly afterwards by an even stormier one with his new Metropolitan Police chief, Sir Charles Warren.[42] Jenkinson expressed his feelings at considerable, and repetitive, length in writing, which, if he was as prolix in his conversation, may have been one of the things which irritated Harcourt, who was in any case an irritable man. Jenkinson found him 'unreasonable', 'changeable', 'impulsive', 'unscrupulous', 'unjust', and 'just like a spoilt child'.[43] For his part Harcourt claimed that the whole problem had arisen from Jenkinson's 'ungovernable' temper and his 'overbearing treatment' of Scotland Yard.[44] But he also felt there were greater issues at stake.

One of those issues was constitutional. Jenkinson's position in London was a highly irregular one, as Harcourt began to see clearly after the panic which had originally led him to bring the Irish spy-master over subsided. At the height of that panic he had made promises to Jenkinson, of powers over the Metropolitan Police Force, for example, which in retrospect seemed rash, and potentially embarrassing if they were discovered by unsympathetic politicians. 'I have pointed out to him over and over again', wrote Harcourt to Spencer in June 1885, 'that the Comms. of Police are the persons and the only persons constitutionally responsible for the protection of life and property in London, and that I have not the right even if I had the wish (which I have not,) to over-ride their authority by establishing a superior or even a concurrent Police authority in London.' This was why he wished to pack the RIC men off home, and to confine Jenkinson's role within London now to a passive one. The task of actively seeking out information there was exclusively Monro's. If Jenkinson 'happened' to come across information in London he was to pass it on to him. Outside London he could take a more positive intelligence-gathering role, but if any intelligence thus gathered bore on London, then that, too, had to be communicated immediately to Scotland Yard.[45] That was the only division of responsibilities consistent with constitutional legality. Jenkinson, with his insensitivity to consti-tutional and political niceties, saw it mainly in terms of departmental rivalries and personal betrayal, but this was not the whole of it. Fundamentally the difference between him and Harcourt was between a professional's and a politician's point of view; or, by another way of putting it, between what was expedient and what was correct.

As well as this, there was one further important issue at stake in this affair. That was to do with concepts and methods of anti-Fenian policing. It was hinted at in Jenkinson's complaint against Scotland Yard for its lack of discretion, which to him seemed just irresponsible, but which in fact was based on a fundamental disagreement over the need for secrecy. This may have derived partly from the old preference for preventive over detective methods in British police tradition. Chief Commissioner Henderson told Jenkinson in June 1885 that Monro shared this preference: that 'He objects to *all* Secret Agents'.[46] It may not have been quite like that: not an objection to secret agents as such, but to the kinds of uses they were put to. Harcourt appears to have gone along with Monro on this. He was certainly less enamoured of secrecy than was Jenkinson, and for better political reasons than the latter could ever conceive.

The problem with secrecy for politicians was that it could get them into trouble. Informers and agents were seldom dependable types of people. One 'greedy drunken fellow' called Mottley caused all sorts of problems for Jenkinson in the summer of 1883 when he started boasting of his exploits and had to be protected by the government in consequence.[47] A more serious case was that of 'Red Jim' MacDermott, who was reported to be under sentence of death from his Fenian colleagues in north America as an informer at around the same time. If he was murdered, wrote Jenkinson, it would be his own fault for being indiscreet; but it would also be 'a most disastrous thing for me'. Every other potential informer would be frightened away, 'and the sources of my informations would be dried up'. He requested, therefore, that MacDermott be arrested on a trumped-up charge, in order to divert suspicion from him.[48] This was done eventually; but Harcourt was not at all pleased. 'It was very near being a great scrape,' he told Spencer afterwards, 'as the processes of the law ought not to be employed for prosecutions which are not *bonâ fide*, and our friends in their zeal are very apt to go slap dash into situations without looking sufficiently before they leap.' It was a small incident, but a potentially embarrassing one, which should serve, he advised, 'as a warning for the future'.[49]

For the men who were ultimately answerable to Parliament for the conduct of the secret service, such risks may have seemed too great. This would account for the differences between Harcourt's and Jenkinson's approach to counter-terrorist work, which were fundamental. Jenkinson should have seen this from the beginning. If he had, then he might have stopped complaining about provincial policemen frightening Fenians off their manors, which clearly did not shock Harcourt half as much. In June 1884, shortly after Jenkinson arrived in London, Harcourt told him how *he* thought he should work. He called it 'picketing'. The idea was that Scotland Yard should put watches or 'pickets' on all the suspects revealed by Jenkinson's secret information, in order to deter them from committing crimes. 'He says', wrote Jenkinson, 'it is the easiest thing in the world to do and if the men are driven abroad they should be followed & picketed there also.' It followed that to be successful the 'pickets' had to be visible. This was totally at variance with the secret service line.

Jenkinson dismissed it as 'impractical'. Even if Scotland Yard were up to the job, which they were not, 'all the picketing in the world couldn't choke off these Dynamiters'. What he thought was needed was information, which it appeared 'Harcourt does not believe in'.[50] The best information was to be got through 'reliable agents of good class'.[51] It was 'quite impossible to find out the plans of these conspirators' merely by watching them,[52] and counter-productive if they knew they were being watched.[53] The only way to keep tabs on them was to spy on them without their knowledge. If that were done in Glasgow, wrote Gosselin to Harcourt in August 1883, then 'nothing could happen for the future' there without its being known to the authorities; 'it being more than probable the same tactics, the same Houses and People would be again used'.[54] That way they would always know what was going on; which was preferable to frightening it into less accessible lairs.

So Jenkinson stuck to his guns. That gave Harcourt an opening against him, when the outrages continued through 1884. 'I have been doing all in my power to make you watch these Fenians *openly*,' he told him in December, '& you won't do it. But if you had followed my advice you would have put a stop to all this long ago.'[55] That may have been unjust, but because picketing had, in Harcourt's words, 'never been fairly tried',[56] it was impossible to tell. All that could be said was that

Jenkinson's method had not proved an undiluted success. Despite its secrecy, the Fenians had tumbled and adapted to it, and become more dangerous – as Jenkinson admitted – as a result. It was always possible to argue, therefore, that the alternative would have been a surer deterrent; as well as being closer to Britain's traditional usages, and less likely to get ministers into 'scrapes'.

That is mere hypothesis. What is less hypothetical, however, and is also important, is the conflict this affair reveals between two very different counter-terrorist policing philosophies of the time. On the one side there was Williamson's and Monro's old-fashioned 'Scotland Yardite' approach, which was rooted (despite Monro's colonial background) in the Metropolitan Police's liberal and Peelite past. Scotland Yard had come to accept the need for detectives, certainly in this kind of field; but it saw their role as not very far removed from that of the uniformed police. So far as possible they should prevent crime, by acting on what they knew as soon as they knew it, even if that meant saving putative criminals from the retribution that would have followed if they had been allowed to mature their plans. They accepted disclosures from informers, but did not go out of their way to cultivate them, and certainly not by means of wholesale deception, like setting spies up in artificial or 'front' occupations. Hence Jenkinson's oft-repeated complaint about Scotland Yard's lack of informants, which he regarded as ineptitude, but for them was a matter of deliberate policy.

This – the spy system – was the Irish practice, which was still regarded with distaste in British police circles, and accounted for much of the ill-feeling towards the RIC. When Jenkinson came he tried to introduce this Irish practice into Britain, which is what set the pigeons fluttering at Scotland Yard. Neither Monro nor Harcourt ever trusted either his effectiveness or, one suspects, his honesty. Their lack of confidence in his effectiveness arose from their differences with him over means; which differences also account for Jenkinson's contempt for Monro's men. Their doubts about his honesty, which they only ever expressed obliquely,[57] were a natural corollary of his whole Irish approach, which seemed actively to encourage moral corruption of various kinds. We shall be dealing with some possible manifestations of this in the next chapter. For the time being it is only necessary to note the battle that was going on for the soul of mainland Britain's counter-terrorist agencies in the later 1880s, which ended in defeat for the new methods – or seemed to – in January 1887, when Jenkinson resigned.

The events which led up to his resignation are obscure, partly because

Spencer's departure from office in June 1885 left Jenkinson without a patron-confessor in whom he could confide.[58] Harcourt's successor at the Home Office was Richard Assheton Cross, who in July 1885 was lulled into thinking that he had repaired the rift between Monro and Jenkinson;[59] but it went on simmering after that. In the summer of 1886 they were at loggerheads again, this time over one of Jenkinson's 'secret agents', a man called Dawson (*alias* Winter), who came under the CID's notice for perjury and fraud. Jenkinson tried to persuade Monro to intervene to protect his man, and when Monro refused – 'correctly' – he tipped Dawson off, so that he escaped abroad. On this issue, which Monro saw as a matter of principle, the Home Office took Jenkinson's part and Warren took Monro's. Warren wrote to the Home Secretary that the episode showed Monro to have been 'perfectly correct in his intimation regarding the impracticality of working in unison with Mr. Jenkinson', in whom he himself had now 'ceased to put any confidence'.[60]

Things could not go on like this. The CID's Irish Branch was particularly seriously affected. Much as Monro and presumably Williamson rejected Jenkinson's charges, and counter-attacked through Harcourt, the affair can have done nothing for its morale. That morale, and the Branch's efficiency, may also have been affected more tangibly by Jenkinson's new role. One of the first things he did on his arrival in London in March 1884 was to hive off nine out of the Branch's original thirteen members to work at the ports, leaving their places to be filled by less experienced men. Those men had their hands full. Two of them were employed searching baggage at Charing Cross and Victoria stations, four of them were on night duty (in two shifts), and one was a clerk, leaving just six men for enquiries and surveillance. Only three of them were Irish. They were not enough. In April 1884 the Police Commissioner requested, and was given, an augmentation of four Irish constables to strengthen them.[61] By August the total number had increased to twenty-two: seven shadowing suspects, eight on night duty, four on 'reserve' at the Office to take up 'enquiries that may come in', and three clerks.[62] Still they found themselves stretched: especially Williamson, who apparently died as a result of this over-work.[63] Although it is difficult to tell, and would be wrong to accept Jenkinson's judgements at face value, they do not appear to have been unusually effective, and were once or twice, as we have seen, ludicrously lax. They were not the government's front-line troops against terrorism, who had their somewhat uncomfortable billet in Room 56. Apart from the name, which became attached to it by popular usage and was never official, there was nothing yet very 'special' about the Metropolitan force's Irish branch. Its day, however, was to come.

It came because Jenkinson's own day came to an end at the beginning of 1887, leaving a vacuum which Williamson's branch helped to fill. There were a number of reasons for Jenkinson's demise, on top of the ones which had nearly provoked it so often before. One general one may have been a relaxation in the (new Conservative) government's attitude of vigilance in the face of terrorism, once the main dynamite campaign had come to an end. Harcourt's successor Cross, for example, was not nearly so obsessed with Fenian affairs, partly because he did not need to be. Lord Carnarvon, who followed Spencer in Dublin, did share most of *his* concerns, including his view that the Fenian dogs were merely sleeping, which made Jenkinson's role as vital as it had ever been. Carnarvon expected, as he wrote to the Chancellor of the Exchequer at the end of 1885, 'very serious trouble before long', which meant that 'it wd be nothing short of madness to weaken in any way the one agency that exists for the detection and prevention of gross political crime.'[64] That appeared to him to be Cross's intention, when he refused to go along with a proposal of Jenkinson's – his old plan, pressed more insistently now – to give him an official position in Whitehall. Jenkinson now argued that he needed this in order to end his own personal uncertainty about his future and his pension.[65] He also wished, by shedding some Irish 'detail work', to be able to devote his whole time 'to collecting information from all parts and weaving it into one whole'.[66] Cross however explained that he had 'no opening for him'.[67] Carnarvon professed himself 'astonished' at his 'treating what may be so serious a matter so lightly'.

> I must suppose that he knows that Jenkinson holds all the threads of these conspiracies, is alone able at present to deal with them, and has repeatedly declared that he can deal best with them in London rather than in Ireland. To set all this aside as a matter of secondary importance seems to me simple madness.[68]

Carnarvon suspected that parsimony might lie behind it. The Chancellor of the Exchequer was certainly anxious to reduce the Secret Service vote, which by 1885–6 had soared to £11,326 for the Home Office.[69] On this particular question, however, the Chancellor assured him that he would raise no financial objection to any arrangement that was decided;[70] and Cross himself denied that he undervalued Jenkinson. He thought, he wrote to Carnarvon, 'very highly' of him. 'It is quite clear that he has a very good knowledge of things abroad, and very accurate information of what is likely to happen with the exception of one solitary instance' (presumably the Burkham case).[71] He was also aware of the possibility of new outrages in Ireland and England 'whenever Mr. Parnell finds that he cannot have his way'. He knew therefore 'that his [Jenkinson's] services are likely to be necessary for some time to come', and he was 'willing and anxious to pay him handsomely'. The difficulty, so far as he was concerned, was finding an 'office' for him in London; and he wondered why the existing arrangement, whereby Jenkinson worked ostensibly for the Irish government, could not continue.[72] The reasons for *that*, replied Carnarvon, were firstly that Jenkinson himself was adamant about it, and secondly that 'the maintenance of him on the Irish estimates will bring upon you & the Govt. in the H. of Commons an enormous amount of trouble'.[73] This, however, was precisely Cross's objection to his being transferred to the Home Office grant.

Lord Salisbury, reading through the correspondence on 'this Jenkinson business', declared himself unable to 'get at the bottom' of it. Both parties professed themselves anxious to keep Jenkinson, but each preferred the other to incur the odium of defending him before a suspicious and hostile House.[74] This may indicate the fundamental reason why Jenkinson left, a year later. It was a combination of two factors. The first was the unpopularity or anticipated unpopularity of his sort of activity in Britain, which had the effect of limiting the scope of that activity as soon as it needed to be officially acknowledged in some way. Liberalism in Britain may have been stretched and strained by some of the things that hit it in the 1880s, but it remained pure enough for political policing and espionage on the Irish pattern still to appear incongruous. The second and related factor was a certain weakening of anti-terrorist resolve amongst ministers, which was probably attributable to the fact that the dynamite danger no longer seemed a pressing one. This made them less willing, as Carnarvon put it, 'to fight [for] an appointment which cannot command much enthusiasm & which may meet with opposition': less willing, for example, than Spencer and (originally) Harcourt had been. Carnarvon was as guilty of this as Cross, though he argued that the latter's parliamentary difficulties would only be a tithe of his. Both regarded Jenkinson as 'indispensable', or said they did;[75] neither, however, would take the political risk necessary to secure him. That can only be because the political risk for the moment seemed more real than the terrorist one. Jenkinson, who resigned in protest with effect from 10 January 1887, felt scurvily treated. Spencer, commenting on the affair to Harcourt, agreed.[76] (Harcourt did not.)[77] But then Jenkinson, as Spencer had pointed out at the very beginning, 'like many Indians' never had properly understood politics.

The government's problem was a real one. Public unease at political policing in Britain still ran deep. Harcourt himself was sensitive to it. To the Queen in the summer of 1884 he wrote of its implications: 'there is such a violent prejudice against that *espionage* which can alone remark these secret plots that the task of detection is very difficult'.[78] He spoke of the same difficulty on another occasion to an audience of London policemen. Replying to criticisms of their detective system he observed that 'Those who complained of the faults of that system were often the first to denounce the very methods by which it could be made effectual', such as 'any organised system of espionage.' That was unfair. People had to recognise that 'if they were called to play an above-board game against men who played against them with loaded dice and marked cards, against the midnight marauder, the skulking assassin, and the secret society, they must expect to be baffled and defeated.' At this stage Harcourt seemed to imply that this was not a bad thing. People were right to prefer the 'protective and defensive' role of the British police to a detective system which involved underhand methods. If bafflement was the price of this, then it was an acceptable one.[79] This fitted in with a widespread feeling in Britain at that time: of positive *pride* in her detectives' lack of prowess.

The Queen's secretary expressed this feeling in 1883, when he wrote to Harcourt to congratulate the police on their capture of a dynamitard in spite of the fact that detective work was not their '*forte*'; 'I doubt if Englishmen ever could take up the business as the French do.'[80] That may have been just old English gentlemanly prejudice; but that a lot more could rest upon it was suggested by a long *Times* leading article on the British police which followed the decoration of one of them (a uniformed man) for his bravery at the time of the Palace of Westminster bomb in 1885. As always in this kind of analysis a start was made by contrasting the Continent, where, claimed *The Times*, the police were 'regarded as the natural enemies, or at any rate as the habitual antagonists', of the ordinary man. In England it was different. There,

> The policeman is the friend of every peaceful citizen, and even the less orderly classes do not regard him with active animosity. He guards our houses, he regulates the traffic of the streets, he helps us at difficult crossings, he is the arbiter of trivial disputes, his patience is inexhaustible, and his temper imperturbable. He has his faults, no doubt, like the rest of us;

but it is precisely because he is so much like the rest of us that his mild sway is undisputed. He does not belong to a caste apart, he is not permitted to regard himself as infallible, and he is not inclined to magnify his office. He is not, indeed, by any means infallible or impeccable; he is honest and sturdy, but, perhaps, a little obtuse; he is not very adroit in the diagnosis of difficult matters, being apt to confuse apoplexy and drunkenness, with a presumption in favour of the latter not altogether inconsistent with his actual experience, and his detective faculties are perhaps unduly limited.

But none of this was really a failing. In fact it went, *The Times* claimed, 'to the root of the matter . . . as to the general relation of the police to the community'. There was 'not a little to be said' for both systems: the English, and the 'inquisitorial'. But they were 'not easily combined'.

> In a free country the police is most effective when it is treated as the ally of the community in the common warfare against wrongdoing. It may be less successful in the detection of exceptional crimes; but it is far more successful in the prevention of ordinary misdeeds. A popular police force is thus the safest and least irksome security for the peace, order, and tranquillity of a civilized and law-respecting community. If any proof of this is needed we only have to point to the police of London and to the unexampled ease and success with which its duties are discharged.[81]

Obtuseness was thus more than a tolerable failing in the British police. It was almost a prerequisite of their particular sort of success.

This consideration may have acted as a genuine restraint on the effective development of political detective work in mainland Britain: in 1884–7, for example, when it tied the government's hands in relation to Jenkinson. But it also had another effect. As well as discouraging certain kinds of policing, it also strengthened the argument for their concealment, if despite these prejudices they still emerged. That concealment in turn could have acted as a protective cloak beneath which they could emerge more easily: which meant, ironically, that the feeling against political detective work may indirectly have encouraged its growth. This was likely, if not inevitable, in a situation where the priorities of the public and of the professionals were so very far apart. *The Times*, speaking for the public, may have found PC Plod reassuring; but Jenkinson and Harcourt both knew that he was no match for the cunning and unscrupulous conspirator with his bomb. Guile had to be met with guile; and if the public would not swallow guileful methods then those methods would have to be hidden from them. This was the only way, at a time when popular expectations of the police and consequently of the Home Office were so unreasonable. Harcourt's outburst to the cabinet about being expected to fight Rossa with his hands tied could have been addressed to the general public too. The Home Secretary was responsible for internal State security, but he was also supposed to be responsible in another way to Parliament, and the two seemed to conflict. There was no other way of seeming to reconcile the two duties, than a shabby but necessary secrecy.

There was another shabby advantage too: though it was probably a minor one. This was that it provided the government with an excuse, if things went – as they often did go – wrong. If Britain's political policing was not known about, then it followed that it could not be blamed if it failed. This was a bonus for the CID, which was the butt of a great deal of general criticism at that time. Any successes it had in this area were all the more laudable in view of the liberal restraints it was supposed to work under; when it did not succeed so well, those restraints could be trotted out as an excuse. We have seen Harcourt giving them a canter in the summer of 1881. This was always a convenient alibi, which the revelation of any extensive police 'espionage' might have blown.

Of course there were other, and better, reasons for secrecy. The two best were to protect informers, and to avoid forewarning miscreants. When Anderson agreed in March 1883 to widen his circle of agents, he did so on the understanding 'that I will not divulge their names to any one without their consent, & that in no case, without their consent, shall they be required to give evidence in a Court of Justice'.[82] This was clearly sensible. It was never 100 per cent effective. Most Fenians and socialists were fully aware that they were being watched. So far as the socialists were concerned, especially foreign socialists, this was partly because they were predisposed to believe it anyway. Some of them would have been hurt to think they were not being watched, which would suggest that they were not being taken as seriously by the authorities as they took themselves. It also confirmed the view of many of them, derived from first principles, of an oppressive capitalist police. But there was more to it than this. The Fenians and socialists not only sensed they were being spied on; they knew the faces and names of their spies. We know they knew them because they wrote about them in their newspapers; about Hagen and von Tornow, for example, who in 1882 came in for a torrent of personal vilification in *Freiheit*.[83] Later on the fullest descriptions anywhere of the work of the Metropolitan Police's political branch are to be gleaned from the Anarchist press. If it was these people the government was trying to fool, then it did not altogether succeed. So far as they were concerned, the deception was only skin-deep.

But by another way of looking at things this situation was ideal.

British police philosophy had always put prevention first. One way to prevent crime was to deter it, by letting it be known that there were police about. This was the rationale behind the practice that had been instituted quite early on in the detective department of sending plain-clothes policemen, when they had nothing else to do, out on patrol.[84] If the Fenians and anarchists had suspected nothing at all about the government's political sections, then they would have been more carefree, and presumably more dangerous, then they dared to be. The best of all worlds would come about if they could be persuaded that government surveillance of them was in fact more ubiquitous than it really was. This was what a skin-deep deception achieved. They knew something but not everything of what was going on. What they did not know they imagined. One favourite subject for their imaginings was the activities of informers and traitors in their own midst. Most con-spiratorial groups were continually riven by mutual suspicions among their members of spies and *agents provocateurs*. Jenkinson thought this compensated for the other advantages they enjoyed. One of the results of his activities amongst the Fenians, he wrote in 1884, was that they were 'all now working much more secretly than they did before', which made them harder to detect; but it also made them 'distrustful of one another. No man feels sure that his most intimate friend is not a traitor, and they find it exceedingly difficult to get workers.'[85] Even the leaders did not escape: like H. B. Samuels, the editor of the Anarchist *Commonweal* in 1893, whom his erstwhile comrade David Nicoll suggested was put up to his fieriest fulminations by the police.[86] Later Lenin himself was apparently set upon in London by Russian comrades who had been told that *he* was a spy, and had to be rescued by a British detective.[87] This is why Anarchist press accounts of political police activities, though full, are also undependable. From the authorities' point of view, however, this was no bad thing. In this area an imperfect secrecy was better than absolute secrecy, or no secrecy at all. It got the revolutionaries thinking and worrying, which in the circumstances was easily the best that could be hoped for.

Government secrecy thus had many advantages. It made its quarry nervous and confused. It protected its agents. It provided an alibi. It permitted activities, necessary ones in the government's eyes, which might not have been sanctioned in the clear light of day. It enabled quick and resolute executive action. It kept everyone reasonably happy, by allowing them to be persuaded, according to need, that either more or less was being done. It could be justified on grounds of national security, without any details needing to be scrutinised. It consequently pervaded the whole system of political policing in the 1880s, all the way up and down.

Even at the top very few people knew what was going on. We have already come across Harcourt keeping his cards very close to his chest; Gladstone apparently absenting himself from a cabinet meeting in order to avoid having to report its discussion of the Secret Service fund to the Queen; and Lord Spencer refraining from writing to his leader about detective measures in 1882 because he felt that as few people as possible should be in the know.[88] Inter-departmental memoranda were careful to avoid any but the vaguest references to secret police work, which the Home Office in particular appears in any case to have shown little interest in.[89] Nothing – or nearly nothing – was ever committed to paper; which meant that when governments changed hands the briefing on these matters had to be by word of mouth. When Gladstone's government fell in June 1885, for example, its successor found 'no mem[orandum] describing the system in existence', and the new Home Secretary had to be filled in verbally.[90] Over in Ireland Carnarvon was similarly briefed in the strictest confidence, after which he wrote to Cross that 'There are several things I want to say rather than write', and asked him to call.[91] The circle of the initiated was very small indeed; and none was anything like as initiated as those who actually did the work. Outside them there was nothing but mystery and deception: which because it extended to posterity, affects the historian too.

In spite of this there is very little mystery about the outlines of the earliest origins of Britain's vigilant state. We know when its distinctive agencies were founded, why, and by whom, and when one of them – Jenkinson's – came to an end. What we cannot be so sure about is exactly what they did: the methods they employed, how effective they were, and the extent to which they kept to 'the rules'. These are some of the important questions, and they are ones that the secrecy of the time still to a great extent obscures. Scarcely any of the evidence is dependable, because it was not intended to be. We are left therefore with surmise. That is the nature of the animal, in this cloak-and-truncheon world.

CHAPTER 5

Secrets

However necessary secrecy may be in dealing with political crime, it has three unfortunate effects. The first is to provide a cover for roguery, and perhaps a temptation to it. The second is to arouse suspicions of roguery, even if the temptation is resisted. The third is to make it difficult for the historian to find out for certain whether or not roguery has occurred. This is a serious problem, because in this field the question of roguery has more than a merely intrinsic importance. It may have a bearing, for example, on the causes of the growth of political policing in Britain, if the political police used improper means – like provoking crimes – to perpetuate themselves.

Roguery is relative, depending as it does to a great extent on the standards of a time. By the standards of that time, which were very exacting, there can be no doubt at all that Britain's political police went further than they were supposed to: but that is not saying very much. There was considerable disapproval then, for example, of what was called 'espionage', some of which we have met already, especially over people who were not suspected of particular crimes.[1] That disapproval was shared by many in the Uniform branches of most police forces, and even by some officers of the Metropolitan Police CID. At least one 'Special Irish Branch' sergeant found the practice 'in little accordance with the usages of a free country', and claimed that his chief inspector was against it too. That chief inspector apparently instructed his men 'never to join in any political movement for the purpose of obtaining information', on the grounds that it was 'degrading to the service for any official to play the part of a spy'.[2] If this advice was widely followed, it may be one of the reasons for the Irish Branch's ineffectiveness during the early 1880s, by comparison with Jenkinson's less principled bunch. The latter was essentially a spy organisation, with few of the other functions of a police force. Jenkinson described its methods in outline in a letter to Harcourt in September 1883.

We try to find agents in the first instance. Then from them we endeavour to obtain a thorough knowledge of the Fenian organisation in Great Britain. Out of this grows a knowledge of the men who belong to the organisation, and by watching and obtaining information about the men who hold the most violent and extreme opinions, we by degrees shall find out the groups or sections who are plotting assassinations and explosions.[3]

Jenkinson himself apparently wore disguises, which was another thing old police hands like Williamson disliked.[4] All this was kept from people, partly because of the protests it would be sure to arouse. That is not to say that anything much more protest-worthy went on. It is useful to know that the authorities used spies against the Fenians, but scarcely surprising or highly significant. The important question is how much further they went: whether they invented conspiracies, planted evidence, or initiated terrorist crimes.

The evidence for this sort of thing ranges from the theoretical to the circumstantial. The theoretical argument is that secrecy is *likely* to foster wrongdoing, by its nature. Lord Acton, in one of his less celebrated aphorisms, wrote that 'every thing secret degenerates'.[5] The reason for this is that secrecy diminishes accountability, which is normally a vital check on conduct. People need to have an unusual degree of personal moral probity to continue to act morally if they are not going to be found out. If they do not accept the prevalent definition of 'morality', then they are even less likely to restrain themselves. This may have been the case with political agents and policemen who regarded the rules they were supposed to be bound by as unreasonable, against an adversary who acknowledged no rules at all. Unreasonable rules, like unreasonable laws, call out to be broken. Secrecy makes it easier for them to be broken with impunity. This makes it theoretically possible, if not probable, that the conventions governing the conduct of Britain's secret police and intelligence agencies in the 1880s were sometimes seriously bent.

It depended largely on the probity and vigilance of the men to whom those agencies were secretly responsible; but even that was no guarantee of rectitude. Often they could not know what was being done under them. Occasionally they may not have wanted to know. One reason why the Home Office, for example, seems to have taken very little interest in the detailed activities of its political intelligence sections may have been to avoid embarrassment.[6] If a Home Secretary was wise enough to know no evil, then when he was questioned about it in the Commons he could tell no lies. But in any case his agents had reasons of their own for keeping the truth from him. One was that they did not know the full extent of the truth themselves. This was inevitable, in their particular line of work. Most of their information was gleaned not directly, but from informers. Informers were deceivers by trade. They were also valued in proportion to the importance of the intelligence they dispensed. This was doubtless a temptation to them to make the most of any intelligence they had. It may also have tempted them to fabricate conspiracies, or to initiate them. Another temptation was the need for credibility amongst their co-conspirators. For the most successful infiltrators – men like Henri Le Caron amongst the Fenians in America – this must surely have been difficult to resist. A leading revolutionary who did not at least once in a while initiate a revolutionary plan was bound to come under suspicion. Le Caron seems never (apart from one little indiscretion early on) to have been suspected. This by no means proves that he, or any other informer or spy, acted as an *agent provocateur*.[7] What it does indicate, however, is that his superiors could never be sure.

Those superiors were perfectly aware of the danger. 'I have to confess', wrote John Littlechild, who was one of the CID inspectors engaged on dynamite cases in the 1880s, 'that the "nark" is very apt to drift into an *agent provocateur* in his anxiety to secure a conviction, and therefore he requires to be carefully watched.'[8] His colleague George Greenham wrote in his memoirs of how easy it was for the detective to be deceived by the 'voluntary "informer"', especially 'foreigners with shady surroundings', for money.[9] For this reason the founder of Pinkerton's Detective Agency in America, in a letter of advice to Gladstone after the Phoenix Park murders, recommended the British police to do away with informers altogether, and to eschew rewards, 'as I consider them as incentives to crime'.[10] The same point was made in a Home Office reply in 1884 to the City of London Court of Common Council, which had asked the government to offer a bounty in connection with the London bombings; 'Instances have recently occurred', it went on, 'where crimes have actually been concocted with the object of securing a reward which it was anticipated would be offered for its detection.'[11] Patrick McIntyre, who was one of the original members of Williamson's Special Irish Branch, wrote in 1895 that political informers were generally 'worthless', and sometimes 'even provoke crime, instead of preventing it'.[12] In order to avoid this Robert Anderson, who was Le Caron's 'control' throughout the 1870s and 1880s and a man who set great store by moral probity, used to pay *his* spies regular salaries, rather than by results; but it must have been clear to any informer that a salary would not be continued long that did not seem to be justified by results. Besides, there were other considerations to be borne in mind. Anderson described his own practice, he wrote, 'for the benefit of others who may hereafter have similar duties to discharge'. But he felt 'bound in honesty to add', significantly,

> that if they consult their personal interests they had better not follow my advice. In secret service work *kudos* is not to be gained by preventing crimes, but by detecting them, and successfully prosecuting the offenders![13]

Kudos was one likely motive: either for the individual, or – in a situation of great rivalry and even enmity between different police agencies – for a particular Force. From this point of view the risk of indirectly and perhaps unknowingly provoking crimes may have been thought worth while. With confidentiality sacred between detective and informer, no one, after all, was ever likely to find out.

Another likely motive was the need to persuade both the politicians and the general public of the value of the services the political police provided. That value was not always appreciated. Even during the Fenian bombing campaign in London we have seen that people's perception of the danger to them was surprisingly low, and not enough to jolt them out of old liberal prejudices which were a bar to the development of political intelligence work. Both Jenkinson and Harcourt feared that the end of the campaign would lull them into apathy again.[14] Those who, like Harcourt, believed that the Fenian menace was a continuing one which required to be watched just as closely while it was slumbering as when it snarled and bit, were often irritated by their countrymen's short memories and shallowness. For those who were professionally employed in secret work, such attitudes threatened their livelihoods too. Le Caron, writing of his experiences in 1892, was especially bitter towards 'the ordinary British citizen who laughs at dynamite and pooh-poohs the existence of things calling for a more elaborate Secret Service'. One day, he went on, 'a big thing will happen, about which there will be no leakage beforehand': and then the people would realise the perils of stinting in this field.[15] Another way to bring them to this realisation would have been to provoke 'a big thing', or to encourage it, or to delay nipping it in the bud. This was always possible, while there remained this tension between the perceptions of the professionals and of the public, and while the activities of the professionals were shielded from the public by secrecy.

The tension arose partly from the professionals' greater proximity to the source of the danger; but another reason for it may have been that they were atypical sorts of men. They were atypical in a number of ways. They were bound to have at least slightly different values and standards from the majority of the people they protected, otherwise they would not have been in that job at all. We have seen that the moral reputation of even 'ordinary' detective work was not a very elevated one at that time, least of all in other police circles; which made it difficult to recruit into the detective force generally, let alone its 'Special' branch, any policeman with a conventional reputation to lose. Anderson, whose regard for his own conventional reputation we have noted before, claimed to regard this part of his work with distaste, which only his sense of a higher national duty could overcome.[16] Others seemed to revel in it. This marked them off from the majority of people, in a society which had not yet learned to accept fully the morality of the spy.

They were also marked off by their backgrounds. For many of those in the lower ranks – agents, informers, detective-constables and sergeants – that background was Irish, as was to be expected in view of the nature of the chief enemy. Scotland Yard's Special Irish Branch started off mainly English, but became more Irish as time went on, and in the 1890s (when the Fenian threat was only secondary) became dominated by Irishmen. Higher up, Robert Anderson was Anglo-Irish, but all the rest of those who officered Britain's secret services had military or Indian colonial backgrounds. Brackenbury and Gosselin were both old soldiers. Brackenbury in addition had been private secretary to the Indian Viceroy for a year. Jenkinson's Indian Civil Service career has been remarked upon already. Vincent was army; as were the two Metropolitan Police Commissioners between 1869 and 1888, Henderson and Warren. James Monro, who took over the CID from Vincent in 1884, and later took over Jenkinson's secret service work, was in the Bengal civil service for twenty-seven years before he came to Scotland Yard. To help him with the secret work he chose Melville MacNaghten, whom he had known as a planter in India, and whose firm way with the natives he particularly admired.[17] The line continued after the 1880s, with Sir Edward Bradford, the Chief Commissioner in the 1890s, serving in the Madras army and with the 'Political and Secret Department' of the India Office before he joined the Yard; and Edward Henry, his head of CID from 1901 and then his successor as Commissioner, having got *his* previous experience running the Bengal police. None of these men had English police backgrounds. The backgrounds they did come from may not have been incompatible with liberal values, but they were less likely to nurture them than most. The empire was coming home. Liberal Britain was being policed by outsiders; or at least by men from its fringes, where that sort of liberalism ran very thin.

Of course illiberalism and roguery are not at all the same thing; and none of this 'evidence' of wrongdoing is worth very much on its own. At best it establishes some possible motives, and an opportunity; but even the most innocent of us have motives and opportunities for crimes that have not been done. What is needed to prove that the secret services seriously exceeded their powers in the 1880s is a body with a dagger in it: and that is not at all easy to find.

Not that there is any shortage of candidates. The 1880s is littered with corpses which would do very well, if only they could be proved to be the victims of foul play. The most promising is probably the case of John Daly and James Egan, who were convicted of treason felony and dynamite offences at Warwick assizes in August 1884. Daly had been arrested by RIC and Liverpool detectives on Gosselin's orders at Birkenhead station on 11 April. He had on him parcels containing parts for grenades. He had been betrayed by an informer, who told Gosselin that the grenades were intended to be thrown into the House of Commons. Egan owned a house in Birmingham where Daly had lodged. He was arrested at the same time by the City of Birmingham police, who found a canister of nitroglycerine buried in his garden and incriminating documents in his house. Daly was given a life sentence and Egan twenty years.[18] Before many years of those sentences had been served, doubts were cast on the propriety of the whole proceedings from what seemed an impressive, if not impeccable, source.

That source was the Chief Constable of Birmingham, Farndale, who had been having Daly shadowed since October 1883 and was responsible for Egan's arrest. In the autumn of 1886 Farndale told a member of his watch committee, Alderman Henry Manton, according to the latter's recollection, that 'the explosives found on Daly were planted on him by the police'. Later on he elaborated. The grenades, he claimed, had been purchased in America with money supplied by the Irish Police, and placed in Daly's coat pockets by a confederate, 'Big Dan' O'Neil, in their pay. He added that he believed that this was done 'with the knowledge and sanction of the Home Secretary'. It was because he was so shocked by this that he decided to spill the beans. Manton also suspected, on the basis of information from another source, that the nitroglycerine found in Egan's garden was 'planted'. In this case the offenders must have been members of Farndale's own Birmingham force, whose detective branch Farndale himself had claimed a few years before was 'the most corrupt and unreliable force in the country'.[19] On hearing all this Manton wrote to Gladstone, who

73

said he could not interfere, and then to the ex-Irish Chief Secretary, Home Secretary Matthews, and Parnell. (He claimed later that his letters to Parnell were intercepted at the Post Office, and never got through.)[20] In September 1890 his accusations reached the newspapers, and in August 1891 and February 1892 were debated in the House of Commons.[21] On one of those occasions the Nationalist MP Tim Healy suggested that Daly was being 'poisoned' in Chatham prison, perhaps to get rid of him before he could reveal more.[22] Manton fought the case for ten years, but without its ever being cleared up. The Home Office never admitted impropriety, and Manton and his supporters could never prove it.

The truth is no easier to come by today. Internal Home Office files contain no great confession, but no evidence either that any really searching inquiry was made. The first thing Matthews did after receiving Manton's petition was to contact Farndale, who contradicted some of the details of Manton's account but confirmed the bulk of it. He believed that Daly was *generally* guilty, but that the evidence which had convicted him had been a 'plant'.[23] Farndale's letter was then passed on to Gosselin, who gave 'emphatic contradiction to each & all of the allegations made' about Daly's case, though he thought Egan (whose arrest he had not been involved in) might have got a raw deal.[24] Matthews then quizzed Gosselin face to face, raised the matter with Monro (who wrote to Gosselin), and had interviews with Manton and Farndale at the end of January 1888.[25] It was all quite thorough in its way; but it never tried to prise beneath Gosselin's own testimony. On the basis of this Matthews assured the House of Commons in July 1891 that he had 'gone with all possible minuteness and impartiality into an investigation of every circumstance connected with the conviction of Daly', and had satisfied himself of the groundlessness of Manton's charge. Harcourt also denied it.[26] But doubts remained.

They were bound to, in view of the circumstances of the case. Matthews himself had not been in office at the time of Daly's arrest, and so could have had no first-hand knowledge of it. Harcourt might have had; but if *he* knew of any wrongdoing it was not likely that he would admit it, in view of the very great seriousness of the charge. In a letter to Spencer in November 1887 he emphasised that 'nothing of the kind' had 'ever come under my notice' while he was at the Home Office, and that 'anyone who went in to the "agent provocateur" business in my time was dismissed without benefit of clergy'.[27] He also, however, possibly to establish an alibi, denied ever knowing any of 'the details of Daly's case'.[28] Gosselin was another who would have had to have borne some responsibility for it if it was true, and so was not likely to let on. In a letter to Jenkinson, retailed to Harcourt, he confessed to feeling 'uneasy' about it all.[29] Later on one of Jenkinson's agents in Ireland, William Joyce, claimed that Gosselin had admitted to him that Daly was one of a number of men entrapped by '*agents provocateurs* in the employment of Anderson and Jenkinson'; but it is difficult to know how much credence to attach to that.[30] Jenkinson, who would probably have had to have been in the know, had left by October 1887, and does not seem to have been officially approached. Nor does Anderson. No one else was brought in to Matthews's 'investigation', which consequently would have been fairly easy for a skilled operator to hoodwink. And Jenkinson, in particular, was highly skilled.

Even Harcourt was not quite sure about *him*. Clearly he would not put such villainy past him. 'Jenkinson is such a rash and headstrong fellow that one never knows what he may have done', he wrote to Spencer. He might had added that Jenkinson was under considerable pressure from Harcourt himself to come up with results at just this time, which may have constituted a motive.[31] 'However', Harcourt went on, 'as he asserts that there is no foundation for the statement we have only to be satisfied with that.' Is there a hint of scepticism here? Harcourt also felt that 'the uneasiness of Gosling' (sic) was a 'suspicious feature' of the case.[32] But he delved no deeper. Both he and Matthews were hampered by their reluctance to question the word of a gentleman. That was in spite of the fact, which they must have been aware of, that neither Jenkinson nor Gosselin could have been a real gentleman, from the nature of their work.

Then there is the persistent problem that none of these men needed to have known about it, for chicanery still to have taken place. 'Gentlemen in their position', as a Nationalist MP pointed out in August 1891, 'are unaware of the machinations of their subordinates.'[33] That may have been true. Harcourt himself, for example, wrote of 'Jenkinson's inveterate habit of bottling up everything in order to get credit for himself'.[34] Anderson was another one who was less than frank; Harcourt once said of him that his 'idea of secrecy is not to tell the Secretary of State'.[35] The same may have happened lower down the hierarchy. Daly was certainly betrayed by a police informer: but who was to know for certain whether or not that informer had entrapped him first? All of which gave a certain *prima facie* attraction to Farndale's evidence, which despite all the government's denials he persisted in.

The Home Office took that evidence seriously enough to feel that they needed to explain it away. Under-secretary Lushington reported to Matthews that the answer was probably simple jealousy. Farndale, he wrote, 'would have liked to have had the credit of arresting Daly in Birmingham'. Gosselin's 'secret police', however, insisted on waiting until he had the bombs on him, '& I dare say did not admit Mr. Farndale to the whole of their confidence'. When Daly was eventually arrested it was away from Farndale's patch, and with all the credit going to the Liverpool force and the RIC. Lushington suggested that 'This may have mortified Mr. Farndale'; who did, as it happened, complain on these grounds when he met Matthews in January 1888.[36] There is also evidence of bad feeling between them from the beginning of the Daly case.[37] Another consideration is that because Farndale missed out on Daly's arrest, he could have no first-hand knowledge himself of how it was done. His own sense of conviction suggests that he regarded his source as dependable. But he could be no more certain of it than anyone else outside the tight little circle of 'secret police' directly involved.

The Home Office may have been no wiser. But Lushington, for one, was convinced that it had 'a very strong case'. He was also anxious to demonstrate it publicly, in order to stop the matter snowballing: 'for if the doubts raised in Daly's case against the good faith of Government agents are not quieted, an agitation is sure to spring up for re-opening other Fenian cases of the same date.'[38] (The first was likely to be that of Whitehead, one of the Gallagher team of dynamiters rounded up in Birmingham and elsewhere in April 1883, which Manton said he had always had his doubts about.)[39] But the Home Office was subject to certain restraints. Letters which Lushington felt would greatly strengthen the government's case against Daly, for example, could not be cited for fear of raising 'awkward question as to how they . . . got into Government hands'. For similar reasons 'the S of S must decline altogether to say' who the government's informants were.[40] Considerations like this made it necessary to maintain what *The Times* called 'A certain reserve in reference to the facts',[41] which was not necessarily to the advantage of the government. However good its case, it could not make the best use of it, because of the way its intelligence had been obtained. The House of Commons would have to be satisfied with the Minister's word. The problem with that, of course, for the cynics in the House, was that it was exactly the line a minister would take, in the 'national interest', if he were trying to keep the cupboard door closed on a skeleton.

In any case the door remained shut, whether there was a skeleton behind it or not. Jenkinson probably threw the key away in 1887, when he destroyed all the papers relating to his secret service work.[42] Without them we are unlikely ever to get to the bottom of the Daly affair. On the surface it looks suspicious, and the more so the deeper we probe. A tantalising glimpse of the way the case was worked comes in a letter from Jenkinson to Spencer just after it, where he talks of his 'arranging to have the bombs passed to Daly', in order to have him caught red-handed. That suggests, strongly, that the secret agent involved may not have confined himself merely to spying and reporting back. The same letter admits that Jenkinson kept this information back from Harcourt, who would, he said, have wanted him to intervene earlier 'to frighten Daly away'. That would have deprived Jenkinson of his *coup*.[43] This is probably the nearest we shall get to positive proof. It makes it more probable that some element of *agent provocateuring* was involved in the Daly case, than that it was not.

But it is impossible to be sure. Jenkinson's letter can be taken another way. Most of the other evidence is inherently unreliable. We are dealing here with an unsavoury world of dishonesty and deviousness on all sides. Most of our testimony comes either second hand, or from professional liars who could not be relied on ever to tell the truth. Harcourt was never above a little dissimulation;[44] and Jenkinson's and Gosselin's careers were built on it. That undermines the defence. But the same is true also of our Queen's evidence: the testimony of members of the secret service who later welshed on it, like William Joyce and Patrick McIntyre. McIntyre, a Special Irish Branch man, was not concerned in the Daly affair; but he claimed he knew that *all* of the Fenian conspiracies bar one (Gallagher) were 'got up' by *agents provocateurs*.[45] This looks like horse's mouth stuff: but it is hardly the most reliable breed of horse. McIntyre was content to go along with the Irish Branch's activities and methods for eleven years until he was caught fiddling a time sheet, was demoted, and resigned.[46] It is never wise to accept uncritically the word of a turncoat with a grudge. Chief Constable Farndale also had a grudge, of a different kind; and one or two possible skeletons in his own Birmingham cupboard, like the Egan case, and his Head of Detectives, James Black, who was in charge of that case, and in 1892 had to leave the Force under a cloud.[47] All the testimony is tainted. The only transparently honest man in this whole affair was Henry Manton, whom Farndale dismissed as 'very old and childish',[48] and who may have been misled.

Others may have been misled as well. Secrecy can be a cover for neglect and incompetence, as well as for excess of zeal. It may have caused the degree of political policing in Britain to be exaggerated. From certain points of view this could be advantageous. Robert Anderson, for example, probably kept his Home Office job for years by virtue of a largely imaginary spy network in America, until Jenkinson rumbled him. Some of Anderson's own agents may have made a good living by persuading him that they were more effective than they were. Even Jenkinson was not above being hoodwinked occasionally: as in June 1885 when a man called Burkham in America was found to have been drawing a salary for revealing an entirely spurious plot.[49] In that case the harm was undone; but in others agents might have gone on for ever feeding wrong information up the line. This was serious for a number of reasons; one of which was that it gave a false impression of the extent to which the secret service had matters under control.

As well as the money to be made out of this kind of dissimulation, there was also a reputation of sorts. Anderson was one of those who clearly loved being taken for a man of mystery and power: one who knew far more of vital importance than it was possible for him in the national interest to divulge. This reputation was highly prized by a certain kind of secret policeman: those who published memoirs, for example, which peppered in the main rather dull narratives with tantalising references to state secrets and sealed lips and Tales that Never Could Be Told. There are a number of these, though they were all written later.[50] They hint at a particular secret service psychology which might be interesting if it could be analysed. One of its features was a mild paranoia which mirrored in some ways that of the secret police's adversaries. Plots and dangers were seen where none existed, and trifling threats blown up into world-menacing conspiracies. Against these conspiracies they – Britain's thin invisible line of secret political agents – stood as civilisation's constant and only defence. This view of the magnitude of the threat clearly enhanced their idea of their own importance, and by implication, if the threat was contained, of their powers. It may have encouraged them, unwittingly, to make too much of themselves.

This, however, was not an important factor yet. There was little cause for political policemen to inflate their self-importance in the early 1880s: rather, if anything, the reverse. Despite all the conspiring that went on, conspiracy theories of events generally found little favour in Britain then, by contrast with other countries. The secret police do not seem to have exaggerated the danger of subversion particularly, or their own role in combating it. Neither does the press. This is still too early for the spy-master and the (anonymous) political policeman to be the subject of admiring articles and interviews in the newspapers, or to feature in sensational novels, as they did quite frequently in the following decade.[51] People were not yet ready to find this sort of thing reassuring, or even to need reassurance at all. Consequently if exaggerated ideas about the methods of the secret police did get abroad, it was not the fault of self-advertisement by the secret police.

In fact exaggerated ideas did not get abroad very much; even in radical circles which might have been expected to be on the look-out for police misdeeds. Radical newspapers seemed either ignorant of secret police activities, or unconcerned. One early exception was the *Reynolds's Newspaper* columnist 'Northumbrian', who in May 1881 launched an attack on Harcourt for 'making Scotland-yard an official kind of "Third Section"' in connection with the *Freiheit* affair.[52] The paper also voiced very mild suspicions, which it did not pursue, about the Daly case.[53] Generally speaking, however, socialists and working-class radicals in the early and mid-1880s took no interest at all in this particular repercussion of the dynamite campaign. Nor did anyone else. As yet there seems to have been no very great awareness of secret service and secret police activities anywhere outside Fenian and foreign anarchist circles, and no great tendency, therefore, to imagine monsters lurking behind the mask of secrecy.

This in itself must be counted a success. From the authorities' point of view it would not have done at that particular time to alert people to the growth in Britain of what was still widely regarded as something oppressive and alien. This was one of the two major justifications for the degree of secrecy which surrounded Jenkinson's and Gosselin's and Williamson's agencies between 1883 and 1887; and which may possibly, though we cannot be certain, have given rise to abuse.

CHAPTER 6

Between Deluges
1887–90

During the Fenian bombing campaign of 1883–5, the Special Irish Branch of the Metropolitan Police had a relatively minor role. Most of the work of detecting dynamite conspiracies was done by Jenkinson, Gosselin and their agents, with the Scotland Yard section sharing the work of acting on the information they received from these men with provincial forces and the RIC. It was only after Jenkinson left in January 1887 that this began to change. His departure was followed by a period of confusion, out of which the 'Special Branch' proper of the Metropolitan Police grew.

The confusion was not only Jenkinson's doing. The period from 1886 to 1890 was one of very great difficulty for the Metropolitan Force generally. The difficulty was highlighted by two entirely different series of events, which cast widespread doubts on the competence of the police. The first of these was the wave of serious rioting which hit London between 1885 and 1887: beginning with increasingly disorderly open-air socialist meetings in Dod Street, Limehouse, and culminating in two violent clashes with the police on 'Black Monday' (8 February 1886) and 'Bloody Sunday' (13 November 1887) in and around Trafalgar Square. These touched the police's public order function. Their handling of them alienated nearly all sections of society, from the middle and upper classes who thought the police could have been firmer, to working-class radicals who accused them of brutality. 'Black Monday' was the cause of the resignation of Sir Edmund Henderson, who had been Metropolitan Police Commissioner since 1869. The second series of events reflected more on the CID. This was the notorious Whitechapel, or 'Jack the Ripper', murders of 1888–9, which the detective department never did get to the bottom of. They added to the barrage of complaints which assailed the police from all sides in the later 1880s, and stimulated a fundamental scrutiny of their organisation, methods and top personnel.

One of the leading scrutineers was William T. Stead, the first modern crusading journalist, who launched a series of major campaigns against the Metropolitan force between 1886 and 1888. The first of these, published in Stead's *Pall Mall Gazette* in the wake of 'Black Monday', attacked just about everything from the dinginess of Scotland Yard's premises to corruption (drunkenness and immoral living) in its higher ranks. Its main complaint, however, was against the very top men in the force, whom it characterised as 'Dodos' and 'an assortment of living antiquities'. The only exception it made amongst the Commissioners was the CID chief James Monro, who was 'the one competent' man, chiefly because his experience before joining the police had been detective rather than military. The least competent was Henderson, whose resignation on 20 February consequently delighted the *Gazette*.[1] During the interregnum that followed it suggested several names to replace him, including Brackenbury and Jenkinson;[2] but was entirely happy with Sir Charles Warren when his appointment as Chief Commissioner was announced. Warren, it enthused, was 'a man after our own heart': lacking a little perhaps in 'gaiety of spirit and genial humour', but more than making up for this by his 'deep religious conviction' and his stern views on prostitution and drink.[3]

Warren's holy glow wore off, however, over the next eighteen months or so, during which the *Pall Mall Gazette* grew progressively less enchanted with him. It attacked him powerfully over 'Bloody Sunday', and over what was taken to be his assault on the right of public meeting generally,[4] which led Stead and Annie Besant to set up a 'Law and Liberty League' to protect the public against police excesses in November 1887.[5] The controversy over Warren's public order methods was aired in Parliament, and in a wider campaign in liberal and radical circles on behalf of 'free speech'. Harcourt, among others, voiced the fear that under Warren Britain's old consensual police tradition was being violated by a new military-style 'gendarmerie'.[6] Another complaint was that Warren's obsession with public order was leading him to neglect ordinary crime. Warren disputed this; but his case was not helped by the sudden outbreak in September 1888 of one of London's worst ever 'ordinary' crimes. The Whitechapel murders, and the police's failure in the face of them, added to the force of the many calls for his resignation, which were answered in November 1888.

One of Warren's main problems before he resigned was his relations with his detective department. By nearly all accounts the CID seems to have been in a bad way in the later 1880s. The *Pall Mall Gazette* claimed that by October 1888 it had 'collapsed'. The fundamental reason for this was that Warren was stifling its initiative with 'red tape', some of which was ludicrously unsuited to a detective department: like the rule which excluded from it men under five foot nine inches tall. 'There is no room for clever little ferrets of men', commented the *Gazette*, 'among the London detectives.' Another 'extraordinary rule' was the one which made it compulsory for all CID men to have served in the Uniform branch, where the criminal classes had a good long chance to get familiar with them, and where they acquired, apparently, the characteristic Scotland Yard 'gait'. (Warren, it is only fair to say, denied all this.)[7] They were then reduced 'to a condition of motionless paralysis' by other regulations, like the one which insisted they get permission from the Chief Commissioner before pursuing a criminal out of town. There were also restrictions placed on rewards for informers. 'Under these circumstances it is not surprising that our detectives do not detect.' At the root of it all lay the twin evils of over-centralisation, and military-style discipline. These were entirely inappropriate for a plain-clothes branch. 'Battalion drill avails nothing when the work to be done is the tracking down of a midnight assassin, and the qualities which are admirable enough in holding a position or dispersing a riot are worse than useless when the work to be done demands secrecy, cunning, and endless resource.' This sort of regime was a recent development, claimed the *Gazette*; for which Warren was mainly to blame.[8]

Monro also held Warren to blame. A furious row between them dominated the final twelve months of the latter's tenure of office. It started with a complaint from Monro in November 1887 that his department was over-worked and under-manned. 'The result has been,' he wrote, 'that Mr. Williamson has broken down, and that I am in a fair way to break down also.'[9] (Williamson was granted three months' sick leave in February 1888 after being certified as 'suffering from debility and fainting attacks'. He died in December 1889 at the age of fifty-eight, mainly as a result, said Monro, of his 'especially arduous labours' against the Fenians. One of his children suffered from 'weakness of intellect'; that too, Monro claimed, was 'a direct consequence of Mr. Williamson's connection with Fenian inquiries, under circumstances which I shall explain verbally'.)[10] Monro asked for a new post of Assistant Chief Constable to help them both, but Warren failed to give him his full support. Instead he suggested remedying the situation another way by shedding some of the CID's duties.[11] The Home Office took Monro's side, and agreed to the appointment of Melville MacNaghten to the post.[12] MacNaghten was Monro's nominee; 'I saw his way of managing men when I was an Official in India,' he wrote to Warren, 'and was struck by it, for he had a most turbulent set of natives to deal with, and he dealt with them firmly and justly.' This was supposed to reassure Warren as to his 'officer' qualities.[13] Warren, however, was not convinced. At the end of March 1888 he threw a spanner into the works by suddenly revealing an incident in MacNaghten's Indian career in which he was supposed to have provoked some usually mild-mannered 'natives' into attacking him. Considering his lack of obvious qualifications, the number of ICS and military men who *were* qualified, and the fact that 'he is the one man in India who has been beaten by Hindoos', Warren wrote to the Home Office, it would surely be unwise to appoint him.[14] The appointment was consequently rescinded for the time being: a decision which led to a great deal of unpleasantness, because Monro had already told MacNaghten that the job was in the bag.[15]

Relations between Warren and Monro worsened thereafter. Warren resented Monro's independence, and the direct access he was allowed to the Home Secretary: of which more anon. He claimed that it imperilled 'the safety of the Metropolis'.[16] Monro retorted that it was Warren's unprecedented *interference* with the CID's independence which undermined its efficiency. Consequently, 'with the restrictions now attempted to be imposed on my action as Head of the Department, I must, in justice to myself disclaim all responsibility meanwhile for any unfavourable results, to which the system now initiated will lead.'[17] That let him off the hook for the Whitechapel murders, which started just three months later. Before then, in the middle of August, Monro resigned in protest against the 'change of policy and system' Warren was trying to impose.[18]

The clash between these men was more than one of personalities. Two different police ideologies were involved. Warren was a military man, who saw policing in terms of order and discipline. This was the reason for his appointment, after Henderson's laxer methods had failed. He diagnosed the police's problem as one of command, and to rectify it created five new top posts, all of them filled by army officers.[19] He clearly thought very little of detectives. In an article he published in *Murray's Magazine* in November 1888 he repeatedly emphasised how unimportant the CID was – 'a drop in the ocean' – compared with the Uniform branch. To support this he appealed to the police's original *preventative* function, which was far better exercised, he said, by uniformed men. In any case detective work was not suited to the 'genius of the English race'.[20] Policing should be open, visible and by the book, rather like cricket, where everything was governed by the rules of fair play. Plain-clothes policing was like taking off the bails at the bowler's end without a warning while the batsman was backing up. It was also a constant temptation to corruption, as history showed very well. This sort of attitude from a superior was clearly difficult for a dedicated detective like Monro to live with. Detectives knew that life was not like cricket, and especially among the criminal fraternity. Corruption was the risk you had to run to be effective, and not half so dangerous as the stultifying effects of red tape. This was really the hoary old dilemma of the British police since its earliest days: how to reconcile purity with results. Warren and Monro represented the Scylla and Charybdis between which the Metropolitan force had tried to steer for years. In the 1880s it steered on to both of them; with the result that several poor women in Whitechapel got drowned.

The Whitechapel murders are no concern of ours (unless they were politically motivated, which is unlikely, but was suggested at one stage).[21] The general condition however of the Metropolitan Police in the later 1880s is, because it had a number of important implications for its counter-subversive work. It was bound to affect its morale. It brought the police into the political arena, and to the critical attention, especially, of radicals who had taken little interest in it before. Lastly, and more directly, it had a specific and significant bearing on the development of the 'Special Branch', which was one of the main causes of the quarrel between Warren and Monro in 1888.

The precise course of the Special Branch's evolution over these years is not always clear. In Jenkinson's time – to recapitulate – there had been five separate major counter-terrorist bodies in Britain. Firstly there were the mainly uniformed Metropolitan police on 'protection duty': men guarding public buildings and figures in London. These reached a peak of about 1,000 men in January 1885, but in the next three years were reduced by about a half.[22] Secondly, there were the 'port police' sent out of the Metropolitan force to guard ports of entry in Britain and of exit on the continent, who remained steady at about 45–46 men. Fifteen of these were plain-clothes.[23] Thirdly, there were the 'special duty' police stationed at Central Office – the 'Special Irish Branch' – who comprised two inspectors, four sergeants and twenty-two constables in 1886, until two of the constables were taken away towards the end of the year.[24] Fourthly and fifthly, there were Jenkinson's and Gosselin's intelligence sections, whose numbers are impossible even to estimate. Beyond all these there were the RIC, some of whose officers were in Britain reporting to Jenkinson; and the various provincial detective forces. That was the 'system' in January 1887, when Jenkinson's departure threw it into some disarray.

It is clear that Jenkinson was only allowed to go because the Fenian menace was not felt so acutely as it had been; but still it was accepted that he needed to be replaced. The manner of his replacement, however, made a considerable difference to the structure of his organisation. Instead of choosing a man – like Gosselin – to take over that organisation as it was, the work was handed over to Monro, who as we have seen had been angling for it since 1884,[25] and who now combined it with his ordinary duties as Assistant Commissioner in charge of the CID. This brought the post right into the middle of the Warren–Monro maelstrom, and created other problems besides.

A problem for the historian is that the arrangements and 'explanations' for Monro's new role were only made 'verbally',[26] with the result that less hard information survives about it than about Jenkinson's role before him. One or two points, however, can be established with a fair degree of certainty. Monro had the title, though perhaps not an official one, of 'Secret Agent' in connection with this work.[27] He brought Anderson back out of the cold to help him with it, at an annual salary of £400. This was 'in spite of objections from Mr. Lushington', the under-secretary, who as things turned out was wise to be wary.[28] At the beginning of February 1887 Monro was also given a staff of 'special' high-ranking police officers: one chief inspector and three second-class inspectors.[29] These men were intended as substitutes for 'the private anti-Fenian agents employed by Mr. Jenkinson'. What happened to those agents we do not know. For 'purposes of administration' their replacements had to be members of the CID, '& not be ostensibly distinguished from other Constables [sic] of that Force'; but they were financed (secretly) out of imperial and not Metropolitan Police funds.[30] The Chief Inspector was John Littlechild, who was taken from the Scotland Yard 'Irish Branch', and not replaced there.[31]

This group was consequently now formally part of the Metropolitan Police, as Jenkinson's had not been; but it was still kept separate, at least for some purposes, from the Irish Branch. On most of the returns that were made of 'special duty' CID strength thereafter, right through to 1911, it appears as a distinct category, known as 'section D', as against the Irish Branch, which was known as 'section B'. ('Section C' was the port police.)[32] It was also referred to as the 'Special Section formed in 1887', the 'Special Confidential Section', the 'Special (Secret) Branch', and, on some printed notepaper in November 1887, as 'Home Office. Crime Department. Special Branch'.[33] These details may be tedious, but they are important in view of the confusion that has arisen in the past in the minds of those who have assumed that there was always only one single 'Special Branch'. The *first* Special Branch which bore the name was this little cadre of four police inspectors under Monro, who took over Jenkinson's duties in February 1887; and not the 'Special Irish Branch' of the CID, which at this time was – at least on paper, and for accounting purposes – quite different.

Four things in particular seem to have distinguished the new 'Special Branch'. The first was its extreme confidentiality: which has the incidental effect of making it difficult to be sure about its other distinguishing marks. The second was that it was a *national* police arm, intended for political work in the provinces as well as in London. This was kept highly secret, because Britain was not supposed to approve of centralised police authorities; and it was the reason why it was paid for out of national funds.[34] Its third distinctive feature was that from the beginning it was briefed to take care of 'the observation of anarchists' as well as of Fenians, if a report by a much later Head of CID is to be relied upon. This appears to have been a new departure.[35] Lastly, 'Section D' was directly answerable to the Home Secretary rather than to the Metropolitan Police Commissioner; which was the aspect of it which caused all the trouble with Warren in 1888.

Warren, with his military regard for hierarchy and his mania for centralisation, hugely disliked the fact that there was this little corner of Monro's activities which was not under his control. In April 1888 he wrote to the Home Office that it was 'eating into the heart of the discipline of the Police Force having a system under which the Assistant Commissioner can go to the Secretary of State direct without reference to the Commissioner'. This may have been his main reason for wishing to separate Monro's two responsibilities again, as in Jenkinson's time, though he suggested it to Monro first (in February) as a solution to his repeated complaints about over-work. He used the same argument to the Home Office. Monro, he wrote, claimed 'that he is overtaxed and strained by the various duties that have devolved upon him and yet he is able to do the duties of Secret Agent in addition to the duties which overtax him'. Warren considered that it was:

due to the efficiency of the Criminal Investigation Department that the Assistant Commissioner should be allowed to devote his time and energy to his legitimate work, and that he should not be burdened with the care and anxiety of duties which previously occupied the whole of the attention of an officer of undoubted experience and ability at a very high salary.

He also made the point that 'The Secret Agent as a matter of his existence must be an alarmist', which Warren believed was detrimental to his other, CID role.[36] It was a telling riposte to all Monro's talk about imminent 'breakdowns', and elicited a somewhat weak defence. The Secret Agent work, Monro said, did not come into it. It never detracted from his 'ordinary' work because 'If there is pressure the Special work suffers first.'[37] If that was intended to calm Warren, then it may not have calmed the government so much.

The government nevertheless supported Monro to the hilt,[38] without however being able to prevent his resignation later in the year. That resignation had the effect of separating the two jobs for a while, though not in the way Warren had intended. Anderson took over at the CID; but the Jenkinson mantle did not pass to him. Instead Monro took it with him, retaining his control of 'Section D' from a room in the Home Office.[39] Apparently there was an arrangement between them that if Monro ever wished to return to the CID Anderson would move over for him, back to the Home Office.[40] In the event, however, it worked out differently. At the end of November Warren resigned and Monro succeeded him as *Chief* Commissioner; and possibly – though there is no direct evidence for this – kept the Special Branch in his hands. When *he* left to go to Bengal in June 1890 there is no saying what happened to it. The most likely possibility is that Anderson took charge. Or it may have passed to Gosselin for a while.[41] Gosselin was certainly still working, very much behind the scenes, well into the 1890s. So was the other 'Special Branch' (Section B) with a steady establishment now of one inspector, four sergeants and twenty constables.[42] The relationship between these different agencies is unclear. It is highly likely that they worked closely together, as two sections of what was in practical terms one body. For that reason they will hereafter be referred to collectively as *the* 'Special Branch'. What is clear is that in the later 1880s, despite all the tribulations which beset the Metropolitan Police Force more generally, that Special Branch kept its own little corner of the peace. This may have been a tribute to its effectiveness; or it may have been due to the fortunate fact that, with the main Fenian bombing campaign now over, the peace was easier to keep.

The Special Branch also succeeded in resisting any pressures that might have been put on it in these years to reduce its numbers on the ground that the peace was easier to keep. Whether those pressures were ever explicit is uncertain. In June 1885 the Chancellor of the Exchequer, Hicks Beach, had expressed the 'hope' that the secret service budget could be cut. In 1888 there were Treasury complaints about the 'practically uncontrolled' special police expenditure.[43] Warren was ever eager to reduce the number of his constables on 'protection' duty, and in April 1888 did actually reduce them by sixty-eight, to the annoyance of the Home and Irish Offices who felt they should have been consulted.[44] In December 1890 the Irish Office proposed reducing the number of RIC men at British ports.[45] A year later, at the Home Office's request, the Metropolitan Police Commissioner recommended a reduction in the strength of the (Section B) Special Branch by four.[46] There may have been other hints of proposed cuts; or a feeling amongst those who made up the Special Branch that the lull in terrorism might tempt a parsimonious government to lower its guard. They countered this by insisting on the continuing danger from Fenian extremists, both generally, and in the form of specific plots.

The most sensational of these specific plots was the one which was to have spoiled Queen Victoria's Golden Jubilee celebrations in 1887 by causing explosions in Westminster Abbey and elsewhere during her thanksgiving service on 21 June. The originator of the plot was the Fenian F. F. Millen, assisted by four others. At the time a great deal of uncertainty surrounded it. The popular story was that the Special Branches were tipped off two months before, watched the conspirators closely, and frightened them off. Two of them, Callan and Harkins, were tried in February 1888 and sentenced to fifteen years' imprisonment.[47] Everyone connected with the secret service regarded it as a great feather in their caps.[48] A report by Monro singled out Littlechild, Melville, Quinn and McIntyre of the Special Branch for particular praise. Williamson was also prominently involved.[49] But there were always doubts. One was voiced by a clerk in the Home Office, who wondered about the true seriousness of the affair. Of course, he minuted, 'good work has been done, in that the conspiracy was prevented from coming to a head at all, but for that very reason it is not clear how much danger to the public was really involved.'[50] Much later on some Irish MPs suggested that the whole thing had been either invented, or 'provoked'.[51] The latter suspicion was fed by Anderson's own revelation in 1909 that one of the conspirators had been in the pay of the British secret service.[52] That put a new complexion on it all.

A contemporary report by Monro, preserved among Anderson's papers, confirms that this was also *his* understanding of events. The informer was Millen himself, who had been passing intelligence to the British for years. Monro claimed that Millen revealed the projected plot to his predecessor at the head of the secret service – presumably Jenkinson – even before he told his confederates. He implied that Jenkinson had been content to let the plot develop, in the hope of catching the other conspirators red-handed. When Monro took over in February he only learned of this 'accidentally', and to his very great dismay. Quite apart from anything else, if Millen had been arrested 'he might have made statements on the subject, of, at all events, a most embarrassing kind'. It seemed to Monro 'undesirable in the extreme to prosecute the agents of a plot, while there was even the semblance of justification for asserting that in its inception the Govt. was privy to it.' In his book this came uncomfortably close to *agent provocateuring*. That was why Monro decided to prevent the plot rather than to reveal it: even though revelation 'wd. doubtless have impressed the public' more.[53] Anderson agreed, that in order to achieve what 'would have been ostensibly a brilliant police *coup*', they could not possibly adopt 'discreditable means'.[54]

The 'Jubilee Plot' itself therefore may have had its shady side; but together with a host of other anxieties surrounding the Jubilee it seemed to justify, at least for the time being, the continuance of the secret police. A sergeant in the CID Special Branch, John Sweeney, later described the frenzied activity they put in at this time amongst anarchists and nihilists as well as Fenians, arising from the 'alarming reports' that flooded in to Scotland Yard from all sides.[55] One of the most alarming concerned neither a Fenian nor an anarchist, but an Anglican clergyman called Canon Hurford, who was found to be offering his tickets for the Westminster Abbey service for sale to raise money to pay for the publication of a Jubilee *Te Deum* he had composed. 'What a chance for a dynamiter to get a quiet pot shot at H.M.!' wrote an agitated Home Secretary; adding that in his view it constituted simony, or 'constructive High Treason' at worst.[56] The Jubilee was a worrying time. It appears to have inculcated in the authorities an abnormal sense of vulnerability, out of which respect for special police methods was likely to grow.

The Special Branch may have been right to be vigilant. Many people suspected that the Fenians had only interrupted their bombing offensive momentarily while parliamentary methods were tried, which meant that it was likely to resume – if they could find the men to do it – once Gladstone's first Home Rule bill fell. A highly provocative Irish Coercion bill was passing through Parliament at the time. The Jubilee was an obvious target for provokees. If Millen's plot was partly encouraged by the secret service, as it may have been, then it was in order to bring home to governments and people a danger which really existed, but which they might not believe without tangible evidence. If they did not believe it, then they might not sanction the proper precautions. Over the next four and a half years no other 'plot' was revealed comparable to the Jubilee one; and so the danger, for those who believed in continued vigilance, increased.

Monro was aware of the danger; and it was probably owing to him that the Special Branch survived those four and a half years intact. In December 1887, for example, just six months after the Jubilee Plot, he scotched a plan of Warren's to reduce the number of police stationed outside public buildings from 320 to 150 by passing information to him 'from outside London ... rendering it necessary to continue on protection duty these men ...'.[57] In April the next year Warren returned to the same attack; this time Monro could not cite 'any special danger to public buildings', though he insisted that 'the recent case of *Callan & Harkins*, and the general information received from America show that there are agencies of mischief still active, and ready to take advantage of a relaxation of precautions': which did not persuade Warren but did persuade the Home Office, who overruled him.[58] With Warren gone Monro must have found his task easier; but even then he was found on one occasion writing to the Home Office's explosives expert Vivian Majendie that the notion 'that there is now no such thing as dynamite conspiracies or conspirators' was a 'mistake'. 'The danger from Fenian machinations', he claimed, was 'just as great now as ever it was'; which made it unwise to relax precautions then.[59] In December 1891 the new Chief Commissioner, Edward Bradford, wrote to the Home Secretary that 'information which reaches us from all quarters' indicated a new Fenian offensive soon, which in his view made the moment 'for weakening in any way the "Special Branch" of this Department' inopportune. In spite of this Bradford gave in to Home Office pressure on that occasion to reduce Section B's strength by four constables;[60] from which fate it was temporarily rescued very shortly afterwards, however, by a brand new crisis, real or 'provoked'.[61] That must in a way have relieved the champions of the Special Branch, who since the summer of 1887 had not had anything much more solid than rumours and a general sense of political threat to feed upon.

Despite the lack of solid food all the government's counter-subversive agencies in the later 1880s found things for themselves to do. The port police carried on looking for suspicious characters and helping customs men with suspicious baggage at the main British and nine continental ports.[62] In January 1889 a small exemption to the normal security checks was made in the case of people travelling from the Continent *via* Britain to America, so long as their luggage was carried under bond between English ports; but not, for some reason, for passengers travelling the opposite way.[63] In November 1888 twelve extra constables were put on to examining the belongings of passengers from America arriving at Euston and St Pancras stations.[64] The numbers of police protecting public buildings and ministers' houses fluctuated wildly with every little Fenian rumour that blew, with the result that Warren at one stage lost count of them: 'the question of what men have been augmented for protection duties', he wrote to the Home Office in October 1888, was 'a profound mystery and difficulty'.[65] (His confusion was compounded by a certain lack of logic in the categorisation of these officers as 'inside' and 'outside' men: among the 'inside men', for example, were included the men guarding the Albert Memorial which, as he correctly pointed out, 'has no inside'.)[66] These were the Metropolitan Police's overt precautions against political crime.

The Special Branch also kept itself busy, though less overtly: watching known suspects, following up information received, and guarding public figures. As the Fenian danger seemed to recede, its duties broadened out. Before 1887, wrote John Sweeney in his recollections of the early Special Branch,

> the Anarchists in England had been comparatively quiescent; but they now began to grow restless. They held frequent meetings; there was quite a small boom in the circulation of revolutionary publications. Then, as now, England was a dumping-ground for bad characters, and London thus received several rascals who had been expelled from the Continent as being prominent propagandists, and as being suspected of complicity in various explosions . . . One could never be sure of what these fellows would be up to at any moment, so that Scotland Yard had an anxious time keeping every movement of theirs under surveillance. We knew the addresses of most of them, and the places where they worked, when they did any honest work, and we kept watch on those places; that should anyone be absent, even for a few hours only, we should have no difficulty in cornering him and making him account, if he could, for his absence. It may be imagined how much extra work was thus put on the shoulders of the Special department, which has to deal with this class of criminal . . .[67]

An occasional report of their enquiries among these foreign desperadoes survives. Some of them were negative: such as one on foreign socialists in England prepared in response to Dutch anxieties in August 1886.[68] A rather fuller one on Russian nihilist exiles was sent to the Foreign Office in May 1887.[69] Another negative one on an alleged plot against the German crown prince by means of 'electric machines' was forwarded the next year.[70] Enrico Malatesta, the leading Italian anarchist, was traced soon after he arrived in London in 1890, and his address passed on to the Italian ambassador.[71] A report on Malatesta by Littlechild and Melville of Section D forwarded to the same ambassador in April the next year warned of his recent departure to Italy 'for the purpose of fomenting disturbances'.[72] When foreign dignitaries visited Britain it was the Special Branch's duty to protect them, which it did by travelling with them, and by making discrete enquiries amongst their refugee compatriots. This was done in July 1889 for the Shah of Persia, and in 1891 for the Prince of Naples. (The Shah proved a handful, partly because of his liking for young actresses, and Monro was glad to see the back of him.)[73] This much is known, because it involved correspondence through the Foreign Office, which has kept its records almost complete. The same cannot be said for the Special Branch's activities amongst Irish and British dissidents, of which scarcely any documentation survives.

In the case of British dissidents – anarchists, socialists and the like – this is very likely because there was no great Special Branch interest yet in the sorts of things they did. Of course the police were concerned about certain socialist activities: incendiary speeches and writings, for example, riotous meetings, and other pursuits which threatened 'public order' generally; but these do not yet seem to have been areas where it was felt necessary to call the secret service in. Scarcely anywhere in any official document or private paper or printed reminiscences is there any suggestion that Special Branch methods or personnel were ever employed against British socialists or anarchists or trade unionists before the early 1890s: with one possible exception. In September 1886 the authorities got wind of some socialists 'drilling' in the back yard of the house of Harry Quelch in Southwark Park Road. The police sent two officers to observe the proceedings secretly from a window of the house next door. One of the two (the only one whose identity is known) was a PC Boulter; whose name appears fifteen months later in a list of members of Section B.[74] Otherwise there is no trace of them. When the police were asked by the Austrian government in 1890 about projected May Day demonstrations in Britain, for example, the best they could come up with was a newspaper cutting: which does not suggest any very active surveillance of left-wing groups.[75] When the socialist John Burns was prosecuted for incitement to violence in November 1887 the Special Branch does not appear to have been involved; and it was not called in to assist the policing of demonstrations.[76] In September 1887 there was a bit of a fuss in radical circles about a 'domiciliary visit' paid by two (non-Special Branch) police sergeants to the socialist Lewis Lyons at the dead of night: but it turned out on investigation that it was on the invitation of Lyons, who was a friend. The purpose of that visit, Monro wrote later, was to find out about a procession the two officers thought might be passing through their division after a meeting at Tower Hill the following Sunday. It was done openly, and as a matter of course, in order to decide whether the procession required to be policed.[77] This appears to have defined the limits of the police's interest in socialism. Beyond it there is no jot or tittle of evidence that anyone in the employ of the government ever infiltrated English left-wing organisations, for example, or 'shadowed' socialists like Morris and Hyndman and Burns. Nor did any prominent British socialist suspect that this was so; which means that the Special Branch was either exceptionally clever in this area, or uninvolved.

The Irish of course were different, and a continuing preoccupation of both sections of the Special Branch throughout these years. One presumes that Irish suspects were watched and followed as they had been for years, and informers milked for all the intelligence they could provide. One very valuable informer, according to Monro and Littlechild, was the Jubilee plotter Thomas Callan, who gave information 'of a very useful character not only as concerned the conspiracy in which he had been engaged, but as likely to be a guide in dealing with any future conspiracy' to Littlechild when the latter went to visit him in Chatham gaol in March 1888.[78] Another prison visit Littlechild was said to have made around this time was to a man called Wilson, or Clark, who later claimed that he offered him his freedom if he would testify against Parnell.[79] The special significance of this was that the case against Parnell was not supposed to involve the police at all; who should have remained neutral in what was really a matter between Parnell and his accuser, *The Times*.

The 'Special Commission' to enquire into *The Times*'s allegations that Parnell and other Nationalist MPs had been implicated in Irish crimes met between September 1888 and November 1889. It is highly probable that the government did give more help to *The Times* in this case than was proper, though most of that help came from Dublin.[80]

Littlechild, as Chief Inspector of the Section D Special Branch, may have had some part in it too, though it is difficult to know how much.[81] One attempt by the Radical MP and journalist Henry Labouchere in 1890 to prove that a Metropolitan Police Inspector called Jarvis had been sent clandestinely to America to bribe P. J. Sheridan to give evidence for *The Times* collapsed ignominiously in October, when Jarvis sued for libel and Labouchere, who had clearly been gulled, had to settle out of court.[82] On the other hand this affair worried the Home Office, who were against a public hearing on the grounds that 'if there have been any questionable proceedings on the part of Government or Police Agents, these might come to light in the course of the trial with damaging consequences.'[83] This suggests at the very least that the Home Office were not confident that everyone around them had clean hands. Cleanliness in this regard was especially vital in view of the upshot of the Parnell Commission, which was a disaster for *The Times*, and had indirect repercussions on the secret service work of the government.

The report of the Parnell Commission contained a judicious mixture of 'verdicts'; but by the time it came out this hardly mattered at all. The main impact of the proceedings came through the dramatic revelation, in February 1889, that the most incriminating documents *The Times* had based its case on were clumsy forgeries. Whether or not that exculpated Parnell, it seemed to *inculpate* others more; and it also had a wider effect. By undermining people's trust in 'conspiracy' theories generally – Fenian conspiracies, that is – it may have reacted adversely on those who were charged with countering conspiracies nearer home. If people had known then what they came to know later, that one of the anonymous authors of *The Times* articles attacking Parnell was their new Metropolitan CID chief Robert Anderson, they might have been even more sceptical. Another effect of the Commission was to blow the cover of the spy 'Henri le Caron', who was Anderson's main source. That was a deliberate decision on Le Caron's part: either to help *The Times*'s case against Parnell, or to enable him to retire comfortably after more than twenty years of dangerous secret work, or both. Neither purpose succeeded. Le Caron was given a house and an annuity by *The Times* in return for his evidence, and a regular bodyguard thereafter by the Special Branch; but his last years were in fact anything but comfortable, and when he was reported to have died on All Fools' Day 1894 many people suspected that he had really been spirited abroad to rescue him from the terror in which he lived.[84] His evidence on behalf of *The Times* was by most accounts impressive; but it availed them nothing against the effect of the unmasking a couple of weeks afterwards of the forger Richard Pigott, which turned the 'trial' right around.

From then onwards the whole counter-Fenian effort was very slightly tainted. Pigott and Le Caron became associated together, which may have been unfair to the latter. Le Caron was an object of opprobrium not only among the Irish, but in Britain too. Harcourt (hypocritically) called him a 'miserable wretch'.[85] Parnell's counsel before the Commission, Sir Charles Russell, talked in his summing-up of his 'odious profession', and described his whole life as 'a living lie'.[86] Of course not everyone felt like this about Le Caron. Some shared his own estimate of himself as a brave patriot.[87] Nevertheless his evidence had a mainly adverse effect on the public's view not only of him, but of government anti-Fenian measures generally. It confirmed some of their suspicions that not all those measures were above-board. It had shown, said the anarchist monthly *Freedom*, 'what despicable and cowardly meannesses both Liberal and Conservative governments have been, and are, capable of, to serve their ends'.[88] Le Caron's name became a part of the demonology of the libertarian left, rather as the spy Popay's had been in Chartist times. Of course he was nothing at all to do with the 'Special Branch': but such fine distinctions were not known about then. A chain of guilt by association was formed, running from Pigott through Le Caron and Anderson, which inevitably touched the Scotland Yard Irish section too. At the very least the revelations of February 1889 made people more widely aware of the existence of this counter-subversive underworld: whether they approved of it all, or not.

In this way as well as in others the late 1880s appear to have been a turning-point in people's attitudes towards the police. One reason for this was dissatisfaction with their detective competence – Whitechapel; but another was concern about their growing 'political' role. The police were not entirely to blame for this trend. Their problem was that politics on its edges had become more 'criminal': endangering public order on the one hand, and life and property on the other. Their critics, however, accused them of over-reacting to this, in two different ways.

Both those ways were seen as diverting them out of the old Peelite police tradition, into alien or foreign paths. Monro and Warren had this in common, if nothing very much else. Monro, said a spokesperson of the Law and Liberty League, 'was bitten by the craze of being a political policeman, the head of an English third section' – like the French. Warren was 'bitten by the military craze', and wished to be 'the head of an army of Gendarmes'. Between the two of them, 'the head of the Third Section and the would-be Prefect of Police', the 'proper work' of the Force was neglected. 'Mr. Monro could think of nothing but dynamite and Invincibles. Sir Charles Warren dreams of the threatened Revolution, and sends his horsemen to smash up political meetings. In the meanwhile the thief and the burglar flourish, and a series of horrid murders are perpetrated with impunity and under the very noses of the police.'[89] Comparisons were also made with the Royal Irish Constabulary, another force outside the main British tradition, whose methods and ethos seemed recently to have seeped in. The *Pall Mall Gazette* called the Metropolitan force 'a cockney reproduction of the Royal Irish', not least in its independence, which the *Gazette* deplored, from municipal control.[90] These particular criticisms were new. They seemed however to bear out fears which had surrounded the British police forces since their inception, that they could too easily turn into agencies of repression if left in government hands.

Some critics blamed the top men in the police, who were all, as we have seen, either military or colonial hands, or both. This was the criticism the journal *England* made of Warren when he was appointed in 1886: that he was '*par excellence* a soldier', whose only experience of administration 'has been in dealing with barbarians'.[91] So far as the Special Branch was concerned this was compounded by the fact that its personnel became far more predominantly Irish after its first couple of years.[92] It was a symptom of the trend we have noticed before, whereby liberal Britain came to be policed more and more by men coming from outside the main liberal tradition, as times got harder for her. It was anticipated by the socialist William Morris in 1884, commenting on the fact that Britain at *that* time was still 'free'. She would not, he predicted, always be so.

> It is true that at present Capitalist Society only looks on Socialism in England with dry grins. But remember that the body of people who have for instance ruined India, starved and gagged Ireland, and tortured Egypt, have capacities in them – some ominous signs of which they have lately shown – for openly playing the tyrant's game nearer home.[93]

By the end of that same decade he and those who shared his way of thinking could see the Empire, and Anglo-Ireland, clearly striking back.

That was one change of attitude. But it was not the only one. In other quarters – even occasionally in the same ones – the shift of opinion was the other way. This can be seen with regard to detective work in particular, which at this time seems to have been losing some of its disrepute. One sign of this transition was an aspect of the *Pall Mall Gazette*'s police campaign: championing as it did a loose-reined detective system, against Warren's mid-Victorian propriety and discipline. Another sign is a passage in Robert Louis Stevenson's novel *The Dynamiter* (1885), where one character, Somerset, commends detective work as 'the only profession for a gentleman'. His companion baulks at this, on the grounds that 'hitherto I own I have regarded it as of all dirty, sneaking and ungentlemanly trades, the least and lowest'. 'To defend society?', asks Somerset rhetorically; 'to stake one's life for others? to deracinate occult and powerful evil? . . .' Somerset's view here was the emerging one; his companion's the old.[94] The new view was catered for a little later on by Conan Doyle's Sherlock Holmes stories, the first of which appeared in 1887. That story, 'A Study in Scarlet', also featured secret political societies. Around this time Holmes adopted his earliest recorded disguise (as 'a rude sailor'), though his public were not to be told of this until 1890.[95] By then such ruses appear to have become widely tolerated; as well, of course, as Holmes's addiction to cocaine. His popularity grew enormously in the 1890s, which is hard to imagine ten years before. (Even 1887 was just a little too early; the first edition of 'A Study in Scarlet' flopped.)[96] This may be significant. Values were changing, no doubt under the pressure of material circumstances. Old taboos were lifting, and among them the Briton's old maidenly blushes at the thought of a plain-clothes police.

Whether this would spread to embrace *political* police was yet to be seen. Plain-clothes detection and disguises were only a step away from espionage, but it was still a very long step. Sherlock Holmes never spied on socialists, and the spy story as a genre had not yet been born. Le Caron published his reminiscences in 1892, but was not admired for them, and the next 'police spy' to do the same did it to pander to the public's distaste.[97] It was not until the 1900s that there seemed to be a reliable market for secret police memoirs, which presumably was composed in part of people who approved. Before the 1900s this kind of activity was still controversial, to say the very least. Not that that seemed to matter to the secret police themselves; who continued throughout the 1890s to guard Britain from terrorism and subversion in the best and only ways they knew.

CHAPTER 7

Anarchy

The Special Branch established itself at a time of waning confidence in the intrinsic unsubvertability of the British liberal capitalist way of life. It had its immediate origin in the Fenian bombing campaign, and it was affected by other factors, like foreign pressure and Harcourt's personality and its own internal dynamic, once it had started; but it is difficult to imagine any of these factors sustaining it for long after the Fenian campaign had come to an end, if this had happened in more optimistic and carefree times. The 1880s were far from being carefree for Britain; but the 1890s, and then the 1900s, were worse.

Of course it is common for people in most ages (though not all) to believe that their problems are more difficult to solve than their predecessors': and it is also easy for historians to pick out only the pessimistic trends of a period that might have been more mixed. By some criteria the 1890s were better years than those that had gone before. During the course of them Britain appeared to pull out of an economic 'depression' which by modern standards was not so very serious anyway; production was expanding, exports stable, prices steady, the balance of payments still well in credit, unemployment low in the second half of the decade, and average wages increasing slightly. On the political front, with Gladstone almost gone and firmer hands now on the tiller, there were no more great national humiliations abroad like Majuba and Khartoum, both of which were 'revenged' at the end of the decade, and no more nonsense from the Irish, who after Parnell's disgrace in 1890 retreated in confusion from the front of the Westminster stage. It was also a period of great territorial acquisition, mainly in Africa, accompanied by a national outburst of patriotic feeling probably unparalleled since Waterloo. The 1890s was the decade of the third Marquis of Salisbury, Rudyard Kipling and the earliest flowerings of the genius of Edward Elgar: not men whom it is easy to see as pessimistic figures, in an age which in many ways represented an apogee.

All was not, however, as it seemed. Salisbury was a realist who was well aware of the vulnerability which lay behind Britain's imperialistic bluster at the end of the century; and beneath both Elgar's and Kipling's art there is a sombre descant of uncertainty. As well as these three characteristic figures of the 1890s there were others who even on the surface were less reassuring to anyone: men like George Bernard Shaw, Aubrey Beardsley and James Keir Hardie, who were the embodiments of many of their contemporaries' darkest fears. Scarcely anybody in Britain who thought at all about anything was not fearful of some broad current or other in the national or international life of the time. The objects of those fears varied from person to person and from group to group. Most of them centred on Britain's place in the wider world, which was believed to be under threat commercially from the Germans and Americans, militarily from the Germans, Russians and French, and in the long term racially from the Asiatic hordes who so greatly outnumbered all the Europeans together, even if they could ever come together to resist them.[1] That was the external threat. It was matched by an equivalent threat from within, of various kinds of subversion, whose special significance at this time was that they undermined the nation's ability to meet the external dangers effectively.

'Subversion' was not only seen politically. For some people a far more insidious form was that which infected what was sometimes called 'the Blood'. Racial 'degeneracy' was a favourite subject of speculation in the 1890s, manifested as it was believed to be in rising figures for suicide, insanity and crime.[2] One of the factors sometimes blamed for this was Jewish immigration, which amounted to around 120,000 men, women and children between 1870 and 1914.[3] Others were capitalism, which made men poor, 'socialism', which made them effete, and the pace of life in the age of steam.[4] People argued over this endlessly; but most of them agreed that the 'race' was weakening physically and mentally, to a point which endangered its domination of the world.

A second broad category of subversion was 'immorality', which probably had its effect on 'the Blood' too. Immorality in this context meant sexual, usually homosexual, indulgence. There was widespread concern about this in the 1890s, mainly because of its supposed ravages amongst the English upper classes. In December 1895 twenty boys were reported expelled from Eton for paederasty, and throughout the decade the Home Office worried about 'obscene materials' imported into Britain from Spain and directed at the public schools.[5] Oscar

Wilde's conviction in May 1895 reflected the widespread unease about this kind of thing, as did the lesser-known cases of Henry Vizetelly in 1889 for publishing Zola in translation, and of George Bedborough in 1898 for selling what was intended to be a scientific study of homosexuality. Others who avoided the lawcourts but aroused storms of protest were Grant Allen for his novel *The Woman Who Did*, published in 1895, and Bernard Shaw for his play *Mrs Warren's Profession*, which the Lord Chamberlain banned (the play, not the Profession) in 1898. Behind these British literary figures was seen the baneful continental influence of men like Wagner and Ibsen, whom Max Nordau diagnosed in 1894 as morally insane. These were the real subversives: the men who gnawed away at Britain's *moral* fibre, substituting for it what Oscar Wilde at his lowest point characterised as 'eroto-mania', and what others – hinting at a political connection – called literary 'anarchism'.[6]

There were indeed connections between the new *fin-de-siècle* morality in Britain, and some forms of politics, though they were probably very insignificant. Shaw for example was a socialist, as well as an apologist (in a way) for prostitution. Wilde stood bail for the anarchist John Barlas when he got into some trouble in 1891. (He had known Barlas, who was also a poet, at Oxford.)[7] Anarchists were involved with the Legitimation League, which existed to reform the marriage laws, and the Rational Dress Society, which crusaded against late-Victorian over-dressing by putting its men into little frocks.[8] Anarchists also tended to reject conventional morality generally. None of this was lost, as we shall see, on the Special Branch; but it was not by and large regarded as the major component of the chief political threat to Britain's *status quo*.

That threat was generally felt to come from two directions. One was democracy, which was provoking quite a powerful intellectual reaction against it in the 1890s, from writers who felt it undermined liberty, encouraged class war, and had the 'eagles' of society, as the historian W. E. H. Lecky put it, governed by the 'parrots'.[9] Those parrots were very often socialists, who had made great strides in recent years, both in Parliament, where they now had their own MPs, and in the trade union movement. They were the source of most of the industrial unrest of the period, which culminated in September 1893 in strike riots in the mining village of Featherstone, during which two men were shot dead by the militia. Socialism was regarded as a real menace in the 1890s, much more so than in the 1880s, partly because it was feared that it could become the ideology of the enfranchised majority. The other significant political threat of the time clearly could not. Violent anarchism was only a minority movement everywhere in the 1890s, and probably most of all in Britain; but then violent anarchism had something to make up for its lack of numbers, which was the bomb.

'Anarchism' had two common meanings in the later nineteenth century. One was the belief in a social system in which there were no laws imposed from above. The other was indiscriminate and wholesale murder, in order to terrify. The first is an accurate description of the aims of anarchism; the second describes the means favoured by a very small proportion of those who called themselves anarchists. The second was the slightly more common meaning ascribed to anarchism in the 1890s. The reason for that lies in a number of events which happened on the European continent and in north America from the middle 1880s on.

Those events established anarchist 'outrages' as part of the normal political scene. The *Review of Reviews* in 1893 called them 'the ordinary incidents of government in the last decade of the nineteenth century'.[10] They started in May 1886 during a strike in Chicago, where a bomb wounded eighty policemen, and led to the execution of four – possibly innocent – anarchists. (A fifth blew himself up with an exploding cigar the night before he was to be hanged.) In the next two or three years there were riots nearly everywhere in Europe, some of them involving or exploited by anarchists; and attempted political assassinations in France, Russia and Spain. In 1890 the Moscow secret police chief was shot dead, and the Tsar was forced to leave one of his palaces because it had been mined by nihilists. 1892–4 were the worst years. Paris found itself terrorised by an anarchist known as 'Ravachol', and then, after his arrest in March 1892, by Émile Henry, Théodule Meunier and Edouard Vaillant. They went mainly for magistrates' houses, police stations, boulevard cafés and the Chamber of Deputies. The most notorious explosion was the one which destroyed the café where Ravachol had been arrested, and killed its owner, M. Véry, and one of his customers in April 1892. Spain was another major terrorist centre. The most shocking incidents there were the bomb Salvador Franch threw into the auditorium of the Liceo theatre, Barcelona, in November 1893, and an explosion which killed twelve in a religious procession in the same city in July 1896. The anarchist crime-wave brought several distinguished fatalities: president Carnot of France, stabbed to death by Caserio in Lyons in June 1894; the Spanish prime minister, Canovas del Castillo, shot in Santa Agueda by Angiolillo in August 1897; the empress Elizabeth of Austria, stabbed in Geneva by Lucheni in

September 1898; king Humbert of Italy, shot dead in Monza by Bresci in July 1900; and president McKinley of the United States, shot in Buffalo by Czolgosz in September 1901: besides a legion of generals, police chiefs, minor princelings and magistrates. Most of the perpetrators of these crimes were caught, and then hanged, guillotined or garotted according to national taste, but without significantly stemming the carnage.[11] The *Review of Reviews*, again, called it an 'epidemic . . . almost as mysterious and universal as the influenza', against which 'Police precautions appear to be as useless as prophylactics against the fatal sneeze'.[12]

The same journal remarked a little later on the contrast in England, where, it said, 'Our indigenous development of Anarchism is so mild as almost to provoke a smile'.[13] The problem in Britain arose mainly from her situation as an asylum for foreign anarchists who found things too hot for them in their own countries, and who included Kropotkin, the philosopher of anarchism; Louise Michel, nicknamed the 'Red Virgin'; and some of the Paris dynamitards.[14] The presence of these malcontents created some problems for the authorities, as we shall see; but no real dangers on the continental scale. There were one or two small incidents. There was an anarchist bomb-making 'factory' discovered in Walsall in January 1892, in connection with which four men were convicted and imprisoned in April.[15] There was an explosion in Greenwich Park, near the Observatory, on 15 February 1894, which killed a young French anarchist called Martial Bourdin who appears to have stumbled while carrying a bomb. Joseph Conrad based *The Secret Agent* on this event.[16] Directly after it a reinforced dug-out was built on Duck Island in St James's Park for Colonel Majendie to examine suspect bombs in, though it was never ideal, because – being in a lake – it tended to get damp.[17] A little later the same year a foreign anarchist called Francesco Polti was arrested in a London street with explosives in his possession, intended for the Royal Exchange.[18]

Those were the major sensations. Apart from them there were frequent bomb scares, as one would expect, most of which turned out to be either hoaxes or mistakes. Some of the hoaxes were ingenious: like the case of the Tamworth pair who sent twenty-four copies of a magazine stuffed inside bomb shells to government offices in December 1894 in order to win a prize offered by the magazine for the most original way of advertising it.[19] Items mistaken for bombs included packets of Mazawattee tea, a can of disinfectant, and a new design of baby's feeding bottle.[20] A forgivable mistake was made in 1892 in the case of a Swiss national called Cavargna, whom the Birmingham police disbelieved when he told them that egg-shaped bombs found in his possession were intended to exterminate rabbits in New South Wales. (Cavargna explained that they were egg-shaped in order to fool the rabbits into thinking they were eggs, and that they were to be tied around the necks of the rabbits and fitted with fuses to give them time to scurry back to their burrows to blow up their families. He sued for wrongful arrest.)[21] Other 'bombs' were pure hallucinations. Those which turned out to be real were usually found to have nothing at all to do with anarchism, apart from the fact that anarchism may have given the perpetrators the idea. A bomb which exploded in an Inner Circle underground train at Aldersgate station killing one man and injuring ten in April 1897, for example, was probably put there by an ex-employee with a grievance.[22] Native British anarchists were seldom involved at all in violent acts, apart from the Walsall factory, and Oscar Wilde's poor half-mad friend Barlas, who fired a gun in the direction of the Houses of Parliament on the last day of 1891. If the others caused any trouble then it was in far less fearsome ways. Some anarchist newspapers stepped over the line which divided free expression from incitement to violence, and had to be prosecuted as a result.[23] Some open-air anarchist meetings gave offence to local residents in Manchester in 1893, and were consequently stopped.[24] There were one or two cases of anarchists found thieving, and then pleading political principle (*la propriété c'est le vol*) as a defence.[25] But this was really very little. So far as the British people were concerned the excitement the anarchist crime wave caused was mainly vicarious. What happened in Britain was a pale imitation of the horrors happening abroad.

Not that this deterred the sensation-mongers, especially the gutter press and the writers of fiction. Anarchists feature in several bad novels of the 1890s, not always as villains, but usually as men and women armed with demonic powers. Often they were out either to rule the world, which indicated a curious understanding of what anarchy really is, or to destroy it, by a variety of horrifying means. One common one was disease: released either into the air, or into a nation's water-supply.[26] In 1894 the weekly magazine *Tit-Bits* claimed it had discovered such a plot for a fact.[27] By then another spectre had arisen, which was the possibility that anarchists might win the race that was then going on to conquer the air, and use the power this gave them to rain down destruction on a hapless world. That happened more than once in fiction.[28] As the century drew to a close, the vision became even more hideous. J. S. Fletcher's *The Three Days' Terror* (1901) had socialists using chemistry to dissolve central London to dust.[29] A 1906 novel had Jewish anarchists, in league with Germany and with American capitalists, bringing Britain to its knees by means of a great earthquake.[30] At this point these accounts merge with another genre, of catastrophe novels, which became an increasingly common form in Britain and also in France in the wake of Richard Jeffries' *After London* (1885). Anarchists setting off earth tremors and hurling dynamite from navigable airships were just another variant of the many disasters dreamt up for the world in the 1890s, which included great fires, freeze-ups, fogs, fissures, fevers, military armageddons and colliding planets: almost everything, in fact, save the thermo-nuclear bomb.[31]

This must all tell us something about the British national psyche in the 1890s: probably confirming its feelings of unease under the surface jingoism; but it does not really indicate a widespread and genuine fear of the non-fictional anarchist at this time. Reactions to him (or her) ranged from sympathy, even admiration, to rank hostility, but without indicating any sense that Britons were under threat. Even in novels the anarchists' 'leaders' were very often treated favourably. Some of them were brilliant, charismatic men, who had been turned bitter against the world by tortures suffered at the hands of the tsarist police, generally below the waist.[32] Others were beautiful and aristocratic-born women with noble souls, who had also been tortured, but not so that it showed so much. One of them, called Zalma, was enticingly portrayed with 'pulsing busts, which hid behind the down of fur and lace, as though they were moons about to appear from masses of feathery clouds'. If her creator wanted to make her an unsympathetic character, he did not succeed.[33] Another, Natasha in George Griffith's *The Angel of the Revolution* (1893), was the leader of an organisation dedicated to helping the Anglo-Saxon race save the world from Russian despotism, American money-power and British party bickering by means of terror, and then to rule it along Lockian-cum-communist lines. The book ends with a description of the dawn of this new age, and of Natasha's 'loveliness softened and etherealised by the sacred grace of mother-hood'.[34] In Robert Cromie's *A New Messiah* (1902) the hero's aims are treated sympathetically, but not his methods.[35] Other anarchist heroes and heroines were less successful, and less admired, but generally excused on account of their sufferings. One showed glimmerings of goodness when he was persuaded to leave off massacring the population of London by a letter from his dying mother in Islington.[36] Only a few were unmitigated monsters, like Vitroff in Hume Nisbet's *The Great Secret* (1895): 'a man with a nature like a venomous snake' and 'the face and the spirit of a devil'.[37] All the men, incidentally, or nearly all of them, had piercing, jet-black eyes.

Away from this world of fevered imaginings, real-life anarchists and nihilists were regarded more soberly. There were one or two exceptions to this in the periodical press, but generally they were in articles written by foreigners. One notorious one was a contribution to the *New Review* in January 1894 by 'Ivanoff', which tried to tar Russian dissidents in Britain with the anarchist brush.[38] There were others who also confounded the two movements, whether honestly or otherwise, especially in those political circles where dispossession was regarded as the greatest conceivable crime. 'Internationalism, Red Republicanism, Communism, Socialism, Nihilism, Anarchism,' wrote the *Globe* newspaper in July 1895; 'who shall draw the line between the meanings of these appellations? Their central object is always found to be identical; the taking away from those who have for the benefit of those who have not.'[39] That however was a minority view. Most writers made a clear distinction between anarchism and 'nihilism' in particular, if only on the grounds, as the novelist 'Ouida' put it, that 'the latter has the reason of its being in the most brutal government that the world holds'. That – its Russian autocratic adversary – provided a justification for 'nihilism' which anarchism could not claim; but even in anarchism 'Ouida' found qualities, like 'resolution, patience, *sang froid* and absolute indifference to peril', which 'we have been accustomed to consider virtues'.[40] A distinction was also drawn between anarchism and socialism, helped along perhaps by Stepniak's teasing definition of anarchism as 'middle class individualism pushed to the ultimate',[41] and by an article in the *New Review* for September 1894 by one of those ultimate middle-class individualists (an advocate of what ninety years later would have been called the 'privatisation' of the police and the fire service) which he entitled 'A Defence of Anarchy'.[42] This was perhaps a rather precious point; but it indicates the dispassion which pervaded the discussion of anarchy in Britain at this level.

The same objectivity appears in most informed commentators' reluctance to see all anarchists as terrorists. 'There are, as we must always remember,' said the *Review of Reviews* in March 1894, 'Anarchists and Anarchists.'[43] On the one hand there were the Ravachols and Vaillants, whom most people regarded as beasts. On the other, however, there were men like Kropotkin, whom Oscar Wilde once described as 'possessing the soul of a beautiful white Christ'.[44] Most informed critics took the point that anarchist objectives did not necessarily indicate a penchant for violent means: that as a letter to the

Morning Post put it in September 1898, 'Murder is no more an essential part of Anarchism than is a Dr. Jim raid of South African Imperialism.'[45] Another correspondent, to *The Times* in February 1894, put the proportion of violent men among anarcho-socialists at 2 per cent; though he also warned that this might increase if the readers of *The Times* continued to perpetuate a social and economic system which he claimed was 'breeding dynamitards'.[46] Very few people thought it had come to that yet. Journalists describing visits to anarchist clubs in Britain painted a mainly ressuring picture of gatherings of oddities who talked fierily but when it came down to it were really very tame. One of them who was shown round a Whitechapel anarchist den in 1894 reached the conclusion that 'this club is no more dangerous to the State than a Mission-hall'.[47] Even some of the magistrates anarchists were hauled before in the nineties spoke up on their behalf. In October 1893 a Dr Sinclair of Manchester expressed himself full of sympathy for them: 'young men who, with some slight variation in the accident of upbringing, and with a somewhat different mixing of the emotional and intellectual in their composition, might have been officers of the Salvation Army, or teachers of Sunday Schools.' A sense of injustice had pushed them instead into a vague, theoretical sort of millenarianism, with no clear idea of how they were to achieve it, except that 'physical violence has no part in their scheme'.[48] 'Anarchists', ruled another magistrate, a Mr Cluer, in December 1896, 'are very often very mild and quiet individuals. Most of us are better than our opinions.'[49] This revealed a calm discrimination, which in harder-hit countries was inconceivable.

Just occasionally the most violent anarchists were actively defended, even in the 'respectable' press; or at least (and more often) excused. In September 1894, for example, the *Fortnightly Review* carried a defence of them by Charles Malato, who portrayed Ravachol as a kind of latter-day Robin Hood and professed to prefer his 'savage revolt', which was at any rate 'sincere', to the crimes of some of history's more favoured sons.[50] Not many others went quite this far; but there were dozens of commentators in Britain who were willing to plead mitigation for the worst anarchist outrages. A ninety-year-old Earl Grey, for example, attributed them to 'the hard conditions of life' of the working classes, which in turn were due to tariff barriers abroad.[51] The *Review of Reviews* blamed 'the mal-adjustment of social conditions'; and – if anarchism ever caught on in Britain – the kind of anti-social activity which had depopulated much of Scotland in order that a millionaire 'may have solitude for his deer'.[52] The sensational novelist William le Queux, in a book of stories about Russian nihilists published in 1896, reiterated the old British notion that 'Revolutionaries are the creation of circumstances, of the general discontent of the people'; and its logical corollary, that 'Discontent only grows the more when it is repressed'.[53] The organic analogy was often brought into play here: for example by a contributor to the family magazine *Good Words* in 1894, who argued that 'Just as a carbuncle proclaims disorder in the human body, so Anarchy proclaims some disorder in the body politic'.[54]

Others made the case that governments perpetrated worse crimes than anarchists: like taxation, according to Auberon Herbert, who cannot have been entirely serious;[55] or legalised violence on a much larger scale. 'For every drop of blood shed by those whom society calls "evil-doers",' wrote one apologist in 1898, 'rivers flow by the hand of "the community's representative"; for every sorrow inflicted by a burglar or an Anarchist, towns are desolated by "Her Majesty's Ship Blunderer."' [56] The *Review of Reviews* made a related point when it drew attention to the puniness of the anarchists' efforts by the side of other causes of tragedy. 'Tuberculosis, which slays two thousand babies every year in Paris, is a far deadlier foe than dynamite'; as were the railway train, which killed scores in Britain every year, and coal mining, which claimed 340 lives in a single night at the Albion colliery in South Wales in June 1894. 'Anarchy will have to multiply many times before the Anarchist risk can be counted as more than a small percentage of the risk which every miner faces without a thought, and without even feeling himself a brave man for doing so.'[57] A glance through the pages of any popular newspaper of the time lends credence to the *Review*'s case. Anarchist outrages anywhere were mere drops in an ocean of murder, suicide, infanticide, epidemic, accident and other 'natural' horrors, which Britons suffered almost as a matter of course in the 1890s. This may not have justified the former, and was not intended to; but it had the effect of throwing them into a kind of perspective.

The same lines of argument are found in British anarchist newspapers of the time, which only very rarely supported the excesses of their comrades abroad.[58] Generally those excesses were explained away as 'the natural consequences of a society based on violence and on the exploitation of man by man',[59] but condemned both morally and tactically. The only substantial difference was that anarchists regarded colliery disasters as *culpable*, because they were caused by capitalist 'cupidity'.[60] So were other forms of working-class suffering. 'Violence is bad,' commented 'Diogenes' in *Freedom* in 1896; 'but starvation, degradation, and the habitual subjection of man by his fellows are a thousand times worse, and if violence can help to remove these, then up with violence. The real argument against it, however, is, that in very few cases is it really helpful.'[61] This applied to Britain in particular, where (claimed the *Torch*) 'there is no occasion for bombs . . . So long as the propaganda by speech and press is possible, it is much better understood and more fruitful.'[62] That was also H. B. Samuels's answer to the question he posed in the *Commonweal* in March 1894: 'Why do not Anarchists throw bombs here in England?' Fundamentally it was because of 'the freedom of speech, pen and platform we enjoy', and which made more drastic measures unnecessary.[63] Of course all this may have been a front, but it was a remarkably uniform one. Anarchists in Britain took very great pains to distance themselves from outrage, and from the image of the half-crazed bomb-throwing fanatic which seemed to have taken hold of the popular mind.

All of which – if it was to be believed – bolstered a venerable liberal prejudice. 'The bomb', wrote Samuels, 'is the direct result of the throttling of free speech';[64] which was the simple reason why it so afflicted the Continent. It followed that further throttlings would make things worse. Consequently liberal opinion in Britain was highly critical of European over-reaction to the anarchist crime wave,[65] and anxious that its own government should not fall into the same trap. 'There is no reason for making a fuss about it', urged the *Review of Reviews* in 1893 after a bomb had killed a policeman in Dublin. 'It is a disagreeable incident, and of course very deplorable', but not all that significant in the wider scheme of things. 'The right thing to do is simply to treat it as all in the day's work.'[66]

Parliamentarians generally agreed with this. Demands at Westminster for strong measures against terrorists were rare. The most serious was in July 1894, when Lord Salisbury moved a bill to empower the state to prevent the immigration of dangerous aliens, to which the Liberal government's response was that unless it were 'absolutely required . . . You would have great difficulty in passing it', and to refer Salisbury to the precedent of 1858.[67] No other pressure got even as far as a parliamentary bill.[68] If anything the events of the 1890s made this less likely, by emphasising anarchism's marginality. When they were flushed out into the open, these conspirators looked poor creatures indeed. Scarcely anyone took seriously the notion that the structure of British society could possibly be threatened by them: to think so savoured of paranoia. Nor did it occur to anyone that they might be behind any of Britains's other social and political troubles: the strike wave, for example, or pulling the strings of the ILP. Violent anarchism was an irritation, but tolerable in Britain, whatever it was like abroad. It was certainly more tolerable than Fenianism, which liberal Britain had weathered well. It would probably blow over. In the meantime there was no cause for panic. Old values died hard, and were not yet felt to require jettisoning in order to make life marginally, even questionably, more secure. The only effect of that would be, as a Liberal Home Secretary put it in 1893, to give free and much sought-after publicity 'to a handful of insignificant men'.[69]

It was not, however, quite as simple as that. Asquith's was the cool, dispassionate, liberal response to the anarchist wave of the 1890s; but there was a growing minority of people who believed it was a foolish one. They believed that for one of two reasons: either because they had changed, become less liberal; or because the circumstances had. They usually claimed it was the latter, as people in such situations are prone to do. Violent anarchism was a new phenomenon, quite distinct from anything that had gone before, and nullifying the old liberal rules. This was Balfour's case for wanting anarchist meetings banned in 1893, and his uncle Salisbury's for wishing to withdraw the right of asylum from foreign anarchists the following year. In the first place, as Balfour pointed out in response to Asquith's gibe about their 'insignificance', numbers did not matter any more. Dynamite had seen to that. The anarchists' 'power for evil' no longer depended on how many they were, but on two things: 'their own indifference to life, and . . . the brutal courage which they may be able to display in using the resources of chemical discovery for the most brutal form of destruction of innocent men, women, and children.' This was unprecedented; as was the extremism of their aims. Those aims were to destroy 'all forms of social order',[70] quite indiscriminately, and with nothing to put in their place. It was not just a question of violence. The anarchists' argument that States inflicted more violence than they did, which was true, nevertheless cut little ice amongst people who believed that everything, including killing, should be governed by rules. Anarchists acknowledged no rules at all, not even ones of their own. That may have been their basic fault. It was certainly something which marked them off from their revolutionary predecessors. That was why the Orsini affair of 1858 was not felt to be a fair precedent. The revolutionaries of that time were quite different. 'My whole case', Lord Salisbury told Parliament when the parallel was raised in 1894, 'is that everything has changed since the days of Kossuth, Mazzini and Garibaldi.' They could agree with these men, or not; 'but it is an insult to them to mention their names in the same breath as the men who raise our horror to-day.'[71] The Liberal Lord Rosebery agreed. 'The Anarchists do not represent to us any of those revolutionary graces which in old days recommended many political refugees to our shores.'[72] They were quite unlike the breed of freedom-fighter for which the policy of asylum had been forged in the middle of the century, and consequently beyond the pale of a reasonable toleration now.

That pale may just possibly have been shrinking anyway. Toleration is easy in optimistic times; it was much more difficult in an age as fearful of so many things as the 1890s. Anarchism was not one of those things, but it may have suffered at the hands of a hostility which was engendered by other terrors, like socialism or democracy or collective trade-union power. This was how the Russian exile Stepniak explained the reaction against it in Britain: by the fact that its outrages were associated with a disturbing 'idea'. No one feared the outrages, but the idea was something altogether more dangerous. The erosion or overthrow of liberal capitalism, by other more subtle methods than the bomb, was coming to seem possible, if not inevitable.[73] This naturally aroused apprehensions, and undermined the confidence which had been at the heart of the older toleration. Anarchists like the Walsall Four, who were punished out of all proportion to their offence, were the victims of a relative intolerance and a hatred which gathered their emotional strength from these more general qualms.

That was one thing against them. Another was the sense of obligation British governments felt to their neighbours, who were harder-pressed than they. From this point of view the fact that the anarchists did not appear to want to threaten Britain was not the end of it. In a way it was to their discredit. *The Times* believed there was a reason for it: which was to avoid endangering the policy of asylum which gave them the freedom in England to plot their dastardly deeds abroad.[74] That view was shared by foreign governments. Britain was the only country in Europe which had no means at all of excluding any foreigner who wanted to come to Britain for any reason: no Alien Act, and extradition laws which explicitly favoured political fugitives.[75] The result of this was predictable. Political fugitives used Britain as a kind of sanctuary when things got too hot for them abroad, which irritated the authorities which were making it hot. Their irritation seemed to be justified by Lord Salisbury's claim in introducing his 1894 bill that anarchist outrages were 'to a great extent prepared and organised on this soil': which got him into trouble with the Liberal Prime Minister, who regarded it as an unproven slur.[76] Continental governments preferred to believe Salisbury. They did not hide their resentment. In St Petersburg in November 1897, for example, the Russian foreign minister drew the British ambassador aside to speak to him of it. Of course, he said, there were many material differences of interest and opinion between their two countries; but quite apart from these 'there was one very serious matter which led, on the Russian side, to a feeling of dislike & distrust towards England. This was that we harboured and gave hospitality to a group of men whose open and declared aim was the destruction of Law and Order in Russia.' The ignorant, he went on, attributed this to English antipathy towards Russia, which he knew to be 'nonsense'; but still he felt that there was 'a limit to the indulgence which should be shown'.[77] Russia was not alone in thinking that Britain's indulgence recently had strayed over that line.

This was probably the biggest source of pressure on Britain in the 1890s to take action against anarchists and nihilists. That pressure was felt all the time. Its mildest form was the application which foreign governments periodically made to the British authorities to enquire into known anarchists living in Britain, or to put men on to watch them.[78] Ideally, however, the Continent would have liked her to do much more. One of the most persistent requests was for her to join in arrangements with them to return anarchists back to their own countries when they fled abroad. Other ideas put to Britain were for closer police co-operation across national boundaries, and for the outlawing of anarchist doctrines. Specific proposals along these and similar lines came from France in 1892, from Belgium and Spain in 1893, from Austria in 1894, from Italy in 1898, from Russia in 1900, and from Russia and Germany in 1901, 1902 and 1904: a barrage of petitions, for every one of which the British authorities felt some sympathy.[79] Even if they had not, the demands would have had to be taken seriously. The 1890s were highly dangerous years for Britain diplomatically. They were not a time when she could afford to risk making enemies abroad, for little or no tangible return.

All these circumstances boded ill for the kinds of freedom, or licence, anarchists and other revolutionaries had enjoyed in Britain until then. Lord Salisbury believed they cast doubt on her whole tradition of asylum. Hence his 1894 bill, which was designed to undermine it. On the debate on that bill, Lord Rosebery also expressed the opinion that 'we are hampered too much by traditional watchwords about Great Britain being the asylum open to all nations'.[80] *The Times* in February the same year agreed: that in view of the anarchists' and nihilists' designs on 'foreign and friendly governments', it was 'possible to carry the theory of "liberty for everybody on British soil" a little too far'.[81] The will was there to change this, on the part of some of Britain's leaders. But there was a stumbling-block.

The stumbling-block was 'public opinion'. This was believed to be an insuperable obstacle to any anti-anarchist measure which required *legislation*. This was what Lord Rosebery told his ambassador in Madrid in November 1893: that 'all legislation of this kind was regarded with the most jealous suspicion in this country'.[82] That was partly because of the country's attachment to the principle of asylum, and partly because it did not trust foreign courts (especially Russia's) to deal fairly with politicos. 'I am afraid English public opinion', minuted a Foreign under-secretary on another occasion, 'will not sanction any arrangement for the punishment of such offences unless under the immediate pressure of alarm and indignation at the perpetration of them here.'[83] Salisbury himself in 1898 admitted to his minister in Berne that in England 'great objection would be felt to any attempt to meet the dangers of the anarchist conspiracy by restraining or encroaching upon the liberty of the rest of the community.'[84] He felt bound to make this crystal clear from the beginning of an anti-anarchist conference held in Rome at the end of that year to all the other governments who participated in it, so as not to arouse expectations which could not be satisfied.[85] He said the same in reply to Russia's and Germany's entreaties in 1900.[86] In February 1902 the Turkish sultan was fed an identical line when he asked for Turkish exile meetings in London to be banned: 'I replied', reported the British ambassador to the Porte, 'that the question of political asylum was a very delicate one and that any govt. that attempted to curtail the immunity granted in England to political refugees would have a very serious question on their hands and evoke an outburst of public opinion which would probably considerably shorten their existence.'[87] And so on. Each time legislation against anarchists was mooted, this was the excuse that was trotted out. Popular prejudice would not allow it. That may not have been true. It is impossible to know for sure, because the public mind on this issue was never properly tested. Nevertheless it was thought to be a likelihood. At the very least, minuted Salisbury's successor as Foreign Secretary in 1901, new laws against anarchists 'would be formidable fences to ride at'.[88] They might be able to jump them, or not; but in the domestic political circumstances of the 1890s and early 1900s, with so much residual mid-century liberalism about, it seemed wiser not to try.

This then was Britain's dilemma. Her governments could not legislate against the new terrorist threat, especially at the behest of foreign countries, for fear of offending their own constituents, who did not feel threatened by anarchism. On the other hand they could not do nothing, for the sake of those abroad who did feel – and were – under threat. The problem seemed insoluble; but there was a possible way out. That was for Britain to demonstrate that her *existing* laws and law-enforcing agencies were adequate in the face of this particular form of crime. That way her foreign critics would be mollified, without the need to legislate. It was a sensible strategy, and, as we shall see, successful to a point. But it also had the effect of putting a heavy burden of responsibility on the shoulders of those already charged with combating political crimes in England. These included magistrates, judges, and government law officers; and also, in particular, the Special Branch (or Branches) of the London Metropolitan Police.

CHAPTER 8

Consolidation
1890–1903

This, then, was Britain's situation in the 1890s. Violent anarchism touched her only slightly. It was a problem for her mainly because of the presence in England of foreign anarchists who posed a danger to governments abroad. This danger created pressure on Britain to co-operate with foreign states for the control or suppression of anarchism, which the British people were either deaf or antipathetic to, partly because of the lack of danger to them, and partly because of their devotion to the policy of asylum. The effect of this was to place British governments in a quandary, from which there was only one escape. That was to demonstrate convincingly that one of the reasons for their failure to co-operate with foreign governments was the fact that no such co-operation was necessary. Britain could cope with anarchists and their deeds to the reasonable satisfaction of everybody: both those at home who wanted her traditional liberties to be preserved, and those abroad who wanted the liberties of the most threatening anarchists to be curtailed.

How far government ministers genuinely believed this is open to question. Salisbury's 1894 Aliens bill indicates that he, at least, was not entirely content with things as they were. A few years later his government drew up two new pieces of legislation which were designed to plug gaps. The first extended the 1883 Explosives Act to cover explosive materials acquired for use abroad; the second amended the extradition laws to exclude political assassination from the list of offences previously thought to be exempt.[1] Both these bills arose out of promises made to the 1898 Rome Anti-Anarchist Conference, at which the British representatives came in for a good deal of criticism for the objections they raised to just about every practical proposal made.[2] In the end the government felt unable to pursue even these very mild measures, which were dropped before they came to Parliament;[3] but this did not mean that ministers were truly persuaded of their redundancy. It is rather more likely that they accepted the fact of their impotence in this regard only with reluctance, before presenting as a virtue what was really a necessity.

Nevertheless this was the line they took. At the start of the Rome Conference Lord Salisbury had predicted that 'our system will be much attacked', and saw it as the British representatives' 'main duty . . . to give good reasons for refusing to change it in any essential point'.[4] The chief reason given was that change was unnecessary;[5] which by the end of the Conference the leader of the British delegation claimed he had persuaded everyone of.[6] This was Britain's consistent position throughout the 1890s and into the new century. 'H.M. Ministers are of opinion', wrote Rosebery to the Spanish ambassador in 1893, 'that the present law is quite adequate for dealing with this class of crime and are therefore unable to enter into any international engagement . . .'[7] In August 1894 Asquith told the House of Commons that he thought 'the measures taken in this country for dealing with anarchists to be at least as well-considered and effective for this purpose as those adopted elsewhere.'[8] In response to the Russo-German proposals for new police measures against anarchism in 1901 the Home Office advised the Foreign Secretary to reply 'that the organisation already existing in this country works well & seems to us sufficient for the purpose'.[9] In this case the Home Office had the backing of the Metropolitan Police, for reasons of their own.[10] Publicly at least, this was where Britain stood. There was no necessity for her to compromise her liberalism in the face of anarchism, because that liberalism had not yet been shown to have let her down.

Of course this did not mean that Britain needed to take no action at all: only that such action should keep within the existing law. Sometimes that law had to be stretched a little. One law which was so stretched was the law on extradition, which was a problem because of its ambiguity on the question of 'ordinary' crimes committed for political motives. In 1890 an extradition order on a man called Angelo Castioni for muder was quashed on appeal on the grounds that the murder was political.[11] That would have let anarchists like François and Meunier, who were captured in England and charged with complicity in the Café Véry bomb outrage in Paris in April 1892, off the hook too. This was precisely the point the proposed amendment of 1899 was designed to clear up. Without such an amendment the law appeared to be defective. The difficulty was circumvented, however, in October 1892, when the magistrate François was brought before decided that the Café Véry bomb was not a political act but one of personal revenge for the arrest of Ravachol.[12] Two years later the extradition of Meunier was allowed on appeal, on the somewhat specious grounds that anarchism could not be defined as 'political'. A political motive, ruled Mr Justice Cave, implied the desire to replace one government by another. This clearly excluded anarchists, who were against governments of any kind.[13] That ingenious distinction plugged the most serious hole in Britain's legal defences. But it would not do for lesser crimes, where people might not take kindly to refugees being trapped by a lawyers' dodge.

Some of those lesser crimes could never come within the purview of British courts, because they were not culpable in English law. This applied to expressions of revolutionary opinion, including anarchist opinion, so long as they did not directly incite to crime. This was the reply Britain gave on more than one occasion to foreign governments who objected to anarchist propaganda in England;[14] together sometimes with little homilies on the function of free speech as a 'safety valve'.[15] Free speech, however, went too far when it advocated murder, which was the point at which anarchist propaganda rendered its disseminators liable, not to extradition, but to prosecution and imprisonment in England. This happened in one celebrated case in 1898, when the Russian dissident Vladimir Burtsev and his Polish assistant Clement Wierzbicki were arrested and charged with incitement to murder after articles commending terrorist methods had appeared in an emigré journal Burtsev edited. That prosecution was undertaken at the behest of the Russian government, and was at first looked on rather nervously by the British authorities, in case a Russophobe jury might regard anything written against the Tsar as fair comment. But they persisted in it, to please the Russians, and were rewarded with a 'guilty' verdict and a sentence of eighteen months hard labour for Burtsev: which he served at Pentonville and Wormwood Scrubs.[16]

Continental governments seem to have been reassured and even impressed by the outcome of the Burtsev case, as they were intended to be. They may also have been impressed by Britain's treatment of her own relatively minor anarchist problem, which was firm whenever that problem looked like becoming a genuine threat. English courts did not spare anyone who was caught red-handed with bombs on British soil, for example; or any Englishman found inciting to violence. Walsall was the prime example. Three of the defendants in that case were given ten years' penal servitude, and another five years, for being in possession of castings for bombs which they maintained – but the judge chose not to accept – were for the use of revolutionaries in Russia.[17] In May 1894 Giuseppe Farnara and Francesco Polti were sentenced to twenty and ten years' imprisonment respectively, for plotting to blow up the Royal Exchange in London in retaliation for the annual British tourist invasion of Italy.[18] After the Walsall trial the anarchist David Nicoll published an article in the *Commonweal* asking rhetorically whether the men who in his opinion were responsible for it – the Home Secretary, the judge, and police Inspector Melville – were 'fit to live', and was promptly punished for that with eighteen months in gaol.[19] A little later two more English anarchists, Thomas Cantwell and Carl Quinn, got six months each for being taken to imply at a meeting to mark the opening of the new Tower Bridge that they thought the royal family ought to have their throats cut.[20] Neither the verdicts nor the sentences in any of these cases may have been entirely fair. Nevertheless they were an earnest of the British authorities' need to be seen to be tackling the most dangerous manifestations of anarchism, without recourse to continental methods of control.

Not all the government's prosecutions of anarchists were so successful. One fish that got away was a German anarchist called Fritz Brall who was found in 1894 to have quite a little chemical laboratory in his lodgings in Chelsea, but not enough to convince an unusually charitable judge that explosives were the only recipes that could be concocted there.[21] As well as this, many cases never came to court. Some inflammatory speeches could not be prosecuted because of lack of conclusive evidence. Others were adjudged to be too marginal, or too trivial. Liberal governments felt that the best strategy anyway was to ignore them. In February 1894, at meetings of the unemployed at Tower Hill, the socialist John Williams talked of the police being 'sent to heaven by chemical parcel post', and an effigy of Asquith was paraded suspended from a gallows: yet the Home Office's advice to Asquith, which he followed, was not to take any of this seriously.[22] Such discrimination – like picking the bad balls to hit – probably served the government better than a wilder anti-anarchist broadside would have done. A few severe sentences on the grossest offenders at especially sensitive times – the Walsall and Nicoll trials came at the height of the worst bomb campaign in Paris, Cantwell and Quinn's prosecution just after the assassination of President Carnot, and the Burtsev case at a particularly delicate moment in Anglo-Russian relations – made Britain's point about the adequacy of her laws very effectively.

That was something; but it was not all. Laws were useful to punish in extreme cases, and maybe to deter more generally, but by themselves they furnished no certain guarantee to anyone that terrorism was being kept under control. They were not the British government's main line of defence against anarchism. That line was a thin plain-clothes one, provided by the various police forces of the country, and spear-headed by the Special Branch of the Metropolitan CID.

It was during this period that the Special Branch really came into its own. In the 1880s the Special Irish Branch had played second or third fiddle to other agencies like Jenkinson's and Gosselin's; but this seems to have changed with Jenkinson's departure and the shift of counter-subversive emphasis away from Fenianism and towards the anarchists. That shift was reflected in the fortunes of Gosselin's counter-Fenian organisation, which still functioned in the 1890s, but on a much reduced scale. He was now in charge of operations in America, where in March 1892 he employed one secret agent, seven informants, and two 'sub-agents' to act as what he called 'buffers' (to preserve anonymity) between them. The cost of that operation, he claimed, was a good deal less than it had been formerly. At 'Home' he had 'agencies' in Paris, Dublin, Newcastle, London and Manchester, and eleven informants, plus some clerical and London police help. The total bill for this was around £8,200 a year. On 1 April 1892, however, that establishment was cut drastically. All the British and Irish 'agencies' were closed down, leaving just Paris; four of the informants were sacked, and two sent to America, leaving Gosselin with only five at 'Home'. All this saved about £1,200 a year. His account of these cuts to the Home Secretary ended by emphasising that they were 'grounded on the idea of continued quiet in secret Societies', which he feared might not be forthcoming if 'the just aspirations of the Irish Race' to Home Rule were not met.[23] There is no evidence that Matthews was persuaded by this to change his mind, either with regard to Home Rule, or about the cuts. The result was that Gosselin's secret service diminished in the 1890s, in size and probably in importance too.

As it did so, the Metropolitan Police Special Branch established itself more securely. It was cut too, but not quite so drastically, and not for long. At the end of 1891 'Section B' was reduced by four constables to twenty-one.[24] That was the size of the Special Branch which coped with most of the anarchist incidents of the early 1890s, until December 1894 when it was made up to twenty-five again.[25] A few months before this there were reports in the press of plans to make 'a considerable addition' to the 'secret police system', which however are not borne out by the surviving official evidence.[26] Throughout the 1890s the Special

Branch consisted of just a couple of dozen men, headed by the Scotsman John Littlechild until he resigned to go into private practice in April 1893.[27] (One of his first commissions was to procure evidence for the Marquess of Queensberry against Oscar Wilde.) He was succeeded by the Kerry-born William Melville – Member of the Royal Victorian Order, Chevalier of the Order of Dannebrog, Order of Christ, Crown of Italy, Officier de la Légion d'Honneur, Commander of the Order of Isabel la Catolica, Chevalier of the Order of Francis Joseph of Austria, and Knight of the Order of St Silvester of the Holy Roman Empire – who headed the Branch for the next ten years.[28]

Melville's impressive list of battle-honours illustrates the importance that was attached to his personal qualities by the governments he assisted at home and abroad. He was clearly the dominating figure in the Special Branch even before his elevation to its Chief Inspectorate, and may have taken control of counter-refugee operations as early as 1891.[29] He soon became something of a *bête noire* among the anarchists. He was, as we have seen, on Nicoll's blacklist in 1892; Meunier when he was captured in April 1894 was reported to have shouted 'To fall into your hands, Melville! You, the only man I feared, and whose description was engraved on my mind!';[30] and Giuseppe Farnara claimed he was out for Melville's blood when *he* was charged a little later, because he had 'arrested, or caused to be arrested, too many of my comrades'.[31] No doubt Melville found this flattering. He appears to have been a dedicated and ambitious detective, though according to the *Police Chronicle* he did not look like one.[32] His *Who's Who* entry, and contemporary recollections of him, record no leisure interests at all, as they do for Littlechild (a founder member of the 'Metropolitan Police Minstrels')[33] and for Williamson (a keen sculler and gardener).[34] Nor do they suggest that he inspired as much affection as they did. He was described as 'a big broad-shouldered man with tremendous strength and unlimited courage', who did not always bother to go through all the strict legal formalities with criminal 'small fry' when a good hiding would do.[35] His official service record with the Metropolitan Police has, oddly, not survived.

There is also no surviving list of Special Branch personnel from this period, which means that it is difficult to generalise about the sort of men they were. Several accounts agree that they were mainly Irish, as most of the best known of them – Melville himself, John Sweeney and Patrick Quinn, for example – certainly were.[36] They had to be good linguists.[37] They fostered a reputation for 'the highest integrity', as of course they would need to, and for unusual, even superhuman, sagacity.[38] One old Special Branch hand wrote of their 'brains keener than Sherlock Holmes's', which was one in the eye for Conan Doyle, whose characteristic portrayal of the Scotland Yard dullard was greatly resented amongst the police; another called them 'master-minds'.[39] Some of them were claimed to have psychic powers: which had already saved John Sweeney, for example, from a messy death on the evening of 30 May 1884 when a sudden unaccountable 'urge' had made him leave his office in Scotland Yard less than an hour before it was blown up by the Fenians; and which should have alerted the authorities to the murder of Sir Curzon Wyllie days before it happened in July 1909, if they had taken proper notice of one of Detective-Inspector Dan McLaughlin's dreams.[40] Melville's own more cerebral skills were illustrated, repeatedly, by one particular story of how during a procession to honour a foreign sovereign he trapped a possible malefactor who was working as a cellar man for a wine merchant, by asking him for a special brand of champagne and then 'with a sudden inspiration' locking the cellar door behind him until the procession had passed.[41] That seems to have impressed a lot of people. Special Branch men were supposed – though there may have been nothing in this – to have a secret sign when they met each other, like freemasons, which was 'rubbing the right ear and stroking the side of the cheek'.[42] Some of them had right-wing opinions (though not noticeably out of line for the period) on subjects like socialism, immigration and Jews.[43]

Their duties may have been spelled out precisely to them, but they have not survived for posterity in any published form. The section of the 1907 edition of the Metropolitan Police 'General Orders' which purports to deal with the 'Organisation and duties of [the] Special Branch' in fact tells nothing at all.[44] There is no clear statement of those duties in any police or Home Office memorandum of the time which has come to light. Ex-Special Branch men who wrote memoirs had differing recollections of them. Basil Thomson, who took over the Branch later, defined its duties as 'to foresee and prevent political agitators from committing crime in order to terrorise the community into granting them what they want'.[45] That put it very precisely, and very narrowly. Harold Brust was under the impression that it had the slightly different but no less limited function of 'shielding the great and the famous'.[46] John Sweeney's version was that the Branch 'dealt with all political criminals, misdemeanants and suspects; watched Fenians, members of the Clan-na-Gael, Anarchists, and so on'.[47] That appears on the surface to be a much wider, or more flexible, brief. On the other hand it may have grown naturally out of the Branch's function as

Thomson and Brust described it. 'The Branch believes', wrote Brust, 'that quiet prevention is better than attempts to cure by the Mailed Fist or the Big Stick.'[48] Prevention involved anticipation, which meant tracing potential outrages to their source. Almost any anti-establishment group or movement could be a possible source of eventual outrage, if you wanted to cover every base. Terrorism could be the ultimate justification for Special Branch interest in nearly anybody who did not conform.

In fact it seems not to have been used as such, save in one possibly exceptional case. The surviving evidence, which is very patchy indeed, suggests that the Branch did not often venture beyond those individuals and organisations which could reasonably be suspected of criminal designs. In the 1890s this meant foreign anarchists, and Fenians. There is no record of any significant Special Branch involvement outside these two groups. Even among the anarchists it picked and chose. Most anarchists it regarded as harmless. This was in spite of recurrent warnings from foreign governments about their activities in England, all of which the Branch treated with reserve. Foreign police forces were notoriously prone to be misled by 'untrustworthy informants', as Anderson put it in response to a French rumour of a plot in 1894;[49] or even on occasion to invent 'a wholly false and dreadful catalogue of crimes' to blacken the name of an exile. This, wrote Harold Brust, was a particular habit of the Russian Third Section, or Okhrana, which in the end 'defeated itself, for nobody attached the slightest importance to what they said'.[50] Most of the Special Branch's enquiries on behalf of foreign governments uncovered nothing, or nothing very dangerous. An investigation by Melville and Sweeney into the activities of James Tochatti, who was active in England, is typical. The Spanish government had heard that Tochatti was plotting to assassinate their king. Sweeney found on the contrary that he was merely 'an extravagant talker', who was not worth taking seriously.[51] 'Reports of this sort are for ever coming to the ears of Scotland Yard', he wrote in his memoirs later. 'Fortunately the great majority of them have no foundation.'[52] This suggests that the Special Branch discriminated. It was less impressed by hearsay than its continental informants, and less apt to confuse sedition with dissent. This may have kept its activities within narrower bounds than might otherwise have been the case; together of course with its smallness, which will have limited its field perforce.

Much of its work was done at the behest or suggestion of foreign governments. Among the scores of anarchists investigated in this way were Enrico Malatesta in 1890 and 1891; Vladimir Burtsev in 1892, five years before his arrest; and countess Clementine Hugo in 1894. (The countess was a sister-in-law of the novelist, and according to Melville became an anarchist sympathiser when her sixteen-year-old daughter was abducted 'for the pleasure of the King of Italy'.)[53] Usually the results were the same as in Tochatti's case, but just occasionally (with Malatesta, for example) the Special Branch's enquiries revealed information which confirmed a foreign government's fears. Such information was always passed back to the continental police, either directly or through diplomatic channels.[54] Several foreign police authorities also issued regular bulletins reporting on the anarchist movement in their countries generally, especially after the Rome Conference of 1898.[55] Those bulletins were supposed to include lists of anarchists expelled to Britain, so that the Branch could check on them when they arrived, but that system never worked satisfactorily. In the first place not all governments sent lists: not, for example, Germany, Russia, Spain or Italy. Secondly, those which did often sent them weeks after the expulsions had taken place, by which time the anarchists had arrived and been able to hide.[56] Thirdly, the lists only covered malefactors who had been expelled officially. 'Many foreign Anarchists,' explained Anderson in 1892, 'anxious to avoid a decree of expulsion . . . have quietly crossed the channel without attracting notice, and are found in the usual haunts frequented by their confederates in London; but at present they act with great caution, and it is a matter of difficulty to ascertain even their names.'[57] This whole question was a delicate one between Britain and continental governments. Britain resented those governments using her as a kind of political penal colony, but was usually told it was her own fault for having no alien laws. Clearly she could not complain if foreign anarchists chose to come to her. It seemed to be a different matter if the continental authorities directly deported them to England: but even this distinction was meaningless whilst there was no other European country they could go to anyway. The French, Belgian and Spanish governments agreed to apprise Britain of anarchists embarking for England, but often seemed to forget.[58] The Special Branch therefore was forced back on to its own sources of information, which included informal contacts abroad.

This screening of suspected anarchists coming to England must have taken up much of the Special Branch's time. A Home Office memorandum of August 1897 described the procedure that was followed. Firstly 'the officers escorting the man to the steamer at Calais would acquaint the Special Police Officer stationed there, who would telegraph to the Officer at Dover that an expulsé was coming over here.' If for some reason that did not happen, then 'the Captain of the Steamer would point out the expelled man to the Special Officer at Dover'. That officer would then 'interrogate the man, & if his destination was London would telegraph to Scotland Yard when the man would be seen & located in the usual way'.[59] What the Branch was interested in initially was an address. It needed to know where all the anarchists lived. Thereafter it must have left most of them alone. It had nothing like the resources to keep watches on them day and night. If it needed to it could put a tail on any one of them later. But that generally only happened where an anarchist was suspected of a particular offence.

The Branch clearly had a very full dossier on foreign anarchists in the 1890s, compiled in the first instance from this source. It was very rarely found wanting when it was asked for information about particular anarchists, either by the Home Office or by foreign governments. That information was supplemented by the results of its own enquiries, and by intelligence gathered from spies. Much of it was got from reading the anarchists' own press, and from interviewing people like landladies and neighbours who knew them. Occasionally officers were put on to 'shadowing' or 'housing' them: watching their movements continuously, and following them.[60] The problems with this technique were that it was wasteful of manpower, with three shifts for each suspect, and unpleasant and dangerous. 'The detective knows', wrote Sweeney, 'that at any moment the man followed may realise himself pursued, and turn on the pursuer with a knife or revolver; the detective does not know when relief may come.'[61] Another ploy was to infiltrate anarchist meetings, though that was scarcely less perilous among men who were perceived as 'possibly half-demented, and therefore more dangerous than anyone save a New Guinea head-hunter'. One means of protection was disguise, which apparently was quite simple among these people: all one had to do was grow a stubble, dirty the hands and face, rumple the hair and smoke 'offensively foul foreign cigarettes'.[62] That fooled them all. Detective Constable Herbert Fitch preferred to hide in cupboards, from which in 1905 he heard Lenin – 'a smooth-haired, oval-faced, narrow-eyed, typical Jew' – preaching 'bloodshed on a colossal scale'. A little later he adopted the more daring ruse of dressing as a waiter at a restaurant where Lenin was dining with a secret society called the 'Foreign Barbers of London', and from which he cleverly smuggled out an agenda, with the result (apparently) that the Russian revolution had to be postponed for another twelve years.[63] Other Special Branch men disguised themselves as sanitary inspectors, rate collectors, motor mechanics, house painters and (as we shall see) free lovers, in pursuit of their anarchist prey.[64] They may not always have enjoyed their experiences at the time; but they enjoyed recounting them, and possibly embellishing them, when it came to penning their memoirs later on.

There is very much less in those memoirs about agents and informers, probably because they do not reflect so sensationally on their authors; but it is likely that these were a far more significant intelligence source. One renegade revolutionary claimed in 1906 that the 'ranks of Anarchy' were 'simply honey-combed' with them.[65] They were also a highly secret source, even between detectives, which is why they do not figure large in the surviving official documents either, and still might not even if more official documents survived. Each detective had his own private circle of informers, whom he paid out of his own pocket, and then claimed for on his expenses. 'No receipts are given,' wrote a leading detective chief inspector in 1893, 'for obvious reasons, and it is looked upon as an unpardonable violation of duty to disclose such an informer's name.'[66] If it were disclosed, explained the Police Commissioner Sir Edward Bradford in 1902, or an informer feared it might be, then people in a position to supply information 'will refrain from doing so through dread of the vengeance of comrades which would follow upon their connection with the authorities being suspected'. This was one of his main objections to the kind of co-operation with foreign police forces which would have them pooling their sources.[67] Many of these informers informed on a regular basis, and so shaded into the adjacent category of secret agent or spy. A memorandum by Bradford in April 1902 acknowledged that the Special Branch did rely heavily on 'private agency' of this kind for much of its information, for the simple reason that 'the difference in habits and language makes it difficult for any but a few specially qualified officers to continue mixing with these aliens without being detected'. It also recognised the main pitfall of the system, which was that information gathered in this way might not always be trustworthy.[68] Depending as they did on 'a system of espionage', confirmed Sweeney, 'it is clearly inevitable that there should arise constant gossip and fabrications, harassing and perplexing the authorities.'[69] For this reason Bradford assured the Home Secretary that 'The London police are careful not to act on it to the prejudice of the persons affected until they have tested it':[70] which however did not greatly undermine the essential value of the information acquired in this way.

What was done with that information depended on circumstances. Usually it was merely stored away for future reference. If it seemed important, then it could be passed on to a foreign government, which then, presumably, would take some kind of action of its own. Alternatively the Special Branch might take action itself, by finding and arresting people, if they were suspected of indictable crimes. Another common form of action was to 'harry' the anarchist community, mainly for its deterrent effect.[71] The most spectacular harryings came when the Branch 'raided' anarchist clubs and newspaper offices, which it did quite often. David Nicoll's *Commonweal*, for example, was raided by a squad of men led by Littlechild and Melville in April 1892, and then again in June 1894. On both occasions the police were reported to have opened letters and broken up type. The second raid did so much damage that the *Commonweal* was forced to stop publication, which may have been one of the aims.[72] In 1894 the Special Branch raided the 'Autonomie' Club off Tottenham Court Road the evening after the Greenwich bomb. The raid was done quietly, so that members could continue to be interrogated as they arrived.[73] Raids were a method of keeping the Branch's files up to date, and of letting anarchists know that the police were around. In this latter regard they were a great success. The anarchist press in the 1890s was obsessed with policemen; though it may be that it would have been just as obsessed without the harrying. Anarchy and policing are, after all, singularly antithetical ideas. In any case, whatever the reason, anarchists in Britain were keenly aware of the fact that the Special Branch had its eye on them: which may well have encouraged them to behave.

The Special Branch's other main function was the protection of royalty, both British and foreign, by sniffing out conspiracies against them, and by providing bodyguards. This was clearly the plum job, especially when it took Special Branch officers, as it sometimes did, abroad. Memoirs are full of it, and of the ordinary human kindnesses bestowed by these great people on their humble guards.[74] Those guards were prouder of this duty than of anything else they did; as they had every right to be, in view of their 'absolutely unbroken record of success' – not a single royal lost or even damaged – in this field.[75]

In fact the Special Branch in the 1890s and early 1900s appears to have been pretty successful all round. It missed very little, possibly because there was not much in Britain to be missed. It was not prone to exaggerate what signs of conspiracy there were, or to be gulled by false information or hoax bombs. It had few obvious failures. Its one serious one was Bourdin's Greenwich bomb, which it failed to anticipate or prevent even though Bourdin was a member of a well-known anarchist circle, which the Branch would have had under surveillance for months. That, however, did little harm. In 1901 Melville apparently lost an exciting chase through London's East End after three Russian anarchists who had designs against the German Kaiser and the Belgian King, who were in England for Queen Victoria's funeral. Again, no harm came of it, and it may be that the whole incident (which never became public until the German spymaster Steinhauer 'revealed' it in his memoirs in 1930) was overblown.[76] A more serious failure concerned the Italian anarchist Gennaro Rubini, who was caught trying to assassinate King Leopold II in Belgium in November 1902, six months after the Special Branch lifted its surveillance of him. Melville's excuse for this reads a little lamely, and may indicate a touch of naïvety. Rubini had been watched closely from 1897, shortly after he arrived in England, until May 1902. In that month, however, he was accused by his fellow anarchists of being a spy for the Italian secret police, and confessed to it. 'Being satisfied that Rubini was in the service of a foreign police officer stationed in London,' wrote Melville, 'and knowing that he was denounced by his companions in consequence, the surveillance at one time exercised over him by London Police, was relaxed, his employment as above being considered a natural guarantee of bona fides.' Edward Henry, head of the CID, thought this 'very reasonable';[77] but it was an error of judgement all the same. Another error was Cavargna's rabbit-bomb; but that was surely not culpable.[78] Other failures were trivial, or could be rectified later on. Some, like the Brall case, and the affair of the Fenians Tynan and Bell, who were caught on the Continent in 1896 but could not be extradited, could be blamed on legal quibbles, which were always a bugbear for the police.

To put against this the Branch had some great catches, like the Walsall conspirators, the Paris bombers, and Farnara and Polti; together with the pre-eminent fact that Britain in these years suffered nothing like the scale of outrage which was so common a feature abroad. Compared with the Continent Britain escaped the anarchist onslaught of the 1890s very lightly indeed, with one serious explosion, which however did not harm any innocents; a few trivial and amateurish ones; and two conspiracies nipped in the bud. One of those conspiracies (Walsall) and the Greenwich bomb may not have been directed against Britain in any case. There are a number of possible explanations for this relative immunity. One was that anarchists meant no harm to Britain. That may have been for reasons of their own: to avoid provoking Britain into legislation which would allow her to expel them, for example, or because 'they appreciated their freedom and co-operated with the police to secure order and preserve their good name as good citizens in London'.[79] Alternatively it may have been because they were deterred by the skill and vigilance of the police.

The police themselves naturally liked to believe, or to persuade others to believe, the latter. Anarchists had as evil designs on Britain as on her neighbours, but were prevented from carrying them out by the vigilance of the Special Branch. Governments also had an interest in propagating this version of events, if only to alert the public to the need for strong executive measures against anarchism. If that public did not feel itself to be under threat, then it might be less happy to have all this done merely for the convenience of foreigners. That may be one reason for the solid insistence of the police and the Home Office that both the Walsall and Greenwich bombs were intended for use in England. This was an important point in connection with the Walsall anarchists in particular, whose defence made much of the submission that their bombs had been commissioned by nihilists in Russia for use there.[80] The same was claimed for Bourdin's Greenwich bomb. The Observatory was merely a meeting-point, said his friends, between Bourdin and a Russian courier.[81] That was widely considered to be an extenuating factor, if it could be proved. Russian despotism was thought to excuse or even justify almost any revolutionary means. Attacks on liberal Britain, however, were something else. They were far more likely to arouse public anger, and consequently appreciation for the work of the police.

Because neither the Greenwich nor the Walsall bombs went off when they were planned to, it is impossible to say whom they were intended for. The police were clearly wise to entertain the possibility that some anarchists might have their sights set on Britain, as well as on countries abroad. If Walsall and Greenwich were ambiguous, Farnara's target was not. There was every indication that in that case the Special Branch had prevented an outrage at the Royal Exchange – or maybe Farnara meant the Stock Exchange – which could have cost dozens of 'bourgeois' lives. Reports came in to it regularly of other plots against public figures in Britain, which it would have been irresponsible to ignore. A group called 'Individual Initiative', for example, was rumoured to be preparing explosions in London in retaliation for the extradition of François in 1892, which was by no means inconceivable.[82] There is a certain amount of evidence, though none of it is reliable, for Britain's being in some danger in the 1890s from anarchist terrorist attacks. If that was so then much of the credit for averting that danger must go to the Special Branch.

That was its own view: or at least, the view its ex-officers presented to the world. Melville MacNaghten, who had a lot to do with the Branch in the 1890s, claimed that 'In anarchist circles our information was always so good that, had a plot been in the hatching, I think the Yard would have got wind of it within twenty-four hours'; though he admitted that they could not always guard against 'the individual initiative of some crank.'[83] Harold Brust wrote that the Special Branch had 'made Great Britain famed as one place where not only its own rulers but those of foreign countries may walk in safety'.[84] Herbert Fitch credited the Special Branch with having saved Britain from 'paralysis' and the world from 'catastrophe' on more than one occasion, which he was unable to give detils of, because of the Official Secrets Act. 'Do not think I exaggerate', he went on; but it is possible he did, just a little.[85] Men like this were clearly impressed by the power and importance of conspiracy in politics, against which the Branch stood as Britain's only protection. In their view the history of the world was a constant struggle in the dark between the secret agents of anarchy and those of order, with the Special Branch representing order, and having so far kept the dragon at bay.

More to the point is that this opinion of themselves was shared, though not perhaps quite so extravagantly, in high places. Lord Rosebery, for example, told the House of Lords in 1894 that because of the Branch's efforts 'it is rare, I think, that we do not know what they [the anarchists] have in contemplation'.[86] By and large this also seems to have been accepted abroad. Brust reported King Louis of Portugal's view of the Metropolitan Police as 'A fine body of men with a worldwide reputation' in political matters; 'I wish our own police', the king went on, 'were more like them.'[87] Queen Christiana of Spain told the British ambassador in Madrid in 1906 that she thought 'the Spanish police had much to learn from the British police force' after the Special Branch had alerted the Spanish government to a plot against her life. She also suggested sending some Spanish police officers over to Scotland Yard to learn how it was done.[88] That came to nothing, because Henry feared that their presence might 'stir up excitement and feeling in quarters where it is best that excitement should not exist';[89]

but Spain's continued admiration for British political police methods was reflected a year later in the city of Barcelona's appointment of an ex-chief inspector from Scotland Yard to head and reform its own anti-anarchist force.[90] Later on the Russian Okhrana recruited Chief Inspector Powell, who was recommended by Quinn, for the head of its operations in England.[91] 'There is something about the British detective', wrote Fitch, who cited other examples of the same thing, 'that seems vastly to appeal to kings and queens from overseas. Perhaps it is that we are trained to be quiet and unostentatious; that we never intrude.'[92]

Whatever the reason it must be seen as a compliment, and a sign, together with the lack of any serious complaints against the Special Branch, that foreign governments were in general satisfied with the way it coped with the anarchist threat. This will have done a great deal to emolliate those governments' resentment against Britain for harbouring their political desperadoes: which was, after all, half the object of the exercise.

CHAPTER 9

Revelations

That is one side of the picture. Another, of course, is the anarchists' own. They viewed things differently, in the first case because they were prejudiced against the police, and secondly because they were the targets of most of the Special Branch's activities. From their accounts it appears that the successes of the Special Branch were achieved only at a price. That price was a wholesale betrayal of all the cherished moral principles of the British police, in order to entrap innocent idealists with every conceivable kind of 'dirty trick'.

Those tricks ranged from setting 'corner boys' to attack speakers at anarchist rallies, to initiating bomb plots by means of *agents provocateurs*. In between they included raiding anarchist presses without warrants and smashing machinery; leaning on landlords to evict and employers to sack known anarchists; coaching witnesses and tampering with juries at anarchist trials; and 'moonlighting' at generous under-the-counter fees for foreign police agents.[1] The *agent provocateur* charge first appeared in connection with the Walsall plot of 1892, which was the incident most amenable to this kind of interpretation. It centred on the role in it of Auguste Coulon, who was implicated, but never brought to trial. When Melville was asked in court whether any of the conspirators was in his pay, he refused to answer, and was protected in his refusal by the judge. Everyone on the left of British politics, right up to the ILP parliamentary fringe, thereafter assumed the worst. Some suggested the bomb itself was a 'plant'. 'The police', commented the *Commonweal*, 'are very clever at finding these things, especially when they have previously placed them there.'[2] The more common line, however, was that the Walsall men had been duped into manufacturing the bomb by an agent of the police.[3] That was the first of these typical pieces of skulduggery; but it was not to be the last.

After Walsall almost every single outrage in Britain was attributed by the far Left to *provocateurs*. 'Doesn't it strike you', asked *Justice* in April 1894, for example, that there is something queer about this Anarchist business of Polti and Farnara? Of course they may be the desperate ruffians they say they are, and their intention to blow down half London may also be beyond dispute. But somehow it does seem to us that the great Melville has possibly engineered the whole thing. We don't say that he has, of course. Nevertheless, we cannot but remember that a serious Anarchist plot in England would be very convenient just now, especially an Italian or French Anarchist plot. The Walsall affair showed how far our high-minded police are prepared to go in order to get up a scare at a critical time.[4]

The Greenwich case bore all the same signs. David Nicoll, once editor of the *Commonweal*, suggested that the only Greenwich 'conspirator' not in the pay of the police was poor Bourdin himself; which explained why no arrests were made there.[5] The motive behind it was to create 'a prejudice against Anarchism',[6] which would then be used for the police's own ends. 'All legal bodies', wrote Nicoll, 'make work for themselves, to justify their existence.'[7] This was the origin of all these 'outrages', none of which would have occurred if it had not been for 'le vile Melville' and his 'gang'.

It also explained much else. *Liberty*, for example, claimed that the most violent 'Anarchist' pamphlets and manifestos found in London were 'inspired by Melville with the object . . . of preparing public opinion for the expulsion of foreign refugees'.[8] Nicoll suggested that his successor as editor of the *Commonweal*, H. B. Samuels, might have been in the pay of the police when he published a notorious article welcoming one of the bloodiest of the Barcelona outrages in November 1893.[9] 'Anarchists', asserted *Freedom* in 1901,

> do not make plots in these days; they know that in every case where bomb throwing is advocated the suggestion comes from a police pupil or a police dupe – that is, from men in the pay of those who know that the breath of Liberty is in the air, [and] that Liberty spells loss of power and empty pockets to them.[10]

The *Torch* in 1895 claimed that when Cantwell had been arrested the year before for using seditious language at a public meeting, the police had faked their reports of his speech.[11] They also invented incidents, floated alarmist rumours, and put the worst constructions on real events. This was why they insisted that the Walsall and Greenwich bombs, for example, were intended for England: in order to frighten the public into thinking that it was in more danger than it was.[12] It was the Special Branch, too, which was responsible for the most sensational 'revelations' of anarchist conspiracies printed in the newspapers, like the *Tit-Bits* article, written in the form of an interview with a 'gentleman holding a high position in the detective force', which claimed that anarchists were plotting to wage war on society with bacilli.[13] In the autumn of 1896 there was another spate of bomb scares in London, which all turned out to be hoaxes: but originating where? British anarchists believed they knew.

> One thing is pretty certain: the officials of Scotland Yard *are* looking after Number One and have been for many years, and are very smart at the business, and they intend to keep the ball rolling if they can. For this reason we read of 'Bombs in South London', 'A Bomb thrown from a Tram Car', 'Discovery of a Dynamite Factory', 'Threatening Letters to the Officials', and all the rest of the dramatic effects necessary for the biggest fraud on earth.

'Innocent readers', *Freedom* went on, 'may wonder why all this should be. Well, this is Scotland Yard's "struggle for existence", we suppose.'[14]

To anarchists, of course, none of this was surprising. Police of any kind stood for everything they stood against: the sort of authority which a properly ordered society would have no need of. Even in an improperly ordered society they were of little use in detecting real crime: like, for example, the Whitechapel murders, which were the Metropolitan Police's great failure of the later 1880s, and which *Freedom* believed would have been solved without any trouble at all if the community had been left to police itself.[15] Their true function was as an instrument of class repression: in which role they could hardly be expected to be over-scrupulous towards the champions of the repressed.

> How can a man be brotherly and honest when it is his business to be a human blood-hound hunting down to their destruction the unfortunate and erring among his colleagues? How can he be just when it is his duty to maintain, by any means that fall short of raising a public scandal, the outward appearance of order, where disorder is only the natural and healthy revolt against deep-rooted injustice and wrong? The paid guardians of class rule and the monopoly of property are, after all, men of the people who have thoughtlessly turned traitors to the popular cause, and sold themselves to do dirty work that the masters are ashamed to be seen doing for themselves.[16]

This initial prejudice was bolstered by a long tradition of working-class hostility to the police on many grounds; and by some recent experiences, at unemployed demonstrations and strikes, when the police were felt to have used excessive force. Anarchists had little reason to like the police, and little reason consequently to give them the benefit of any doubts there might have been.

It was partly for this reason that their testimony was not by and large taken seriously outside their own little circles on the Left. Another reason may have been that very few people outside those circles were aware of it. Socialist and anarchist newspapers had tiny circulations in the 1890s, and scarcely impinged on the general reading public at all. The only proper newspaper to raise these questions seriously was *Reynolds's*, which was not so set against the police in principle, but was always on the look-out for impropriety. It gave prominence to the Walsall suspicions in 1892, largely no doubt because of its editor's other role as defence barrister at the trial – it was he who put the famous question to Melville about his 'spies';[17] and in 1895 it published two sets of 'revelations' by ex-policemen which purported to show the authorities using *provocateurs* against both Fenians and anarchists in the past.[18] In the wake of those revelations it also printed a number of letters from readers, some of them claiming to be detectives themselves, describing other forms of police corruption, like blackmailing ex-convicts for money (this was attributed specifically to the 'Secret Service' branch), and employing young boys to trap homosexuals.[19] *Reynolds's* also asserted, however, that *upper-class* homosexuals were *protected* by the police hierarchy;[20] which may give a clue as to why such accusations raised no great storm.

The fact was that the Special Branch in particular was very careful about the sorts of circles in which it operated. Its targets were nearly always poor foreign anarchists, who had little contact with any other classes in Britain, and elicited scarcely any sympathy amongst them. The reason for this was not devious or sinister: clearly if there was a terrorist threat to Britain, this was the sort of area in which to look for it; but it had the effect of leaving the vast majority of Britons entirely untouched (except on the elevated level of general principle) by any abuse of its powers the Special Branch may have resorted to. In earlier times this would scarcely have mattered. In Palmerston's day an offence against a foreign refugee was regarded by a large body of radical and liberal Englishmen as equivalent to an offence against them;[21] but that kind of spirit was not nearly so widespread now. The Victorians' liberal generosity was contracting. They did not necessarily approve of *agent-provocateuring* against others; but they were less anxious to know about it, or about anything to do with the Special Branch, than before. This may have been because it would have been ideologically unsettling for them to believe that such things could be; or because they were more content than in the 1850s to trust the police.

This studied ignorance was aided by the secrecy with which the Special Branch surrounded its activities. In the 1890s that secrecy was not absolute, and indeed it would have had to have been adjudged absurdly ineffective if the object had been to conceal those activities entirely from the public; but of course its real purpose was not to conceal, but to confuse. The main targets of that confusion were potential political criminals, who it was felt would be more likely to be deterred this way; but a side-effect was that the innocent public had no very clear idea, either, of the real nature and power of their political police. What was reported to them in their newspapers was a mixture of truth and fiction, with the truth never being officially acknowledged or the fiction denied, so that none of the information coming to them could be regarded as dependable. One response to this was to disbelieve all of it: which was not unreasonable, and was preferable if you did not like the idea of an English 'Third Section' anyway.

The result of all this was that concern about the Special Branch in Britain was very largely confined to the political outside Left. Some people felt this was short-sighted. The *Labour World*, for example, warned as early as 1890 that the methods which the authorities were accused of using against Fenians might be directed at the Labour movement next. Labour, it claimed, was now 'enlisting the hopes and the aspirations of the working classes everywhere'. As such, it was bound to 'excite the alarm and opposition' of those in power.

> Every effort that money can purchase will be made to crush or to cripple it. Divisions will be fomented, weak and treacherous men, who are found in all movements, will be bought in order to betray their comrades, and the *agent provocateur* will also be sure to make his appearance in the ranks of Labour combinations. He will be found advocating violence and dynamite, and urging excited men to base their hopes upon physical force alone. This is what has happened already in Belgium, Germany, France, and America . . . We want to warn the working men of these countries against the dangers which experience tells us will confront the cause of Labour in the United Kingdom when once that cause has taken definite shape.[22]

It might not, said *Freedom*, even stop there.

> Who of us, whether rich or poor, whether private people or public agitators, even among the members of both Houses, who is it that can say with certainty that he is safe in his own house from the intrigues and violations of the police? Who can guarantee that the agents of the new jesuitical order, invested with power, supported by the government, and whose ranks are

filled with the dregs of all classes, that the agents of this brotherhood do not, in the role of servants, commissioners and so forth, ransack their houses, taking copies and photos of the most secret documents, of the most intimate correspondence with their beloved ones? Nobody and nowhere. Without exaggeration, can it be asserted that even the aged Gladstone is not swarmed . . . by some disgrace of humanity of the type of Jones?[23]

But the argument did not strike home. It was not heard in the upper reaches of society, and if it had been it is doubtful whether it would have been heeded. It seemed inherently incredible; it did not relate to most people's – even Labour politicians' – experience; and it was contrary, in any case, to what the middle classes wanted to believe.

For this reason the fact that nearly all the contemporary charges against the Special Branch come from the extreme Left is of very little consequence. The Left's interest in discrediting the political police was no greater than the middle classes' interest in defending or ignoring it, and should not be used to dismiss its testimony out of hand. In some cases it is the only testimony that would ever be likely to surface: in those pettier instances of persecution, for example, where a policeman or an agent was acting on his own. In others it may be the only evidence that has survived. We may never know for certain how the Special Branch acted in the 1890s. But we can, if we are careful about it, surmise.

That the Special Branch exceeded its strict legal powers in the 1890s is certain. Proof of it comes in the form of a number of confidential statements made by top police officials of the time which read like 'confessions', though of a very imprecise kind. Those 'confessions' had their origin in suggestions made at the Rome Conference of 1898 that Britain might strengthen her police powers against anarchists to bring them into line with the Continent's. The response of British police chiefs to this is instructive. They baulked at it not because they objected to stronger powers, but because they felt that legislation designed to strengthen them would have the opposite effect. The reason for this was that laws which extended the police's authority would also have to define its limits, in a way which would make it more difficult than it was at present for the police to exceed them. The clear implication was that in the 1890s the police already did more illegally than any conceivable new legislation would ever permit them to do.

In case there was any doubt about this it was spelled out quite unambiguously to the Home Office in December 1898 by the head of the CID. He wished to state 'emphatically', he wrote, that in recent years the Police have succeeded only by straining the law, or, in plain English, by doing utterly unlawful things, at intervals, to check this conspiracy, & my serious fear is that if new legislation affecting it is passed, Police powers may be thus defined, & our practical powers seriously impaired.[24]

'Utterly unlawful things' was plain English indeed; plainer, in fact, than Anderson felt able to employ a month later in another memorandum on the same subject, and to the same end.

I am clear that the measure of peace & order wh. we have been able to maintain in recent years has been due to action taken by this dept wh. was (if I may coin a word) extra-legal: I hesitate to use the ordinary word wh. seems applicable to it.

Whatever word was applied to it, however, Anderson regarded it as essential. Experience proved it. Whenever in the past the police had gone by the book, he explained, then the anarchists had invariably 'assumed a menacing attitude, & taken to dangerous plots'. He cited one occasion when they had even gone so far as 'to insult the officers in the public streets'. Then, he went on, 'some "extra-legal" action has been adopted by the Police', with the result that the anarchists 'have at once grown quiet & timid'.[25] When Anderson left the CID in 1901, his successor Edward Henry repeated the same argument. It was a clear admission that the Special Branch regularly flouted the rules.

But which rules? Neither Anderson nor Henry was very specific. The only example of flouting they gave on this occasion was what Henry called the 'more or less sustained observation' of anarchists by plain-clothes policemen or their agents, which he admitted was 'not sanctioned by express provision of the law'.[26] A few years earlier Anderson confessed to searching an anarchist's house illegally.[27] It may have gone no further than this. 'Utterly unlawful' seems strong language to describe shadowing and searching, but at that time one never knows. Both were sensitive issues in the 1890s, which the authorities would have wanted to conceal.[28] If they also wanted to conceal anything worse, they did not say. That is our problem. Our best police witnesses to the existence of foul play do not make clear exactly how foul it was.

Our other police witness is more specific, and more incriminating; but is unreliable on other grounds. He is Patrick McIntyre, who in 1895 published a series of 'revelations' in *Reynolds's Newspaper* which went much further than any other police officer ever did in public in attributing underhand methods to the Special Branch. The problem with him, however, is his grievance: which arose originally from his demotion in September 1893.

By most accounts that was harsh. McIntyre had been an experienced and valued detective. He was one of the founder members of Williamson's original Irish Branch in March 1883, and was one of only two of them (with Melville) to carry on into the Special Branch in the 1890s.[29] In sixteen years in the force he had gained twenty commendations for 'zeal, tact, and energy in the performance of his duty', which was well over the odds, and more than £30 in rewards.[30] When he was demoted, from first-class Sergeant to Constable, it was apparently on the eve of his promotion to Inspector.[31] Ostensibly the reduction was for 'making a false report of the date of his return to London from special duty', which seems a trival offence:[32] according to his own account all he had done was to get back a day early from a job, but not report to Scotland Yard until he was expected. This, he claimed, 'was a frequent custom with officers out of town, when their work is finished, although it comes under the head of a technical breach of duty'. But in any case he reckoned that it was not the real reason for his punishment. That was the suspicion Anderson had, but could not prove, that McIntyre might be entering into 'a liaison' with the daughter of an anarchist. That suspicion was fed by 'certain interested persons, who were hostile to me', and who he claimed included Le Caron, with whom he had quarrelled while he was his bodyguard. McIntyre clearly had a capacity for making enemies. Another one may have been Melville, who had once reported him for 'insolence', and who was made up to head of the Special Branch in the very month of McIntyre's disgrace.[33]

It was more than a demotion. McIntyre was drummed out of the Special Branch entirely, and sent back to pounding the beat in Kentish Town, where he had 'the humiliation, after all my years of experience, of being coached by a youth who, six months before, had been behind a Norfolk plough'.[34] That rankled, and a police surgeon who saw him soon afterwards described him as 'nervous, worried, and depressed', and 'obviously extremely anxious to leave the force'.[35] He did leave shortly afterwards, but only after more controversy. He fainted one day while on duty, and was given a month's sick leave; when he returned to work at the beginning of October 1894 he insisted he still was not up to it. The surgeon did not believe him, and ordered him back on duty, at which point he resigned (to become the landlord of a Southwark public house).[36] He then claimed back his 'rateable deductions' (a kind of levy made on every policeman's pay as a surety of good conduct and given back to most of them at the end of their service) but was denied them because of his bad conduct in the past. He kicked up a fuss about this, until the Commissioner himself, Bradford, relented on the grounds that if he did not it would 'give the Ex-Police Constable a substantial grievance, of which he would not fail to make the most'.[37] He made the most of it anyway: first of all setting a solicitor on to the Scotland Yard authorities,[38] and then, when that failed, getting his own back through the columns of *Reynolds's*. This is the background to McIntyre's 'revelations'. As an under-secretary at the Home Office minuted in 1895: his various disputes with the police authorities 'showed a vindictive temper, and no doubt these revelations are another instance of the same spirit'.[39]

Whether this entirely disposes of them is another matter. On the surface much of McIntyre's resentment seems justified. It ties in with many complaints being made at the time of 'military despotism' and 'arbitrary injustice' at Scotland Yard, which apparently were causing another of those slumps in morale which periodically afflicted the Metropolitan Police.[40] If McIntyre's own personal grievance was soundly based, then it might indicate that his judgement of the matters he wrote about in *Reynolds's* was also sound. But not necessarily. A grievance is a grievance, whether it is reasonable or not. The more reasonable it is, the more aggrieved the complainant is likely to feel. This is bound to affect his objectivity, and might possibly tempt him to perjury. In a court of law McIntyre's feelings towards his superiors would certainly undermine the credibility of his evidence against them. If it was the only evidence against them, they would be acquitted on the ground that it was insufficient. But history is not a court of law, and is not bound by the same admirable conventions. There should be no presumption of innocence in this case. McIntyre's motives clearly gave him an interest in embarrassing his former masters, but they do not invalidate his testimony. That testimony has the ring of truth about it: or at least, of what McIntyre took to be the truth. For the real problem with it arises more from the limits of his knowledge about the things he wrote of, than from the possibility that he was telling lies. This is particularly so in the case of the Walsall anarchists, where even a trusted sergeant in the Special Branch could not know for certain whether *agents provocateurs* were used.

In fact McIntyre never *claimed* for certain that they were. His case against the police in this affair, which was the 'revelation' that made most waves at the time, was that it was *likely* that Coulon, who was in the pay of the Special Branch, had also initiated the plot. This was not new. Coulon had been suspected by the anarchists almost from the beginning. What McIntyre's account added to that suspicion were, firstly, the categorical statement that Coulon was Melville's spy; and secondly, two circumstantial reasons for believing that he was a *provocateur*. They were, that agents paid out of secret service funds could not be trusted *not* to turn into *provocateurs*: he cited the example of another man, one of his own agents, who offered to become one for him; and that the Walsall conspirator Frederick Charles, in particular, who had the local reputation almost of a saint, 'would never have gone of his own accord into any diabolical plot'. He also wondered why it was that Littlechild, who was still head of the Special Branch and had always disapproved of underhand methods, kept so 'aloof from the Walsall case' as he did. For the rest he made it clear that, because Coulon was Melville's exclusive 'property', no one outside the two of them, and possibly Anderson, could conceivably know what use was made of him.[41] That was as far as he went. The confirmation of Coulon's status as an informer was important because it had not been acknowledged from the police side before. Whether it was accepted clearly depended mainly on McIntyre's credibility. His other arguments did not. The general point about the tendency of informers to turn into *provocateurs*, and his view of Charles's character, stood or fell entirely independently. This takes us over the difficulty posed by his motives. They only really bear on the question of whether Coulon was a police *informer*: which may be comparatively easy to corroborate.

In fact there can be very little doubt that he was. The Home Office was convinced of it, whether or not it was ever told it authoritatively;[42] and Anderson in his surviving reports on the case never denied it. In one account he described how he ordered the arrest of Coulon shortly after that of the other Walsall anarchists, only to receive an urgent telegram from the Walsall police chief, Taylor, telling him not to.[43] This suggests two things: firstly that Coulon was being protected, either by Taylor or by Melville, who was in Walsall at the time; and secondly that it was initially without Anderson's knowledge. Home Secretary Matthews had the idea at one point of making 'discreet' enquiries about Coulon amongst the anarchists themselves, but then thought better of it, possibly to avoid playing into their hands.[44] As in the Daly/Egan case, therefore, no proper investigation was made of the affair, before the Home Secretary issued his statement that he could see no cause to suspect the involvement of *agents provocateurs*.[45] That seems to have been the genuine view of the Home Office: that Coulon was an agent, but that there was no more reason to suppose he provoked the crime 'than in the ordinary case of a burglary or van robbery in which the Police are first put on the track by an informer'.[46]

McIntyre's whole point, however, and the view of many other policemen of the time, was that in those cases, and in any others involving informers, provocation *was* always a likelihood. This was why he advocated turning off their supply of secret service money: because there was no means otherwise of stopping the abuse, or even of knowing where it had occurred.[47] For this same reason, it was almost impossible to prove. In Coulon's particular case it was more difficult, because he was so well shielded. He was neither arrested, as we have seen, nor called as a witness at the trial. When the defendants' barrister put questions to Melville about him, the judge ruled that he did not have to answer them. This was a common practice in English courts at the time with regard to informers, in order to encourage them to inform;[48] it was not supposed to matter so long as their evidence was not used directly, but clearly it did in those cases where they were suspected of setting up crimes. Because Coulon was kept hidden in the background, no one was ever likely to get to the bottom of his role. If he was an *agent provocateur*, there would probably be no proof of it; just as there would not, of course, if he was innocent.

The positive evidence against him was highly circumstantial. It mainly rested on the testimony of one of the Walsall conspirators (Deakin) that it was he who had vouched for the mysterious letter another of them (Cailes) had received in October 1891 ordering the bombs. His anarchist colleagues in London were also puzzled by his apparent financial security, which he could not account for, and for which he was drummed out of the Autonomie Club in January 1892.[49] Later on the failure of the police to charge him compounded these suspicions. But of course that – suspicions – was all they ever were. Coulon always protested his own innocence, of informing as well as provoking;[50] and no hard proof ever came to anyone's hands. Of course he had the opportunity to provoke, in some degree or another: for there are other stages as well as the initial one at which a *provocateur* can help a conspiracy on. This one lasted for three months from its inception, and the Special Branch's knowledge of it,[51] to its abortion with Deakin's arrest in London on 6 January 1892: ample time for an agent to encourage it if he was ordered to, or if he thought it would please. But all this is the very flimsiest of evidence on which to build a case.

So far as the Special Branch was concerned, it also had an opportunity, and probably more than one motive for using an agent to provoke a crime. The opportunity arose out of the secrecy which both surrounded and pervaded it, protecting it and its individual officers from what otherwise would have been the consequences of any villainy. If Coulon *was* a *provocateur*, then it is likely that the only other man who knew of it for certain was Melville, together possibly with Chief Inspector Taylor of the Walsall police. Anderson indicated, or maybe wanted to give the impression, that *he* knew nothing of Coulon's work for the police until the telegram from Taylor arrived after the main arrests. If it was a secret between Coulon and Melville, or between Coulon and his God (assuming he had one), then it would have been a pretty safe one. Melville was certainly clever enough to conceal it. There was, wrote George Dilnot of him in 1929, 'none who could better keep his own counsel'.[52] Anderson did not have a great reputation for sagacity at this time,[53] and if he really did known nothing of any police plot he may not have had the wit to probe. Matthews was loath to. That gave Melville his chance.

As to motive, there are at least three compelling ones. One was Melville's personal kudos, as Anderson called it,[54] which was boosted immensely by his Walsall *coup*. A second was the threat that the Special Branch may have felt was hanging over it at this time. Whatever the Walsall case's origins were, it came at a particularly good time for the Branch. Just one week before Deakin's arrest, on 31 December 1891, the Home Secretary had sanctioned a cut in its strength, on the ground that he reckoned the threat of terrorism to be past.[55] The Walsall plot seemed to prove the contrary: this, at any rate, was how the police presented it. At around the same time the Foreign Office was also coming under pressure from foreign governments to take concerted measures against anarchist crimes. The problem with that, as the head of the Foreign Office put it to his minister the day after the Walsall trial opened, was that 'English public opinion' would not sanction it 'unless under the immediate pressure of alarm and indignation at the perpetration of them here':[56] which could almost be taken as a hint. From these three different points of view, therefore, the Walsall affair was, to say the least, a boon. It could have been more of one. Apart from Melville, whose reward was a chief inspectorship, neither of the other two beneficiaries benefited as much as they might have hoped. The Branch's numbers were not made up again for three years. The Foreign Office never got its international accord. Nevertheless there were enough motives here to tempt the Branch into skulduggery, if it was unscrupulous enough to fall.

But of course none of this is enough. The actual evidence for *provocateuring* is circumstantial in the extreme: little more than innuendo, hearsay, and a few odd coincidences. None of it is inconsistent with the much more straightforward explanation: which is that the Special Branch was told of the plot by an informer, probably Coulon, and then when it had enough evidence went in and put a stop to it. That it was all contrived by Melville and his agent is not impossible, but cannot be proved. McIntyre's suspicions were probably genuine, were certainly reasonable, and may have been justified: but there is no saying for sure.

That is highly unsatisfactory: for it would be of enormous value to know whether or not the events which were supposed to justify the existence of the Special Branch in the 1890s were in fact fabricated by it for that purpose. It would throw light not only on the methods of the Branch, but also on its very *raison d'être*. That question, however, has to remain unresolved, at least until somebody finds Melville's Confessions in an old tin box in an attic somewhere. In the meantime we have to be content with scraps of evidence on other matters, and some deductions from them; which will show the Special Branch changing quite radically in Melville's hands in the 1890s, whether or not it changed into quite the monster its adversaries claimed.

One change was in its conception of its role, which broadened towards the end of the century beyond the bounds set for it originally. For a start the Branch appears to have become more dedicated to the suppression of anarchism as a doctrine, as well as its terrorist offshoots, than it had been before. Melville's own personal hatred of anarchism is attested by several of his contemporaries,[57] and by a letter he wrote to a secret Russian police agent in July 1897 which was notably more expansive than any of his reports to his own superiors. That letter spoke, for example, of the nihilists as 'scoundrels', and of the *Commonweal*'s ideas as 'disgusting';[58] which indicated a depth of feeling which was, to say the least, unnecessary for the performance of the duties which the Special Branch had been called upon to undertake before. That feeling was shared by many of Melville's colleagues.[59] It might lead, if it was not kept on a tight rein – and who was there strong enough to hold Melville back? – to an extension of the Branch's activities into areas other than simple counter-terrorism: which would mark a significant stage in its development into a more Continental style of political police.

The letter to the Okhrana is also proof of another clear deviation from established Scotland Yard practice on the part of Melville's Special Branch. For years it had been considered improper for British policemen to work directly with foreign police agencies against political exiles living in London, save in wholly exceptional circumstances. This was because, as Salisbury put it to the German ambassador as late as August 1900, 'The House of Commons and public opinion are excessively suspicious of cooperation between the English & Continental Police especially in regard to political crimes.' He cited the examples of 1844, when a Home Secretary ran into terrible trouble when it was discovered that he had intercepted the mail of some Italian refugees at the Post Office on behalf of the Austrian police; and of 1858, when the sight of some French policemen at Scotland Yard had contributed to Palmerston's fall. Salisbury was making his point in reply to a German request for some Prussian police officers to come and study Scotland Yard's methods at first hand, which was turned down, as such requests at that time invariably were.[60] If this was unwise, then obviously active collaboration with the Okhrana was more so, in view of the latter's almost universal reputation in Britain as an agency of tsarist tyranny. If it were ever discovered, then there was no predicting the storm of outrage that would be likely to follow. As well as this, as someone in the Home Office minuted in 1906, 'An imprudent policeman might land us in a most awkward political situation'; which was why it was 'essential that the govt. as well as the police should know what is going on'.[61] Co-operation with foreign police forces, therefore, had to be done through diplomatic channels in most cases, and in others – in connection with serious crimes, for example – only after being sanctioned at the highest level.

Melville cared little for any of this, probably because he did not fully share the prevalent prejudices of most liberal Englishmen of the time. His lack of sympathy with those prejudices is indicated by this letter, whose object was to show Rachkovskii how they could be circumvented in order to bring Vladimir Burtsev to book. It was this which began the proceedings against Burtsev that led to his conviction in February 1898. Melville's advice – for the Russian ambassador to initiate the action 'via the diplomatic route' – was given gratuitously, and quite irregularly; in order, in Melville's own words, to give him an 'opportunity to stick close to these gentlemen and harry them' which he would not be granted otherwise.[62] So far as is known his part in it was kept concealed from the British government, which was under the impression that it was acting on an initiative taken in St Petersburg.[63]

This incident may not have been unique. Melville's relations with Rachkovskii had been close for some time before 1897; and there are other indications in the Okhrana's archive of collaboration between it and the Special Branch after then.[64] This may explain why Russia did not press its case for formal police co-operation with Britain particularly urgently after the Rome Conference, and it may also be what Anderson and Henry were hinting at when they objected to having that co-operation formalised:[65] the fact that it was – though neither side could afford to spell it out – more or less satisfactory as it stood. That was from their point of view. From others it might have looked different. In some ways what Melville's arrangement with Rachkovskii resembled was the beginning of a kind of covert political 'Interpol'. To a certain extent it was outside parliamentary, and possibly even ministerial, control. It was also independent of the dominant British political mores of the time, which is why it had to be kept secret. It transcended national boundaries and ideologies, in much the same way as the 'international secret societies' it was committed against. In Melville's hands, in fact, the Special Branch may have become less a British counter-terrorist agency (though of course this always remained one of its functions) than a cell in a Europe-wide counter-subversive one.

It also branched out into new fields. One was described in his memoirs by ex-Inspector John Sweeney, who was one of Melville's right-hand men. It is a curious story, and concerns the 'Legitimation League', whose main goal was to remove the stigma of bastardy from illegitimate children. In the spring of 1898 the League held its annual dinner at the Holborn Restaurant in London. For a surprise the secretary, George Bedborough, had arranged for a photographer to be present, 'much to the discomforture', as Bedborough's reformist journal *The Adult* put it, '. . . of at least *one* of the giddy guests, who was completely unknown to the remainder of those present'.[66] It turned out to be Sweeney. 'For a considerable time', he recounted, he had been attending 'all the meetings of the League, reporting the speeches and noting the *coterie* which formed in various corners of the well-appointed rooms where the meetings were held.' He had been led there by anarchists who, he claimed, had infiltrated the League in order to turn it into an instrument for *encouraging* bastardy as a first stage towards undermining the social fabric generally.[67] Sweeney was appalled by this prospect, so he decided to put a stop to it. He could not do it directly, because the Legitimation League was breaking no law. So he decided on an oblique approach.

Bedborough, the secretary, was also a vendor of 'progressive' books. Sweeney went to his house one day in May to ask for a copy of one of the volumes of Havelock Ellis's *Psychology of Sex*. The volume was the one on

THE DYNAMITE EXPLOSION AT WHITEHALL

Fenian outrages in London, 1883–4: bomb damage outside the Board of Trade, in the Underground, and at the offices of the Special Irish Branch at Old Scotland Yard.

[From Kladderadatsch.] THE CROCODILES TAKE REFUGE UNDER ENGLAND'S WINGS. [August 26, 1894.

A cartoon from a German satirical paper illustrating continental resentment against Britain's policy of political asylum, 1894; and a fictional anarchist outrage in London, from a novel published in 1893.

The Walsall bomb, 1892; Colonel Vivian Majendie, the Home Office explosives expert; and the interior of his bomb defusing hut on Duck Island in St James's Park, as it survived in 1985.

DAILY SKETCH.

No. 1,315.—TUESDAY, MAY 27, 1913. London: 45-47, Shoe lane, E.C. Manchester: Withy grove. [Registered as a Newspaper] ONE HALFPENNY.
Telephones: Editorial and Publishing: 5676 Holborn. Advertisements: 10,782 Central.

MRS. PANKHURST TRIES TO GET AWAY FROM THE GUARDED HOUSE AT WOKING, FALLS FAINTING, AND IS SENT BACK TO HOLLOWAY.

Once again Mrs. Pankhurst is in prison! She tried to get away from Dr. Ethel Smyth's house at Woking yesterday. The W.S.P.U. motor-car was waiting when she limped out, supported by Dr. Smyth and a nurse. But the detectives wanted to know where she was going and kept their hands on the door of the car while she argued and pleaded. Then, overcome by the weakness inflicted by her torture in prison, she fell back fainting. The police called a taxi-cab and took her to Bow-street. (1) Mrs. Pankhurst leaving the house. (2) Arguing with the detective, whose hand is on the handle. (3 and 4) Fainting, she is supported on Dr. Smyth's knee. (5) Being put into the detective's "taxi." These photographs, exclusive to the Daily Sketch, are the first ones taken since Mrs. Pankhurst was released from prison. Do you think she looks well enough to be sent back to the house of pain?

Special Branch detectives arresting Mrs Pankhurst in May 1913.

The four heads of the Special Irish and Special Political Branches between 1883 and 1918: (from top left to bottom right) Adolphus Williamson, John Littlechild, William Melville, and Patrick Quinn.

Four leading Special Branch lights: (from top left to bottom right) in the 1880s and 1890s, Patrick McIntyre, John Sweeney; and in the 1900s, Harold Brust, Herbert Fitch.

homosexuality, or 'Sexual Inversion', and was intended as a serious scientific study. Serious science, however, seems to have meant very little to Sweeney, who regarded the book, quite simply, as pornography. When Bedborough handed his copy over to him, therefore, he arrested him on an obscenity charge. (Read out in court later, it accused him of seeking to 'corrupt the morals of the liege subjects of our Lady the Queen', to 'debauch and poison' their minds, and 'to raise and create in them lustful desires', by means of a 'lewd, wicked, bawdy, scandalous and obscene libel'.)[68] Bedborough was terrified by this, as Sweeney knew he would be, having wormed his way into his confidence before. So Sweeney proposed a deal. He would make sure that Bedborough got off lightly, he said, if he pleaded guilty, and also wound up *The Adult* and the Legitimation League. It worked, much to the annoyance of a newly-formed 'Free Press Defence Committee' which had been hoping to make a *cause célèbre* of the case. Bedborough pleaded guilty, which meant that no defence witnesses were called, and was bound over.[69] The League and the journal expired soon afterwards. Sweeney was immensely proud, not least of the delicacy with which he had carried out his task. It was, he wrote, a case

> . . . full of pitfalls, where the least slip would have meant one of two things –
> the growth of a Frankenstein monster wrecking the marriage laws of our
> country, and perhaps carrying off the general respect for all law; or, on the
> other hand, of raising about the ears of the authorities a shriek of popular
> objection to our interference with the rights of free speech.[70]

Indeed it must have been immensely difficult at that time, when people were so little aware of the dangers that lurked behind every progressive cause, for those who had that knowledge, and had society's interests at heart, to protect it against its own innocent liberal will.

These incidents were not unique.[71] They indicate a clear extension of the Special Branch's cares and responsibilities in the 1890s, far beyond its original ones. What is equally significant, however, is the fact that this extension had certain limits. For example, the Branch does not seem at this time to have taken any interest at all in native British politics, outside the extreme anarchist circles which had been part of its legitimate interest for years. It is impossible to be certain; but no trace has yet been found of any Special Branch involvement in socialist or trade union affairs in the 1890s, which means either that it was clever enough not to leave fingerprints, or that it never was involved. This may say something about contemporary perceptions of the nature of any subversive threat to Britain. For the moment political threats to the established order appeared less menacing to most people than the moral poison which seemed to be sapping the nation's vitality (this was how it was put) in a far more insidious way. If there was thought to be a political threat, then it was external: arising from the jealousy and hostility towards Britain of foreign powers. These preoccupations are corroborated by the literature of the day. They may explain the specific new responsibilities the Special Branch took on board in the later 1890s: firstly combating sexual anarchy, and secondly smoothing the foreign feathers that had been ruffled by Britain's toleration of the political sort.

Who sanctioned all this is uncertain. Presumably the Bedborough harassment was officially approved, as it resulted in a prosecution. There are also indications that the government may have known something of Melville's relations with Rachkovskii, though they are of an inconclusive kind. In December 1901, in response to a joint Russo-German proposal, the head of the Foreign Office minuted that 'We cannot *officially* join in arrangements for international police co-operation'; and two months later the Foreign Secretary wrote that 'the arrangements made for these purposes should be made as confidentially and with as little outward appearance of combination as possible':[72] both of which statements, and especially the words '*officially*' (underlined) and 'outward', hint at some degree of collusion from on high. On the other hand, it may be that no one sanctioned the details of the Special Branch's activities, above Melville, or perhaps Anderson (who was just the kind of person to perceive a threat to the national fibre in the encouragement of free love). That would follow naturally from a number of features of the Special Branch's situation in the 1890s, including its secrecy, and the lack of accountability which followed therefrom.

This gave it a very wide latitude, and was yet another reason for the authorities' unwillingness to allow foreign policemen to come over to study its system at first hand. The fact was, as senior policemen testified, that there *was* no system. The Branch's 'efficient performance', wrote Bradford in August 1900, 'depends not so much on a strict adherence to Police regulations, as on the possession by the Officers engaged of a strong fund of common sense', which they could use without 'seeking instructions from superior officers'.[73] When Lord Salisbury communicated the sense of this to the German Ambassador a little later, he added that he himself had been unable to get any more information than this from Bradford, 'because although singularly clear-headed he is a very bad hand at explaining, and the clearer he sees, the less able he is to explain.'[74] Or it may be that even Bradford did not know exactly where the Special Branch's common sense led it. Unlike most of the rest of the Metropolitan Police Force, it was felt to need, and was given, a relatively free hand. This clearly suited Melville, who was frequently credited with great 'audacity' and 'fertility of resource', and with having 'his own ways'.[75] How he used that free hand probably depended slightly more on the Branch's own internal preoccupations, than on those of the political masters it was ultimately responsible to.

Those preoccupations depended in their turn on the composition of the Special Branch, and on the priorities which arose out of its professional concerns. Special Branch officers were different from the majority of the people they guarded, not least, as we have seen, in their immunity from that majority's false sense of security (as they saw it) in the teeth of subversive threats. Their Irishness may have accounted for some of this. Irishmen were born into a society with a very different police tradition from the British, and a daily experience of political crime; they were also in some senses outsiders in London, where the Special Branch was based. For these reasons they could be trusted to be free from most of the sympathies, prejudices and qualms which beset the society they found themselves grafted on to. That was one distinguishing factor. A more important one may have arisen from their pure professional zeal. That will have made most Special Branch officers impatient, for example, with rule-books, especially in dealing with enemies who acknowledged no rules at all. They may also have been less able than most other people to cultivate a balanced view of the importance of their task. Countering terrorism and subversion will have had a higher priority for them than for others, for whom the preservation of what today are called 'civil liberties' ranked as high. Working among 'subversives' every day of their lives may have given them an exaggerated view of the subvertability of society, and of the extent to which the process of subversion had already gone. There are clear signs of all this in the ludicrously extravagant accounts of their exploits published by ex-Special Branch men like Brust, Fitch and Thomson in the 1920s and 1930s, and to a lesser extent in Sweeney's memoirs, written much earlier.[76] These indicate the development in the 1890s and 1900s of a Special Branch ethos which was different from that of the 1880s, and quite distinct from the ethos which had pervaded its parent, the Metropolitan Police Force, for decades.

Ultimately, however, that ethos, and the code of conduct of the

Special Branch, will have been passed down from its leadership; which, significantly enough, had changed wholesale between 1888 and 1893. First James Monro resigned as Assistant Commissioner in charge of the CID in 1888, to return to Bengal in 1890. His replacement was Robert Anderson, the government's old spymaster before Jenkinson, and an Anglo-Irishman. Then Adolphus Williamson died in December 1889, and was followed as Chief Constable in the CID by Monro's protégé Melville MacNaghten, the Indian ex-planter who had had the spot of bother in the past with land rebels in Nischindpore. John Littlechild left the police at the beginning of 1893, apparently through ill-health,[77] and may have given control of the Branch's anti-anarchist activities over to Melville, who succeeded him as its Chief Inspector, before then. Melville was also Irish. These were the men – Anderson, MacNaghten and Melville – who took the Special Branch through the 1890s, and then into the new century.

They all appear to have had different ideas from their predecessors; who had had strict views, as we saw in a previous chapter, on the question of how to combat terrorism. One of those views was that it was better to nip terrorist plots in the bud than to allow them to develop in order to be able to make arrests: which the Walsall affair (quite irrespective of whether or not it was 'provoked') clearly flew in the face of. Another was that it was wrong for the police to employ under-cover agents on a regular basis, which again seems to have gone by the board in Melville's time. Williamson, that staunch bastion of all the old Scotland Yard virtues, was probably turning in his grave; for what this meant in effect was that his old adversary, Edward Jenkinson, had won. It will be recalled how in 1884 Jenkinson had tried to introduce Irish methods of counter-terrorism (secret agents and the rest) into Scotland Yard, and how he had failed in the end against the entrenched conservatism of Williamson and Monro. Those two, with Littlechild, stood for a 'purer' code of police conduct, which survived the Jenkinson episode, and for a few years after; but then seems to have wilted when control of the Special Branch passed into less conservative hands. Walsall may have been the turning-point, with Littlechild keeping 'aloof' from it, and then soon afterwards resigning, for this reason; the point when the incubus of Scotland Yard's traditional scruples was finally shed. That was one stage in the Branch's slow evolution from a preventative counter-terrorist organisation in 1883, to a modern political police force; though it was a very long way from that ultimate outcome yet.

CHAPTER 10

Quiet Prevention
1903–9

Melville resigned from the Special Branch, and from the Metropolitan Police, on 1 December 1903. The reasons for his departure are mysterious. He had served in the force for twenty-five years, which he may have felt was enough. Perhaps he was making too many anarchist enemies. Or he may have received an offer from outside that he could not refuse. Unlike Littlechild and Sweeney, he does not appear to have gone into private detective work. Nor is there any sign that he was employed by his old Okhrana friends. Later on he turns up working for some branch or other of counter-espionage: possibly naval.[1] This may have seemed a fitting new challenge for the man a *Times* correspondent called 'the most celebrated detective of the day'.[2]

What is strange, however, is the silence of the official record on the subject of his resignation. Police Standing Orders record a commendation for 'exemplary conduct' on the day he left, and his grant of a pension.[3] But no correspondence about him with the Home Office survives, and no Scotland Yard personnel file. (Personnel files contained records of commendations for exceptional services, and 'Reports' of transgressions.) In these circumstances suspicions are bound to breed. Melville's police career was controversial. He had been involved in more than one case to which rumours of the use of *agents provocateurs* had attached. He was only fifty-one when he left. His departure appears to have been sudden. His successor, Patrick Quinn, had to be made up to Superintendent in a hurry, and without sitting the usual written examination.[4] That came just seven months after Melville had been given sole charge, for the first time in his ten years as head of the Branch, of the large sum of money which was entrusted to it for secret out-of-pocket payments.[5] One of the very few files from this period to which the Home Office still denies access is one which contained correspondence about the expenses he claimed.[6] His son (born in 1885, when he was on Fenian duty) became Solicitor-General in the second Labour government, which may have made his position sensitive in retrospect.[7] All of this is the flimsiest evidence imaginable that anything was wrong. There are other far more likely explanations for Melville's abdication. He probably got fed up with political police work, at a rather dull time, and decided to move on to pastures new. If this is so, then it is unfortunate for his memory that the available historical record is so incomplete, giving rise to what may be unworthy and are certainly uncorroborated qualms.

The man who took over from him was scarcely any younger, but stayed on a good deal longer at Scotland Yard, taking the Special Branch right through the Great War and a little way beyond. Patrick Quinn's service record *does* still survive, with not one single 'Report' for bad conduct, and commendations galore.[8] He was Irish (like Melville), unmarried, reclusive, and prone to catarrh.[9] He also attracted expressions of respect and admiration from his professional and political superiors of a kind which Melville seems to have managed to escape.[10] When *he* retired, on 1 January 1919, he had accumulated a tally of foreign orders and decorations even more impressive than Melville's; to which was added a British knighthood – the first ever given to a CID officer – shortly afterwards.[11]

By his time the position of the Special Branch was secure. No one who knew about it seemed to object. In 1904 John Sweeney published his recollections of his time in the Branch, to the annoyance of the Home Office, especially when they involved him in a libel suit with an ex-anarchist called Parmeggiani (who lost);[12] but they provoked no outcry against the Branch's existence or methods. Public opinion generally seems to have come to accept it, for two reasons. One was that, despite Melville's possible excesses, the Branch in the past had acted in the main carefully and moderately, and within strictly limited and uncontroversial bounds. The other was the gradual heightening of both official and popular perceptions of the dangers threatening Britain from within during these years. The Special Branch was tolerated by liberal opinion because it was felt to be necessary, in view of the nation's increasing vulnerability to ogres of various kinds.

The shape of those ogres changed. Each age has its own particular, and different, fears. The Edwardians' main fear, if their writings are anything to go by, was of imperial and national decline, fuelled and exploited by foreign rivals. This theme pervaded most of the pre-monitory literature of the time, of which there was an enormous amount. Britain was felt to be weakening. The main cause was the 'physical degeneration' of her people, brought on by luxury, poverty, suffragism, Jewish immigration, city living, socialism, effeminacy, masturbation, and a hundred other things. There was much talk – and not only in right-wing circles – of the decline of manhood, patriotism, discipline, vigour and 'grit'. A few commentators diagnosed the condition as terminal. 'England is grown old, her national virility is exhausted', gloated an Irish MP in 1901. 'She has arrived at the age of senile decay.'[13] Most Englishmen, however, preferred to believe that the trend could be reversed. Baden-Powell's Boy Scout movement was one effort in this direction, among many. If such efforts were not successful, then the future looked bleak. It would not be a question merely of decline or contraction, but probably of invasion and enslavement too. That was a favourite prediction, or warning, from the time of the Boer War on. Britain was surrounded by jealous predators, with not a genuine ally in sight. The first clear sign of internal corrosion and they would start grabbing first her empire, and then her shires. England would sink to the status of a German colony, or an American satellite, or a sub-nation like Belgium at best.[14] This was Britain's recurrent and growing nightmare in the 1900s, through to 1914, when some of it came true.

This mood was by no means universal at the beginning of Quinn's reign, but it became almost so in governing circles by the end. It was not an unreasonable attitude to take. Britain was vulnerable, object-ively, in the 1900s, chiefly due to the collapse of some of the liberal assumptions on which her previous security had rested. One of those assumptions was that her international interests could be safeguarded with minimal force, because they did not threaten or even disadvantage anyone. That may have been true in mid-Victorian times, but it was no longer credible now. Other countries felt disadvantaged and threat-ened, or said they did, and so threatened Britain in their turn. After 1904 the main threat came from Germany. It was probably a real one; and it was particularly ominous for Britain, whose security in the past had depended more on the weakness or disinterest of her rivals than on her own military strength.

Her problem was fundamental. Britain's nineteenth-century success had been rooted in a situation which it was no longer possible to maintain. She had risen in a world where that sort of rise was possible with the minimum of state power, and where indeed minimal state power was supposed to be an essential condition for it. Now that world had changed. Britain could no longer maintain her superiority effortlessly; which might mean that she could not maintain it at all. The new challenges that faced her, both internally and externally, could not be met merely by trusting to progress and enlightenment. Something – probably a lot of things, some of them deeply offensive to her political and economic instincts – had to be done. This was disillusioning. In the fairly recent past Britain's self-confidence had been based on the widespread assumption that liberal capitalism could be trusted to bring everything right, more or less on its own. Both Britain's and the world's future were assured by the impersonal and liberal imperatives of history, with very little left either to chance or to the volition of individuals. In the 1900s those imperatives were beginning to look more than a little shaky. This left an unsettling vacuum, at the very least, for those liberals who had reposed their faith in them before.

One effect of it was to reinstate the role of conspiracy. In a world governed by impersonal forces, conspiracy has little place. This was why Victorian governments had been so little concerned by people who conspired against them, and why they had employed so few conspirators of their own. The fates of nations were determined by larger factors, like, in Britain's case, the liberalism of her institutions, which was proof against any conceivable conspiratorial threat. Hence the relative insignificance throughout the nineteenth century of Britain's political police, who were never widely believed (except perhaps by some of themselves) to be of any great national import. For much the same reason Britain had taken little notice of or part in international military espionage in the nineteenth century, on the grounds not only that it was ungentlemanly, but also that it could not matter much. The feeling of security that was imparted to Britain by her sense of being on the side of history made the machinations of individuals or small groups appear unimportant. That was the Victorian view; but already at Victoria's death it had begun to change.

It changed because Britain's stability seemed much more brittle, once history's support was taken away. As the later Victorians came to lose their trust in the inevitability of liberal capitalist progress, so they found themselves turning elsewhere for security. In a world suddenly restored to a state of high political uncertainty, the actions of individuals came to seem to matter more. Things – even great events – could turn on them. Workers could be subverted, the defences of the nation undermined, or the peace of whole continents shattered by tiny groups of men and women working purposefully and clandestinely. Conversely, the only way these eventualities could be *prevented* was by individual agency. Broad historical currents were powerless to stop the murder of Franz Ferdinand at Sarajevo, but a clever secret policeman might have done the trick.[15] (It is a fact, incidentally, that just seven months before Sarajevo Franz Ferdinand visited Britain, was protected by two Special Branch officers, and was not assassinated then.)[16] The security of governments and peoples, therefore, depended on the wits of just a handful of people acting on their behalf. In this way a new premium was put on the activities of the formerly despised figures of the secret agent, the 'special' detective, and the spy.

The popular literature of the time reflects this. A new genre around the turn of the century was the spy novel. Most spy stories interpreted world politics in terms of the secret machinations of individual men. One very early one, E. Phillips Oppenheim's *Mysterious Mr Sabin* (1898), balanced the fate of Britain between a foreign agent who threatened to reveal Royal Naval deficiencies to the Kaiser, and a nihilist sect which stopped him at the last moment by putting the black spot on him. Neither broad historical imperatives, nor the British government, got a look in. That indicated a precarious situation, as it was intended to. It was compounded in this case by Britain's refusal to stoop to 'underhand' methods herself. Later on this changed. Erskine Childers's *The Riddle of the Sands* (1903) had a German invasion plot foiled by the enterprise of two young amateur British spies, under cover of a sailing holiday among the Frisian islands. That at least gave the forces of good a sporting chance. The point was, however, that this chance rested on individual initiative. Good by itself was no longer enough. Britain needed to have one or two clever and unscrupulous agents: a Holmes as well as an army of Watsons, to protect her from the damage that could be done by the agents of the other side.[17]

Some Edwardians accepted this enthusiastically: the Baden-Powell type, for example, who revelled in the sporting side of espionage.[18] Others accepted it only reluctantly, or refused to accept it at all. The old Victorian prejudice against 'underhand' methods was a resilient one, and at least as powerful in the 1900s as the new morality. Novelists had to tread warily with it. Spies, and to a lesser extent detectives, were not everybody's taste in heroes. Even Sherlock Holmes was not an altogether sympathetic creation, and might not have gone down as well as he did without Watson's more straightforward British virtues to buffer him. Spy heroes were a bigger problem. Erskine Childers's pair constantly agonised over whether what they were doing was right. Novelists like Oppenheim and William le Queux found it difficult to make clear to their readers the distinction they instinctively felt to exist between (bad) German and (good) British spies. One solution was to make the British agents 'gentlemen', but that conjunction jarred a little at first.[19] In 1908, in real life, the British consul in Cherbourg refused an offer (for payment) of plans of French submarines, on the grounds that it was ungentlemanly.[20] The leading German spymaster in Britain before the Great War is supposed to have acknowledged that 'Spying is a dirty business', and to have excused it only on the grounds that everyone was up to it.[21] There was a widespread opinion that espionage – by fuelling mutual suspicions – actually gave rise to wars.[22] As late as 1922 Basil Thomson, who became Quinn's superior officer in 1913, was complaining of the 'number of virtuous people who think it highly improper for a Government to keep itself quietly informed of what is going on in its own and other countries'.[23] Before then there were protests in the House of Commons when undercover policemen were suspected of going too far.[24] Napoleon had claimed that one good spy was worth a hundred soldiers, but it would be a while yet before he was accorded the same esteem. The same was true of the home secret service, which never won the affection of those it protected, or even their respect.

The difference, however, was that now it was by and large accepted as a necessity, which put the Special Branch on a firmer footing than before. There was never any danger of its disbandment in the 1900s, or of its running out of things to do. The climate had shifted in its favour: grown colder and more threatening, and more suited to its sort of approach. In these conditions it flourished and grew under the superintendency of Patrick Quinn; especially in the years immediately before the Great War, when the storm-clouds looked blackest, and some of them burst.

Its growth was a steady one. In the mid-1890s sections 'B' and 'D' of the CID, which made up the Special Branch in London, had a combined strength of twenty-five. It also had men (section 'C') stationed at ports. Over the next ten years sections 'B' and 'D' gradually increased, while section 'C' was cut.[25] By 1909 the latter had nine vacancies, which Quinn was happy to leave unfilled; section 'D' had himself and five inspectors; and section 'B' had one chief inspector, eleven sergeants and sixteen constables: making thirty-four in all. In July that year that figure was augmented by another four.[26]

There is no particular reason to account for this increase before 1909. There were no dynamite campaigns or other dramatic events to provoke it. The Police Commissioner reported in 1904 that anarchism was 'practically quiescent in London', which was a reason, he said, for curbing any 'unnecessary activity on the part of the Police'.[27] Two years later he dismissed the influence of the anarchist press in Britain as 'quite unimportant'.[28] This was corroborated by the anarchists themselves. *Freedom* continually bemoaned what it called the 'dullness' of the times, compared with the 1890s, which had been altogether more fun. It also found itself struggling for funds, which was another indication of slump.[29] In the east end of London there was a flourishing anarchist community of Russian Jewish refugees, with a lively newspaper, but it was not thought to pose a threat to Britain yet either through propaganda or by terrorism. Their worst political crime, so far as Britain was concerned, was an article published in one of their papers in the summer of 1902 which suggested that at his coronation King Edward should be annointed with urine.[30] There was little likelihood of political violence from any other direction. In December 1905 a new progressive government came to power. Both the Irish and the socialists held back until they saw what it would do for them. So did other potential dissidents, like Indian nationalists and the women who wanted the vote. The result was domestic peace and quiet, at least for a little while. Yet the British authorities' vigilance, in the shape of the Special Branch, never relaxed.

This was probably wise. No one in a jungle lowers his defences merely because he has not been attacked recently. The mid-Victorians had done so, but only because they had insisted that the jungle did not exist. There were no doubts about that any more; and no doubts either about the continuing vigour of political violence abroad. In Spain there were attacks on royalty and ministers nearly every year. Fifteen people were killed in Madrid in May 1906 by a bomb intended for the king. There were riots all over Spain in 1907 and 1909 in which anarchists were involved. In Portugal in February 1908 the king and the crown prince were assassinated by two republicans. Political murders were commonplace in Russia, where in 1905 St Petersburg felt a tremor of the earthquake that was to upheave it in 1917. There were also significant outrages and *attentats* in France, Italy, the Balkans and the United States. In October 1903 this spilled over into England, when an Armenian was murdered by another Armenian near Peckham Rye, probably on political grounds. Britain could not ignore all this, just because she was not a target herself. In 1905 and 1906 the registers of letters coming to and from the Home Office record a significant increase in those on the subject of anarchism, which suggests a resurgence of its old 1890s fears.[31] 'One never knows where the Anarchists may break out,' wrote Edward Troup of the Home Office to the Scottish under-secretary in September 1906; 'and, though they are very quiet just now, I think no precaution shd be neglected.'

That was in response to a letter from Aberdeen's procurator-fiscal, passing on information he had received from a prisoner called Albert Bernstein about 'a member of the Anarchist Groop [sic] "The Camera"' who he claimed was plotting to kill the King. MacNaghten dismissed the report as a ruse by Bernstein to secure his release, but agreed to send a couple of Special Branch men to Aberdeen to help out just in case.[32] His vigilance was not unreasonable. In 1900 there had been a genuine attempt on Edward's life in Brussels by a sixteen-year-old anarchist called Sipido, who was released from prison, to the alarm of the Metropolitan Police, when he turned twenty-one in December 1905.[33] There were other threats both to Edward's life and to George v's.[34] These justified the closest of watches on them, especially when they went abroad, when they were invariably accompanied by a Special Branch inspector and sergeant, fitted out with 'special outfits' (presumably smart suits) for the purpose.[35] Occasionally a higher rank went. When George v visited the battle front in the first winter of the war, his bodyguard was Quinn himself, who was fitted up with a 'khaki outfit' for the purpose at a cost of £15.[36] In October 1911 the King was accompanied to India by the Chief Commissioner, no less, who took with him Constable A. Tibbenham of the Special Branch.[37] By then the Branch's duties had been extended to include the protection of cabinet ministers too. Churchill, for example, had a policeman along with him when he holidayed in Venice in May 1913, and Birrell had one for a skiing trip to Switzerland in January 1914.[38] No doubt the detectives selected for these tasks enjoyed themselves hugely; but it was an added burden on the resources of the Branch.

Another was its duty towards foreign notables visiting Britain, who might be vulnerable to attack by their disaffected compatriots living in exile. The Kings of Spain and Portugal, the Tsar of Russia and the German Kaiser were amongst those who benefited from the Special Branch's protection between 1904 and 1910.[39] Some of them even had their feelings protected: like Prince Fushini of Japan, whose visit to England in May 1907 was preceded by an order to the band which welcomed him off his ship not to play selections from Sullivan's *Mikado* in case it gave offence. (They need not have worried; when the welcoming dignitaries arrived they apparently found the Prince's own Japanese band playing a *Mikado* medley to them.)[40] The most tense occasion was probably King Edward's funeral three years later, when half Europe's royalty came, most of them under threat from assassins.[41] In the end all passed off uneventfully, which may well be to the credit of the Branch.

There was another reason for vigilance. It arose out of Britain's asylum policy, and the recurrent criticism it continued to engender abroad. One example came on 30 December 1906, when a member of the Spanish *Cortes* claimed that it made her the nerve-centre of the anarchist conspiracy everywhere. Some of his compatriots apparently went further. 'The fact is', minuted the Home under-secretary in August 1906, 'that the Spaniards have a suspicion that we have a sort of understanding with the Anarchists. They are not to rag us, and we are not to rag them.'[42] This was wounding. Britain could not deny that she sheltered anarchists. Nor could she exclude them, even under the terms of the new 1905 Alien Act, which expressly exempted politicos. She did, however, refute the charge that they plotted their outrages there. This was because, as her ambassador in Madrid put it, 'nowhere are the proceedings of the anarchists so closely and efficaciously watched as in England'; from which it followed that 'nowhere else would the concoction of an anarchist plot be more surely detected and exposed'.[43]

That put a great responsibility on the shoulders of the Special Branch, which in the 1900s, as in the 1890s, it seems to have fulfilled tolerably well. It was not easy. Sometimes it had to steer a delicate path between incompatible demands. The Russians were a particular problem, because of the deep well of public sympathy in Britain their dissidents could tap. (In January 1905 it was announced that a life-size effigy of the Tsar, 'correct to the smallest detail', was being prepared to be hanged at a public ceremony in Smithfield market, after a jury of meat salesmen presided over by Mr Billy Harris, the 'Sausage King', had found him guilty of 'permitting wholesale murder'.)[44] The Branch succeeded here partly through restraint, and partly through secrecy. It kept Russian refugees under surveillance, but was careful about what information it passed on officially to the Russian authorities. When some Labour MPs expressed concern about the presence of two Special Branch officers who had been spotted at a Russian socialist congress in London in the summer of 1907, therefore, it was able to swear blind, and probably truthfully, that none of the intelligence they gathered reached St Petersburg. Whatever the Okhrana learned of the congress must have come from its own agents, who were bound to be far better informed than the Special Branch men: which was why it had not requested, because it did not need, British police help in this case.[45] In other cases it did. Then the normal practice of the Branch was to do what it could, secretly and sometimes unofficially, except in circumstances where action was required which might attract notice outside.

All in all the British police appear to have given less help than most other European police forces to the Okhrana in these revolutionary years,[46] but enough to prevent any serious diplomatic breach. From the Russian point of view their most culpable failure was their refusal to co-operate to prevent the smuggling of arms from British ports to Russia by Lettish revolutionaries in 1907, due to what the head of the foreign section of the Okhrana characterised as a 'pedantic concern' for legality.[47] But they were happy to swap information about the identities and movements of dissidents, especially when murder plots were supposed to be afoot – though they retained their customary scepticism of most of these;[48] and they may have had informal relationships with Okhrana agents behind the official scenes. Special Branch officers were occasionally offered, and accepted, generous gifts of watches, tie-pins, cigarette cases and snuff boxes from the Okhrana's European director, which had always been one of the perks of this sort of work;[49] and when Detective-Inspector Powell moved from Scotland Yard to the Russian Secret Service in 1912 he clearly did not cut himself off from his old contacts in the Special Branch. In any case he was not allowed to. On 3 June 1914 the Metropolitan Police CID held its annual dinner for chief officers and inspectors. One of the guests (whose menu found its way into the Okhrana archive) was Powell; a toast to whom was proposed by Superintendent McCarthy of the Special Branch, after a meal of green pea soup, Scotch salmon, saddle of mutton Niçoise, punch sorbet, roast Surrey fowl, orange soufflé pudding, bombe Trocadéro (which must have caused a *frisson*) and dessert; and before a cabaret which included Mr George Robey, Mr Harry Tate, a ventriloquist, a ragtime composer, a highland dancer, a 'Growing Man', and Mr Gerald Kirby in his latest song, 'Willie took his Flo below'.[50]

What Willie did with his Flo below leaves only a little less to the imagination than what Powell and McCarthy, on adjacent tables, got up to over the coffee and cigars. The British authorities' attitude towards this sort of collusion, where they knew about it, was ambiguous. When they were asked by foreign governments to allow foreign policemen to work directly with the Special Branch, they continued to refuse. Police Commissioners were firmly against it. 'I beg to be allowed to say in unambiguous language', wrote Bradford in May 1902, 'that the assistance we are invited to accept [by the Italians] so far from strengthening our powers of control would materially weaken them and might even lead to embarrassing complications.' The anarchists would be sure to spot the foreign agents, which would put them on their guard. That would make it more difficult for the British police to watch them. Some of those agents (like Gennaro Rubini) used underhand methods which it would be damaging for the British police to be associated with.[51] Foreign police were also clearly less discriminating in their choice of targets than the British were supposed to be. 'The reference in the Spanish letter to "Carlists, Catalans, and Republicans", i.e. ordinary political discontents,' wrote the Home under-secretary in response to a later request, 'further complicates the matter.' In this case Henry even suggested that the Spanish police themselves were riddled with anarchism.[52] The key difficulty was that there was no way of controlling them. Consequently formal co-operation was out.

Communication with foreign police forces was another matter. The government had far less objection to the Special Branch's alerting them to 'any credible news' of plots it found. Continental governments were assured of this repeatedly.[53] This was different, because it retained the control of matters in British police hands. There may have been one exception. In 1906 Herbert Gladstone was asked if it would be all right for Scotland Yard to correspond in cipher about anarchists with the St Petersburg police. Henry objected to this because of the 'additional work that would be thrown upon the Police Department here by the placing of the Russian and Metropolitan Police in direct communication', and because of the 'risk of serious results arising from the possible misspelling of difficult Russian and Polish names'.[54] Another consideration may have been the Okhrana's reputation. In any case the Home Office did not like 'hard and fast agreements with continental police authorities' which would 'fetter' the English police.[55] Every case had to be judged on its political or tactical merits. In each one the government was the best judge of how to pass on information, and when it might be unwise to: because of potential political embarrassment, or because there was 'a risk that by so doing the source from which we derived it may be dried up'.[56]

Nevertheless it helped when it could. A great deal of information passed both ways, between the Special Branch and its equivalents abroad, either through diplomatic channels or bypassing them. The Branch tended to regard its own intelligence as solider than the information it got from outside, which it tested rigorously, and often found to be baseless; but this did not detract from the general value of what by now had become an effective international police network.[57] It gave other kinds of assistance too. Whenever there was a major event abroad like a coronation or a royal marriage or a great exhibition, a couple of Special Branch officers generally went along (at the host government's expense) to liaise with all the other political policemen who were there.[58] Very occasionally something more positive was done. The most famous example before 1909 – though it was not *very* famous – was the case of the Italians Adolfo Antonelli and Francesco Barberi, who were arrested by the Special Branch, and then convicted and sentenced to penal servitude in September 1905 on charges of seditious libel arising out of an article preaching assassination in the anarchist journal *L'Insurrezione* in July.[59] This case stood in a direct line with Most's in 1881 and Burtsev's in 1897. The chief difference was that, unlike them, it aroused scarcely any public protest or interest at all.[60]

This was a relatively unexciting time for the Branch. Most of its activities seem to have been routine (though it was a highly responsible sort of routine) and unspectacular. Occasionally it may have found itself at a loose end. In May 1905 one of its Inspectors was sent to Pau and Biarritz in France to make enquiries into the smuggling of 'toy dogs' into Britain, which seems a long way from its usual work, unless the dogs were involved in an anarchist plot.[61] The reason a Special Branch man was used for this purpose was probably his ability to speak French. For the same reason Maguire and McBrien of the Special Branch were sent to Paris in 1902 to keep observation on 'Colonel' Alfred Lynch, who was charged with aiding and abetting the South African Republic in the recent war.[62] Generally, however, the Branch was kept busy protecting luminaries and keeping a close eye on foreign subversives, mainly for the benefit of continental governments, which rewarded it with gifts and honours.[63] It did this unobtrusively. In left-wing circles, for example, where the Okhrana was a constant butt of criticism, scarcely anyone noticed its (milder) British equivalent.[64] Where it was noticed, it was not always unkindly. Lenin is supposed to have paid fulsome tribute to it when it apparently saved him from being set upon as a spy at a meeting in London's East End.[65] No scandals or suspicions attached to it, as they had done in the 1880s and 1890s. The 1900s, therefore, were the Special Branch's period of quiet consolidation; until around 1909, when things began to get very much more tense.

CHAPTER 11

The Shadow of War
1909–14

It was around 1909 that the pent-up general fears that had been steadily rising in Britain since the turn of the century, if not before, suddenly took on specific and tangible forms. The country entered a period of political and constitutional crisis more serious than any for very many years. That crisis revolved chiefly around the questions of Ulster, labour, votes for women and the House of Lords. Some of these questions had aspects which involved the Special Branch, though in the main they were matters of high policy. Alongside them there were other threats, which were much more the Branch's concern. There was a new series of real outrages in England, for example, involving foreign political refugees. There was the assassination of a government official in London, by an Indian with a gun. Lastly, there was the alarm raised by an entirely different kind of subversion, this time from German spies, who were thought to be plotting to defeat Britain from within. All this took place against a background of deteriorating international relations, economic depression, and a political shift in some circles to the right. For liberals it was a deeply unhappy time, whose natural culmination, in a way, was the outbreak of the war.

Of all these threats the alien anarchist one was the least serious, though it was the most spectacular. It began in January 1909, when a police constable was murdered near Tottenham marshes by two Lettish socialists whom he had surprised robbing a wages clerk. Then in December 1910 another group of Letts was surprised burgling a jeweller's shop in Houndsditch, and after a long chase in which three more policemen were killed, was besieged in a house in Sidney Street, Stepney, where on 4 January 1911 three of them were shot or burned to death.[1] Four days before that the dead body of a Russian Jew called Leon Beron had been discovered on Clapham Common in south London, with the letter 'S' cut into each side of his face, presumably to denote that he had been executed as a spy.[2] These were serious and shocking crimes, which had the effect of bringing anarchism back into the light of a garish publicity.

The Clapham Common murder was probably political: either an act of revenge by the Russian Left, or – possibly – a crime provoked by a Russian right-wing group to shock British public opinion into stronger measures against refugees. Tottenham and Houndsditch may have been part of the same conspiracy.[3] Aside from that, however, they are less likely to have been political, except by a very loose definition of the word. They were committed by people with revolutionary leanings and connections; those leanings may have encouraged or excused crimes against property; and it is possible (though there is no evidence of this) that some of the profits of them would have been put to revolutionary use. On the other hand they were 'ordinary' crimes in every other sense. On the surface they were simple robberies, which had tragic after-effects. They presented no conceivable political threat. Foreign anarchists in London perpetrated no crimes against British political targets in the 1900s, and no overtly 'terrorist' acts. They did not, so far as one could tell, shoot policemen out of principle, but simply in order to avoid being caught.

In the country at large they were not primarily regarded as a political problem, but as a 'criminal alien' one. Most of the criticism of the government they engendered turned on its lax administration of the 1905 Aliens Act. (When Winston Churchill visited the Sidney Street affray as Home Secretary in January 1911, he was apparently regailed with cries of 'Oo let 'em in?')[4] That laxity derived from his predecessor Herbert Gladstone's concern in 1906 that Russian Jews might be unknowingly sent back to persecution and even death if immigration boards insisted on proof of their refugee credentials, which made it difficult to exclude any immigrant who had his wits about him when he disembarked.[5] Political asylum was at the root of it, therefore; but it was not political asylum that was primarily objected to. Most criticism of the government derived from social and racial hostility to east European Jews, whose innate criminality these events were supposed to demonstrate. It was this aspect of them that the government felt pressured into legislating for; though neither of the measures it prepared – a bill to make it easier to deport criminal aliens drafted by Gladstone in the wake of the Tottenham murder, and Churchill's 1911 bill to allow the expulsion of aliens for possessing guns or consorting with known criminals – in the end passed into law.[6]

But the political angle could not be ignored. The Tottenham and Houndsditch murderers were anarchists. That established a link between anarchism and violent crime. Some people in Britain took the Russian line over this: that it was a reason for re-thinking their whole policy towards foreign refugees. One man who suggested this was the editor of *Punch*, in a letter to Herbert Gladstone in February 1909 in which he claimed that the present law of asylum was 'nothing but a monstrous anachronism' which flouted Britain's obligations to friendly powers. The Home Secretary's response was two-pronged. There was, he said, no way they could exclude anarchists which was consistent with their liberalism. It would mean giving the courts powers to deport on suspicion, which 'Public opinion would not tolerate'. In any case it was not necessary. Foreign anarchists came to Britain 'in considerable numbers because there is a freer atmosphere. It does not follow that they are not under a closer and more effectual surveillance here than they are abroad.' Generally it was found that they kept within the law. If they stepped beyond it, then 'prompt action would be at once taken'. 'You will understand', Gladstone went on, 'that this is not a matter for public discussion.' But it was Britain's way of reconciling her asylum tradition with her responsibilities for the maintenance of order both at home and overseas.[7]

This was where the Special Branch came in. How deeply involved it was in the Houndsditch enquiries it is difficult to say. The man in charge of them (and of the Clapham Common case) was Inspector Frederick Wensley, a member of an 'ordinary' divisional CID. The City police also had an oar in. But they could not do without the Branch, because of its particular expertise. Quinn and his men were expected to know about the political circles the criminals moved in. They were also the main means of communicating with Riga in Latvia, whose police authorities thought they could help.[8] At the Sidney Street seige in January 1911 Quinn and McCarthy were found in the front line.[9] It was probably they who followed up the connection with Enrico Malatesta, the Italian anarchist who had allowed his workshop to be used by the leader of the Houndsditch gang.[10] (Eighteen months later they tried to get Malatesta deported by linking him with the crime, but failed.)[11] Tottenham and Houndsditch may not have been political crimes, but they put increased burdens on the political branch, both then and afterwards. Six months after the Tottenham outrage, when Quinn requested an increase in its strength, 'The large number of Russian, Polish, Yiddish and Anarchists of other nationalities, resident in London' was one of the 'grounds' he gave.

But it was not the main one. That same letter also mentioned several other calls on the Special Branch's resources, two of which were new. They were the 'increasing demands upon the Special Branch in consequence of the Indian agitation', and the 'agitation by Suffragettes'.[12] The suffragettes were a problem because of their strategy of physically assaulting ministers, which began in 1908. The Indian nationalists came into the Special Branch's sights after one of them, Madan Lal Dhingra, murdered the Secretary of State for India's political aide-de-camp, Sir William Curzon Wyllie, at the Imperial Institute in South Kensington on 1 July 1909. That was just seven days before Quinn's plea for more men, and was placed at the top of his list of 'grounds'.

To cope with these new dangers the Branch was reorganised. Two sections were formed within it to devote themselves exclusively to the Indians and the suffragettes. The Indian section was the subject of discussions on 13 July between the Indian Secretary and Sir Edward Henry, who wanted the Indian government to bear some of the cost. He also hoped that Morley might provide him with 'one or two good informants', and 'some one who has a knowledge of Indians & of what has been going on there – either an Eurasian or a native', to act as the section's 'clerk'. Without some sort of help from India the Branch clearly felt at a loss.[13] By 1913 it had also taken Egyptian dissidence on board.[14]

The suffragette section was formed just a couple of months after the Indian one, on the initiative of Herbert Gladstone, the Home Secretary, after some suffragettes had attacked his car. What impressed him about the militants was their efficiency. 'These women always go down & prospect. Consequently they frequently outwit the local forces.' Some of them, he wrote to his under-secretary, were 'specially dangerous', either 'from nervous excitability or otherwise'. 'Action by a female Dhingra' could not be ruled out. If the Prime Minister or anyone else were injured, 'there will be dangerous & perhaps savage reprisals by the crowd'. The lesson of all this was that 'concerted police action is necessary on the detective side. I think a branch shd. be formed and special officers shd. be sent beforehand to all places when the P.M. or cabinet ministers are due to speak.'[15] Scotland Yard agreed. MacNaghten responded by setting up 'a small Dept. of the Special Branch' for this purpose.[16] It was staffed with experienced officers, because of the delicacy of their task. The Acting Commissioner (Henry was away) pointed out how 'any tactical mistake would be much criticized and would have the effect of promoting, instead of arresting, the progress of the Suffragette propaganda'.[17] That would never do.

Consequently Quinn seems to have taken personal charge, with Chief Inspector McCarthy and Inspector Powell as his right-hand men.[18] The last-named was particularly recommended by MacNaghten for duty amongst the women on account of his unrivalled knowledge of them, and his *'exceptionally good physique'*.[19]

The suffragettes soaked up a good deal of the Special Branch's strength. The scale of their activities ensured that. One single case of criminal damage by suffragettes in 1911, for example, tied up fifteen CID officers, most of them from the Branch.[20] Police raids on their headquarters, and surveillance of offenders released under the terms of the 'Cat and Mouse' Act, must have tied up more.[21] The duty also had its peculiar aggravations. Quinn once indignantly described how, when he went to visit Mrs Pankhurst, he and his men were regaled with shouts of 'Cowards', 'Pigs', 'Dogs', 'Brutes', 'Syphillis' and 'Gonorrhoea' by a crowd of women outside.[22] This was unlikely to have been the kind of thing for which he had joined the Force.

All this was on top of the Branch's by now traditional duties, which were growing more onerous every year. Royal protection must have been a particular headache in May 1910, on the occasion of the funeral of Edward VII. (One anonymous letter received by the Home Office just before that event warned the government that if they wanted to have a 'piecefull funerall' they should not 'invate King Alfonso The murderer of Mr Ferer the Spanish Sosilist', whose blood would flow.)[23] As well as kings and emperors, more non-royals were coming to qualify for protection, as more came under threat. By 1913 they had come to include judges.[24] At any time the Branch could be called on for 'Enquiries of a highly important nature' by any department of state. Apparently the government of Ireland was particularly importunate in this respect. Then there were the enquiries it had to carry out in connection with naturalisation applications, which 'help to add to the work'. These were some of Quinn's other reasons for requesting more men for the Special Branch in July 1909.[25] They must have been in Henry's mind too when he pleaded with the Home Office in 1910 to allow Quinn to soldier on beyond the normal retirement age on the grounds that 'I should find it almost, if not quite impossible, to adequately replace him'.[26] The split infinitive may be an indication of his desperation. Both Quinn and Henry agreed thereafter that there was 'no likelihood of the duties diminishing', but rather if anything the reverse.[27]

Quinn's arguments for an augmentation of section 'B' by two sergeants and two constables in July 1909 were accepted by the Home

Office, which brought the strength of the London-based Special Branch up to thirty-eight.[28] Its numbers increased steadily after that. There were big augmentations in September 1909 (16 men) and April 1913 (15 men), justified on both occasions by reference to 'the persistence with which the militant section of the advocates of women's suffrage maintain their campaign of violence'.[29] Another three were added in May 1913.[30] That brought the numbers in London to more than seventy. Shortly after the beginning of the war they stood at eighty-one at Scotland Yard, plus another thirty-three at ports.[31] Most of these increases were intended to be temporary, but turned out not to be. By this time the old distinctions between sections 'B', 'C' and 'D' had been abolished, because all three were paid for *via* the Metropolitan Police Fund.[32] (The Branch was now generally referred to as 'CID-s' for short.) Its growth over the past four years had been prodigious; though not so prodigious as it was about to become under the impact of the war.

That peace-time growth may have been influenced by other factors in addition to the ones retailed by Quinn. Suffragettes were time-consuming, and an irritation; but they were not – apart from the slight risk of 'a female Dhingra' – a really serious threat. They were overshadowed in the years immediately prior to the First World War by two far greater threats, or impending crises. The first was the War itself, which was widely anticipated. The other was the prospect of serious civil commotion in Britain, which some people thought was presaged by the 'Great Labour Unrest'. Basil Thomson, who succeeded MacNaghten as head of the Metropolitan CID in June 1913, was later remembered to have remarked then that 'unless there was a European war to divert the current, we were heading for something very like revolution'.[33] That gave some hope, at least, to those who feared revolution more than war, as many of the middle and upper classes did. But both gave cause for concern.

They also gave cause for those responsible for Britain's internal security to strengthen their hands against subversion of various kinds. Their main ostensible targets were foreign spies and saboteurs, but the measures that were taken had wider implications too. Espionage first became an issue in Britain around 1906–7, due largely to the efforts of sensationalists like Le Queux and the new gutter press. The pictures they painted of Britain riddled with German spies and reservists were nearly all nonsense, but they clearly struck a chord in those nervous times. People became convinced that every waiter or hairdresser they met was a German agent, whose mission was to convey information back to Berlin to assist an invasion, and then to cast off his disguise, arm himself from a cleverly hidden cache, and form up with the other waiters and hairdressers as an army of saboteurs. This Trojan horse scenario seemed plausible enough to set thousands of men and women hunting the menace in their midst. This was not easy, as the thing that distinguished a spy was supposed to be his inconspicuousness; but the hunters were not deterred. *The Times*, which was sceptical, noticed in 1908 how 'Every day brings its fresh accumulation of "proofs", rarely in the form of personal observation, generally in the shape of remarks made by some unknown person to some one else.'[34] At his home near the south Devon coast Le Queux garnered together all these 'proofs', until he had amassed 'a file of amazing documents which plainly show the feverish activity with which this advance guard of the enemy is working', which he loyally passed on to the War Office.[35]

Within the War Office there were many who shared Le Queux's fears. For years they had believed that the threats Britain lay under required the military to have what Major James Edmonds, who was head of the Army's secret service, in 1908 called 'reasonable powers' over the civilian population both in peace and war. Since 1885 they had been pushing for such powers, but to no avail. The reasons for this, claimed Edmonds, were the purblindness of government ministers who would not recognise a threat if it sat on them; an over-sensitive regard for the liberal scruples of Parliament; and straightforward 'legal stupidity'.[36]

The tide turned in 1909. The breakthrough probably came in March, when the War Minister, Haldane, was at last convinced – or pretended to be – of the reality of the German spy threat. This had a number of immediate results. One was the formation in the summer of 1909, largely on Edmonds's initiative, of a new 'Secret Service Bureau' which much later became known (and hereafter will be referred to) as MI5. That came about as the result of deliberations by a new 'Foreign Espionage' sub-committee of the Committee of Imperial Defence, which included the Home Secretary and the Metropolitan Commissioner of Police.[37] Other sub-committees were set up at the same time, to look into the problem of aliens, and the defence of naval installations. In April 1909 an 'Interdepartmental Conference' was held between the Home and War Offices to consider 'the Prevention of Civil Trouble in the Metropolis in Time of War'.[38] It was in these various sub-committees and conferences that most of the new weapons against subversion were forged.

One was a register of aliens. This was proposed by the 'Espionage' sub-committee in 1910, and implemented the following year.[39] At one stage the idea was to make it open and official. To this end Churchill 'grafted' on to his post-Sidney Street Aliens bill in March 1911 a couple of new clauses enabling the government to compel aliens to register with the authorities in certain 'designated areas' at any time, and to expel, detain or exclude aliens in time of war or 'imminent national danger'.[40] The new bill was discussed by the sub-committee at the end of March, but dropped on account of the 'formidable parliamentary difficulties' that were anticipated, and the likelihood that it would be easily circumvented by genuine professional spies.[41] Neither of these objections, however, applied to an *unofficial* register. That register was drawn up mainly through the agency of county chief constables. The boroughs were not brought into it at first, on the grounds that *their* police chiefs were 'of a different class – & too much in the hands of their Watch Committees'. In October 1911, however, Churchill extended it to all towns outside London.[42] By July 1913 the initial registration was nearly complete, with dockets for 28,830 foreigners resident in Britain filed in the War Office.[43] It was all to be treated, urged the Home Office, as highly secret.[44] Otherwise both its effectiveness and its legitimacy were likely to be called into doubt.

Two other anti-subversion measures carried through in 1911 were Churchill's authorisation of general warrants, in place of specific warrants, for the interception of mail at the GPO around October;[45] and the passage of a new Official Secrets Act in August. The former was done furtively; the latter involved sharp practice. The Official Secrets bill was presented as a measure aimed solely at foreign spies, and as 'nothing novel', which was not strictly – or even remotely – true. Two or three MPs spotted this at the time; one of them interjected in the House of Commons that 'It upsets Magna Charta altogether'. But very few were vigilant or even perhaps awake enough, on a Friday afternoon in mid-summer, to care; and so the bill was smuggled through in record time, with only ten MPs (mostly Labour) voting against.[46]

And so the dyke was breached. First the politicians were converted. After that Edmonds's other obstacles simply melted away. Parliament proved to be scarcely any problem at all, at a time of widespread spy mania and with resolute statesmen at the helm. Churchill, in particular, had shown how easy it was to circumvent or manipulate the Commons, if the political will was there. That left only the lawyers; who in these circumstances, however, could be trusted to do what they were told. The military got at least some of what it wanted, in order to be able to protect Britain adequately against what it had long perceived to be the pressing dangers of foreign espionage, invasion and sabotage.

These were its main targets. Political subversion was not amongst them, though some military men may have felt it should be. From the shelter of an officer's mess in the 1910s it was sometimes difficult to distinguish socialism from treachery. When war broke out in 1914 little effort was made to do so: socialists and pacifists were put under the same strict surveillance as suspected German spies.[47] Even before the war some soldiers were found eliding the strike menace with the spy one. A Home Ports Defence Committee memorandum of May 1912 reported widespread German espionage in South Wales, together with the opinion of the local military commander that labour could not be 'relied upon not to utilize the fact of war being imminent to enforce their demands for improved wages or other conditions'.[48] There was even the possibility that Germany might foment industrial unrest to further her belligerent aims. Winston Churchill was sent 'evidence' that a German agent was subsidising the Liverpool dock strike in August 1911; and in November 1917 the head of the Metropolitan CID recalled the case of a Baron von Horst who, he claimed, had been disbursing money left and right to trade unionists, suffragettes and Irish nationalists in 1912–13.[49] All this added a new and frightening dimension to the industrial problems of the time.

Hence the Interdepartmental Conference on the Prevention of Civil Trouble in the Metropolis, which agreed in June 1909 that the police should be armed with carbines and assisted by two army battalions to put down disorder in London after hostilities had commenced. Later on the Army took this to mean that it could take the capital over completely, with soldiers empowered to shoot malefactors on sight, and its own network of 'intelligence officers' reporting back to 'Area Commandants' from likely 'centres of discontent'.[50] These were contingency plans. In the meantime other precautions were taken. One of the outcomes of the Home Ports Defence Committee memorandum of May 1912 was the setting up of a special force of detectives in the South Wales coalfields to watch out for spies and saboteurs, paid for by the Admiralty (because it was the Navy's coal that was at risk).[51] Other vital installations were protected in the same way.

All these measures had a significance which went beyond the narrow realm of counter-espionage. For whatever reason, the state was extending its powers. Most of the extensions were clandestine: either hidden from Parliament completely, like the aliens register, or half-hidden, like the Official Secrets Act. This meant that they could not be properly monitored, except by the ministers in charge. That left them open to abuse, in the hands of ministers who were even less liberal at heart than Churchill probably was. It also made them profoundly undemocratic, and symptomatised a loss of trust by the government in Britain's (limited) democracy. Parliament was not consulted over the matter of the aliens register because it was feared that it might, on liberal grounds, object. But the register was set up regardless. This was because Parliament did not know what was best for it. The country had to be protected not only from German spies, but also against her own liberal good nature. It was a seductive argument, and all the more so, no doubt, after a session with the Army's 'golden tongued' counter-espionage man, Vernon Kell.[52] But it also marked a radical change in political atmosphere, which was there for other counter-subversive agencies to breathe in too.

The part played by the police in all this counter-espionage work was supposed to be ancillary. They compiled the aliens register, and kept their weather-eyes open for suspicious characters. To this end Kell's department issued secret notes of guidance for chief constables in October 1912, with special reference to waiters and hairdressers.[53] Occasionally Kell seems to have bypassed the chief constables and found police officers willing to report directly to him.[54] At Scotland Yard, according to one of MI5's historians, who got it from Kell's widow, he spent 'day after day . . . laboriously searching the files of the specialist departments there, and painstakingly copying out items which interested him'; and in 'long hours with Quinn', who briefed him on the 'apparently innocent societies which were fronts for more sinister activities'.[55]

Kell clearly needed the police, for two reasons. The first was that he did not have the resources himself to make enquiries. When his Bureau started he was on his own, with one clerk added soon afterwards, and possibly the use of 'a retired police detective'. That detective may well have been Melville, who certainly worked in some form of intelligence after 1903.[56] Later the Bureau was augmented, but on the eve of the Great War it still had only seven officers. The second reason was that it had no executive powers. Kell needed the police to make his arrests for him; and indeed preferred it this way, even if it meant the credit going to them. 'We welcome the belief', he said later, 'that "S . . Y . ." is responsible for dealing with spies. It is a valuable camouflage.'[57] Camouflage was vital at the time, though it seems to have irritated Edmonds later on. On a press cutting about the police in 1921 he noted acidly that they 'did naught as regard German spies except providing cells for those D.M.I. caught'.[58] The implication was that the clever detective work was all done by Kell and his men, leaving the Branch to carry out their orders when they wanted a suspect watched or formally arrested. This may have been unfair.

In fact if the German 'spymaster' Gustav Steinhauer's own account is to be believed, it did not require a great degree of cleverness to catch his agents. The traitor Parrott was betrayed to Scotland Yard by his German contact Karl Hentschel out of pique for his efforts to bypass him and send his secrets to Germany direct. Hentschel later gave himself up at Chatham police station, and then when the Chatham police did not take him seriously went around to another police station to try again. Friedrich Schroeder was arrested when he moved out of the pub he ran in Rochester, leaving behind maps of ports and incriminating letters.[59] MI5's main *coup* came when a German officer attending Edward VII's funeral led the three Special Branch men routinely assigned to shadow him direct to the German spy head-quarters in a barber's shop in the Caledonian Road.[60] That gave them access to the whole spy network, which was a good deal smaller than was popularly believed, and apparently rigidly centralised. 'Briefly,' wrote one ex-Special Branch man in 1932, 'the weakness of the German Secret Service in England was due to the Teutonic fondness for standardised organisation.'[61] It was this that enabled Kell and Quinn to neutralise it entirely when war broke out, simply by rounding up the men whose names they found on envelopes in the barber's shop. It was an efficient operation, but not a particularly taxing one. The art of spying had not yet reached the level of sophistication which called for sophisticated methods to counter it.

It may have been the nagging feeling that somehow it had all been *too* easy that persuaded Kell that there still must be some spies left. If there were, then it was clearly worrying, for the spies who remained were likely to be the cleverest ones at concealing themselves, and so the cleverest, presumably, at spying. There was also the problem of sabotage. None of the men arrested in August 1914 admitted to anything more than military espionage. That left Kell's saboteurs still at large. On 6 August the Home Office telegraphed all chief constables to 'keep special watch to prevent Aliens travelling by night by Motor Car for purpose of committing outrages', and to seize any motor vehicles owned by Germans.[62] The first months of the war also saw a massive search and round-up of all known Germans and Austrians in Britain, to try to account for the remaining agents. By 25 November the

Lord Chancellor reported that 120,000 separate enquiries had been made, and 6,000 house searches carried out.[63] The Special Branch was almost entirely diverted to this work.[64] The burden almost crippled it. Thomson complained in November that the strain was telling. There had been no leave for sixteen weeks, two men had gone sick from overwork, and it was becoming 'hopeless to continue the effort further'. He needed, he said, an immediate augmentation of twenty-five men. That was granted in December.[65] But it made little difference. The spies and saboteurs remained elusive. The Special Branch's efforts against them turned out to be one enormous wild goose chase.

The most recent work on pre-war counter-espionage in Britain concludes that MI5's assessment of the danger from German agents at this time was 'ludicrously wrong'.[66] Edmonds later suggested that the Germans may have deliberately 'planted' false information about invasion plans in order to 'frighten' governments.[67] One man they certainly succeeded in frightening was William le Queux, who at the beginning of the war became convinced that the Germans were out to get him personally for rumbling their schemes. From then onwards he was engaged in a running battle with his local police and the Metropolitan Force over the claim he made for special protection. The Metropolitan police's response to that claim may illuminate its attitude to the spy question. Edward Henry regarded Le Queux, as he wrote to the Home Office in March 1915, as a writer of 'sensational' and 'highly coloured' novels who was mainly out for self-advertisement. 'In his own eyes he is a person of importance and dangerous to the enemy.' In reality, however, he was 'not a person to be taken seriously'. The authorities, 'who view him in proper perspective', had consequently seen no need to provide what he asked.[68] Henry's own perspective may have been influenced by what Le Queux thought of *him*. In a book published just a month before Henry's memorandum to the Home Office he had lambasted 'the utter incapability of the Commissioner of Metropolitan Police' and his 'hopeless department' in no uncertain terms.[69] But the row between them is also likely to indicate a fundamental difference of outlook between them, and perhaps between the Special Branch and MI5 too.

The difference lay in their relative degrees of alarmism. Le Queux's alarmism was extreme. He was frequently pilloried for it, to which he retorted that the government was 'suppressing' the truth for reasons of its own.[70] Edmonds and Kell were scarcely less alarmist. Many of their earliest reports of suspected German espionage in Britain were based on Le Queux's 'evidence', which they accepted uncritically. Much of that evidence was risible.[71] Even cumulatively it should not have been sufficient to convince any moderately sceptical person. Yet on the basis of it they constructed an elaborate hypothesis of German intrigue, which seems to have been real to them, and which they kept in their sights until the end of the war. One reason for this was undoubtedly the size of the stakes they were playing for. It was always *conceivable* that a foreign power could try to reduce Britain to impotence in the face of an invasion by blowing up magazines, fomenting strikes and cutting telegraph wires. If that happened, then the results would be dire. It was better to be safe than sorry, even if the price of safety was ridicule. Another reason may have been Edmonds's and Kell's backgrounds as Army officers. The Special Branch had no one (or no one prominent) with a military background. All its personnel were professional policemen, with experience of the civilian grass roots. Many of them came from working-class stock. They were solider, dourer, and generally less silly than the upper-class community who ran the military side. The Special Branch was used to rumours and suspicions, and to discounting most of them. This was one of its hallmarks. It is likely, therefore, and its attitude to Le Queux confirms, that it was wiser and less impressionable in its pursuit of spies in the 1910s than was the infant MI5.

It may also have been less impressionable on other fronts. The labour troubles of the time, for example, seem to have concerned it very little. There is no sign in the official record that when Metropolitan Police were sent to reinforce local constabularies in strike areas after 1909, Special Branch men went with them. If local police and military commanders wanted intelligence of strikers' activities and plans, it did not occur to them to ask Scotland Yard. In most cases they elicited it themselves.

In many of the great industrial disputes of the pre-war years spies and informers were used amongst the participants, but not by the Special Branch, and not in a 'political' way. During the Hull dock strike of 1911, for example, the Superintendent in charge of the Metropolitan detachment there described how he had 'employed P.C. 703 Smithers in plain clothes to patrol about the town and docks to obtain information as to what was transpiring amongst the dockers and others', and how Smithers had come back with valuable intelligence about grievances, solidarity, picketing and efforts to encourage sympathy strikes.[72] But the best people for this sort of thing were undoubtedly the military. They used spies too, and much more extensively. Edmonds, for example, recalled how he had employed them amongst what he called the 'natives' in an industrial dispute in 1911 – rather as if he was on the North-West Frontier. (In this case the natives came from Hackney.) The best men for this work, he minuted helpfully in August that year, were NCOs and lower ranks from the locality, who should be sent snooping around in plain clothes 'purchased on the spot'.[73] But the idea did not originate with him. It was probably the brainchild of General Cecil Macready, who was sent to control the South Wales 'strike area' in November 1910.

Macready's main reason for using spies was to enable him to assess the situation with which he had to deal. No one else could do it. The mineowners, he claimed, tended to be alarmist, and to expect the authorities to take their side. (On occasion they had even gone so far as to demand that the police and military protect working miners, or blacklegs, with no regard for 'how it might affect the strikers'.) Consequently their advice was 'worthless'.[74] The local Glamorgan constabulary were little better. Some of them were in the owners' pockets, and none had any experience of detective work.[75] Their chief constable felt that using plain-clothes men would be 'dangerous', and in any case favoured trying to cow the strikers by meeting them head-on. (Macready's comment on this was that it would 'make matters worse'.)[76] The eight hundred officers of the Metropolitan force sent to South Wales had 'no plain clothes with them', and lacked 'the necessary local knowledge' anyway.[77] So Macready was left to his own devices.

Two days after arriving he asked the War Office 'for the services of three officers to assist in collecting reliable information'.[78] He was given two. They appear to have done their job well, despite the 'personal risk' to them the work entailed: a report early the following year described how one of them, a Captain Childs, was 'for a time laid up as a result of exposure while carrying out his duties'.[79] 'Thanks to the two officers sent me by the War Office,' reported Macready on 19 November, 'I beleive [sic] I have now fair indication of the intentions of the strikers.'[80] Even the Glamorgan Chief Constable was eventually impressed. 'In no previous Strike in which I have had Military assistance', he wrote to Churchill, 'have the officers made such a careful, & serious study of the situation.'[81] When Macready was withdrawn by the War Office in January 1911, Churchill commended him for his 'tact' and his 'natural and unaffected impartiality between the interests of capital and labour'.[82] That was merited. His employment of secret agents among the strikers almost certainly helped. It gave him objective intelligence of a delicate and changing situation. That enabled him to respond confidently, without over-reacting, to each crisis that appeared. The mineowners did not like it; but Macready believed they were merely spoiling for a fight. His task was not to defeat the strike, but to minimise disorder and violence. His network of spies was vital to this – essentially tactical – end.

It did not really, therefore, amount to a system of political espionage. Its main aim was not to detect political subversion, but to scout out the terrain in pursuit of a particular 'public order' objective. Of course that objective was political in a sense. The fact that Macready pursued it calmly and 'moderately' does not mean that his own motives were not highly political. He may have seen the preservation of order by means of conciliation as the best way of maintaining a broader political status quo. He also did interest himself in political opinions, where they seemed to have a bearing on his main task. He expressed concern, for example, about 'the Socialist ideas which are continually preached in this valley', and sent spies out to cover socialist meetings.[83] At one of them he was told that 'A woman sang revolutionary songs in different languages', and thought that significant enough to pass on to the Home Secretary.[84] That bordered on political surveillance. Macready however justified it on the grounds that he had been told that most of the 'premeditated attempts to destroy property' in the course of the strike came from 'young socialists', which made it important to know about their designs.[85] That may have been coloured by prejudice – his own or his informants' – or it may have been true. It nudged the military close to a form of domestic political espionage; but not for motives which were, at least narrowly, political.

The Special Branch kept right out of this. But it did not keep out of socialist politics altogether. We know of its involvement in this area chiefly because of some of the problems it met. In October 1913 Thomson wrote to the Home under-secretary explaining how Special Branch officers had 'lately had great difficulty in obtaining admission to meetings of Syndicalists and Suffragettes', where they had 'more than once been recognised and molested'. When they had tried to avoid this by pretending they were journalists, real journalists had raised objections. Consequently Thomson suggested that a press agency be paid to provide regular reports of such meetings to the police. This needed the Home Secretary's approval, because it involved money. The latter agreed, as an experiment.[86] This clearly marked a failure on the part of the Special Branch. But it also reveals another new area of activity for it – syndicalism; and suggests that there may have been others, which remained hidden because of the Branch's greater efficiency.

The Special Branch – or some other Metropolitan Police agency – also kept a watch on the Independent Labour Party. Again, evidence of this has survived merely because on one occasion it went wrong. In October 1910 Churchill received a copy of a resolution passed by the Bow and Bromley branch of the ILP, protesting against 'the action of the Police authorities in the Boro of Poplar in sending reporters to the Public meetings of the Labour & Socialist Parties' there. 'In consequence of such reports being fragmentary & distorted,' the resolution went on, 'we believe this system of Police espionage to be dangerous to the best traditions of British freedom.' When he was quizzed about it Henry admitted that the practice of watching socialist gatherings was general, and defended it on the grounds that it was 'the business of the Police to learn what takes place at public meetings, otherwise they would not be in a position to supply information if required by Government, or be in a position to take precautionary measures'. On this occasion – because of the fuss – it was stopped.[87] The question remains: for every case in which police surveillance over socialists was discovered at the time, and was consequently recorded in Home Office files, how many were there in which it all went too smoothly ever to be revealed?

However many there were, it is clear that the scope of the Special Branch's activities widened appreciably in the last few years before the war. Its methods may also have changed. The interception of letters and telegrams, for example, became far more frequent from around 1909. That probably started after Sir Curzon Wyllie's assassination in July that year, when the Post Office was given wide powers to detain and open any telegrams and messages between Britain and India 'which you believe from their terms or otherwise to be likely to be sent by the accomplices or friends of the murderers'.[88] Later Churchill issued a general warrant for opening the mail of suspected spies.[89] Under a similar warrant granted by McKenna, his successor at the Home Office, every single telegram 'emanating from or addressed to the Women's Social and Political Union, or individual members thereof' was intercepted, and 262 sent to the Director of Public Prosecutions for 'examination' by March 1912.[90] Other letters may have been opened *without* warrants, if ex-Inspector Fitch is to be taken at his word.[91] It is likely that Special Branch officers acted illegally in other ways. Walter Thompson (another ex-Inspector) indicated this when he wrote that 'whereas the ordinary detective can always feel that the Law stands firmly behind him, the "Special" more often than not lacks this advantage'.[92] The only way you can lack *that* advantage is to act outside the law.

It is possible to detect – though only very faintly – a change of ethos in the Branch at this time. It comes through in those Special Branch memoirs which were written by men who joined it around 1910, and which are imbued with a sensationalist quality rarely found in earlier examples of the genre. Many are plainly absurd, and most betray prejudices which must have hampered a detached performance of their authors' tasks.[93] Some of those prejudices spread to – or maybe from – Basil Thomson, who took over the Branch (in his capacity as Assistant Commissioner in charge of the CID) in June 1913.

Thomson may have been the first man in that post to regard the role of the Special Branch as a fully counter-subversive one, in addition to preventing political outrages and crimes. One of his earliest memories (he must have been nine or ten at the time) was of pictures on the walls of his schoolroom of scenes from the Paris Commune, which later impressed on him the 'havoc a tiny destructive minority can work in a civilized community that takes no thought for self-protection'.[94] No doubt that lesson was confirmed for him by his experiences as a colonial administrator in the 1890s, in the course of which he found a clever way of banning subversive literature from Tonga;[95] and then as a prison governor at Dartmoor and Wormwood Scrubs. His own memoirs make clear that at the time of writing them, at least, he regarded Britain as being vulnerable to 'subversives', amongst whom he included suffragettes, pacifists, socialists and trade unionists. He described the 'Triple Alliance' of miners, railwaymen and transport workers in the 1910s as holding Britain '*in terrorem*', which suggests that he regarded it as a legitimate target for his Special Branch.[96] When he took up the job he was apparently given an 'entirely free hand' by the Commissioner to do whatever he wished.[97] One of the first things he did, perhaps with Tongan memories in mind, was to 'lean' unofficially on the directors of W. H. Smith to try to stop them selling the *Suffragette*.[98]

Under Thomson the Branch altered radically during the war; but it may have needed the war to alter it as much as he wanted. During the thirteen months that he was Quinn's superior officer in peace-time, there is no firm evidence of any particularly radical development of either its methods or its scope. It kept a watch on socialist meetings; but that kind of thing had been accepted practice in times of unrest for years. The only socialist or suffragist gatherings we know it sent officers to were *public* ones, which anyone was at liberty to attend.[99] It did this, ostensibly and probably genuinely, in order to anticipate events such as demonstrations, or law-breaking, which were likely to involve the police in their public order role. None of the available testimony proves anything beyond this. There is no sign, for example, of the Special Branch trying to infiltrate *private* socialist or feminist conclaves, by having its officers pose as members themselves. There is not even any sure sign of its having employed informers. All these things are possible; but the balance of probability is against it. So far as the Branch's central purpose was concerned it is more plausible, everything considered, that its target in the 1910s remained what it had always been: not political subversion as such (despite Thomson), but politically-motivated *crime*. The distinction between the two is crucial, for it marks the true boundary-line, which the Special Branch may not have crossed yet, between a criminal and a proper political police.

One final factor keeping the Special Branch to this fairly narrow path may have been public opinion; which was probably less ubiquitously hostile to the idea of political policing then than it had been thirty years earlier, but whose residual antipathy was, at the very least, unpredictable. Before, it had been the Liberals who had expressed it most clearly; now it was Labour and the Irish Home Rulers. Ramsay MacDonald, for example, opposed the 1911 Aliens bill on the ground (among others) that it would 'let loose' on the country the police spy and the detective: not 'the faithful public servant who parades our streets in uniform' but 'the other gentleman whom you do not know; you find him in the middle of your political refugees, acting as their friend and their prompter'.[100] It was with this sort of reaction in mind that Henry decided not to put a watch on Emmeline Pankhurst's house when she was released from prison after a hunger-strike in April 1913, in case it was 'said to savour of persecution'.[101] The continued sensitivity of this area, wrote Herbert Gladstone in 1906 or 1907, was one reason why there was a 127-year closure on Home Office records at that time, to avoid revealing the 'not very scrupulous methods for obtaining information' which were used in *Napoleonic* times.[102] In April 1910 there was an almighty row in the House of Commons over Robert Anderson's revelations in *Blackwood's Magazine* of the tricks he had played against the Irish much more recently, which stirred to the surface of the parliamentary pond some very old resentments indeed. 'This is a sordid business,' said the Liberal Edward Pickersgill. 'I suppose Secret Service is necessary. But it is dirty work, and when a man has been at the business for twenty years . . . then the hand of the man who has been engaged in this dirty work is imbued with that dirty work as is the dyer's hand.'[103] There was real feeling there. T. P. O'Connor maintained that 'the people of this country . . . have a racial instinct against the spy and the informer' still;[104] and Winston Churchill, in his reply, had to agree. Anderson's conduct, he said, was 'foreign to the whole spirit of the British Government and Constitution'; and he remarked on the dangers of giving 'Secret Service Agents' too much power, when their opportunities for villainy were so great.[105] That staked out the government's position on these matters, right in the centre of the old liberal territory. After this little episode it would be difficult for a Liberal ministry, at any rate, to seek to return to the bad old Irish ways.

Difficult, that is, in peace-time; for the outbreak of war in August 1914 demolished all the old liberal safeguards, one by one. As in most other areas of British domestic life, in this one the war revolutionised everything: interrupted old continuities, and created an entirely new state of affairs. The military, as was natural, and probably inevitable, came into its own. For years it had been putting a powerful case for subordinating the liberties of the individual to what it saw as the more pressing demands of national security. Now that case could hardly be gainsaid. The military's carefully prepared contingency plans were all wheeled out. Some of them were still resisted. London, for example, was not turned into a thorough military state. That scheme, wrote the Home under-secretary to the War Office in March 1915, seemed to have been 'drafted under a misapprehension as to what was agreed'. He insisted that the capital remained under civilian control, with the authorities empowered to call on military *aid* if necessary.[106] The army had to rest content with that. But in other areas its powers mushroomed. One, of course, was recruitment, where military conscription – surely the most illiberal measure it is possible to contemplate – was introduced, probably unnecessarily, in May 1916.

In the field of counter-subversion the mushroom effect was prodigious. MI5 grew from fourteen officers and staff in July 1914 to 844 at the end of the war. The Special Branch expanded from 114 in November 1914 to 700. Their combined budgets rose from £25,000 a year to more than £200,000. Two new departments were created to censor letters and telegrams; by the end of 1915 one of them (postal censorship) had a staff of 1,453. In 1917 it stopped 356,000 letters from reaching their destinations, in case they contained coded messages for the enemy. The pre-war aliens register was made official on 5 August

1914, and eventually carried details of 53,000 enemy aliens, plus 12,000 women who were married to foreigners, and 34,500 British nationals who were suspected of having enemy 'blood'.[107]

It went further. British dissidents who had no connection at all with the enemy were swept into the net. Often it was because connections with the enemy were suspected. Pacifist organisations, for example, were widely believed to be funded by German gold right through the war. This justified the Special Branch's close interest in them, and also in socialist societies and trade unions which might unwittingly further German ends. Dossiers were kept on thousands of left-wing radicals who were guilty neither of deliberate treachery nor of German blood. Pacifists' houses were raided. Potential strikers were watched. In 1916 a new secret intelligence organisation called 'PMS2' was set up to deal specifically with labour unrest. That body employed at least one under-cover man, William Rickard, who used *agent provocateur* methods to compromise socialists.[108] MI5 and the Special Branch were moving in the same direction, though not so far. In the last year of the war, observes Nicholas Hiley, they 'put more effort into the investigation of Bolshevik influence and the spread of socialism and communism, than they did into counter-espionage and the control of enemy aliens'. By the end of it they had 'established their role as monitors of political opposition in the United Kingdom, whether or not that opposition was controlled from abroad or was breaking the law'.[109]

There, if you like, was a proper political police. It came about at the prompting of the military, under the pressure of war. It puts into the shade everything that is known, or even reasonably suspected, of the Special Branch before 1914. The war marked the beginning of a new era for it, and consequently for what today are called 'civil liberties' in Britain. That is why this book ends then.

CHAPTER 12

Conclusion

The Special Branch today has come a long way since its beginnings. At the last official count it had a strength of 379, with provincial Special Branches (which are a modern development) adding another 870.[1] Some estimates put the number even higher.[2] That compares with twenty-five in 1895, and eighty in 1914. It also appears to have spread its net. Its main targets are Irish and international terrorists, as in the 1880s, but there is widespread suspicion that it does not stop there. Its latest 'guidelines', which were made public for the first time in December 1984, include amongst its duties the gathering of information about threats to public order arising from meetings and demonstrations, and the countering of subversive activities, which are defined as 'those which threaten the safety or well-being of the State, and which are intended to undermine or overthrow Parliamentary democracy by political, industrial or violent means'.[3] Some of the Special Branch's critics are concerned that such a definition is capable of being interpreted very flexibly, by policemen who may be convinced, for example, that the well-being of the state depends on possessing nuclear weapons or breaking strikes. There is some plausible evidence of Special Branch men, or else of MI5 which has taken on a counter-subversive role more recently, keeping records of people whose only claim to their attention is that they hold strong, but legitimate and indeed common, opinions, and interfering in the working of trade unions and organisations like CND.[4] The authorities' response to charges based on such evidence is to ignore them, deny them, or attribute them to excessive individual zeal; but while these agencies are still so secretive and so little accountable to the public, it is natural that doubts should remain.

In the early days of the Metropolitan Police Special Branch there were fewer such doubts, and less occasion for them, for the role of the Branch, as we have seen, was far more limited. The main reason for this was the deep popular feeling that existed at the time against secret political police forces generally, and which had acted as a barrier to the creation of one in Britain until the 1880s. That feeling had a number of roots. One was a common distrust of *all* detective police forces, political or otherwise, because of the deception they involved and the corruption that seemed endemic to them. This distrust went back a very long way, and was the reason for the Metropolitan Police Force's emphasis on the prevention of crime by uniformed officers, rather than its detection by underhand means. Scotland Yard had always had a lot of trouble with its detective branches, culminating in the spectacular scandal of 1877, which justified the Victorians' misgivings to the hilt. Another reason for their dislike of *political* policing was its association with foreign tyrannies, which touched their chauvinistic nerve. But it also went deeper than this. The absence of a political police in Britain before the 1880s was part of a pervasive ideology which was peculiar to that place and time. It had to do with the necessary relationship between government and people within a liberal capitalist economy, which left no room, in the mid-Victorians' eyes, for counter-subversive measures.

The fundamental idea was that this relationship should be as loose as possible, in order to maximise everybody's wealth, opportunity and happiness. That wealth, opportunity and happiness would then in their turn make it possible – or so the theory went – to loosen the relationship still more. This made the whole system a self-generating one, lubricated by what was called 'freedom', which in a nineteenth-century context meant freedom from government, and especially – and very decidedly – from *secret* government agencies like a political police. Hence the extreme sensitivity of this particular issue in Britain from the 1840s through to the 1880s: because it went to the heart of this pervasive middle-class faith in which economic liberalism, political liberalism and social stability were all interlocked. As liberal capitalism burgeoned, as it was bound to do naturally and perpetually, so fewer people would come to have any reason to be discontented, and governments would have less cause to fear the kinds of subversion and rebellion which in less enlightened countries were used to justify *their* political police. This was more than just an abstract notion; Britain's whole national experience in the years following the repeal of the Corn Laws appeared to confirm it, with free economic enterprise bringing in its train increasing prosperity, social and political stability, and a consequent relaxation of the internal vigilance of the state. That was how the system worked. Economic and political liberty were symbiotic. This was the grand theorem of the age; to which one of the many obvious riders was that advanced capitalism did not need, and indeed was a good deal safer without, the protection of a Special Branch.

For these reasons, and because she genuinely was not threatened subversively in the 1860s and 1870s, there was nothing even faintly resembling a Special Branch in mainland Britain before the 1880s. Mid-Victorian Britain really was as liberal in this respect (though not in others) as she claimed. She had no political police force, because she did not need one, and because to allow one would have been an admission of liberal failure, or even – if there was anything in the theory that dangerous dissent was caused by illiberal measures – a cause of it. That negative finding is in its way as remarkable as any of the more positive facts and inferences contained in this book. It may also surprise some people: such as those who cannot credit capitalism with so much restraint, or the *Observer* columnist who in May 1985 wrote, with the modern Special Branch in mind, that 'The trouble about a free market economy is that it requires so many policemen to make it work.'[5] That may be true of today, but it will not do as a historical generalisation. It quite demonstrably does not apply to Britain's free market economy at its apogee, before it started getting into the sorts of difficulties to which it may be that all free market economies eventually become prone.

How the later Victorians were seduced out of this resistance to political policing has been one of the main subjects of this book. In the initial stages very little seduction was involved at all. The Scotland Yard 'Irish Branch', which is generally taken to be the origin of the Special Branch, was very different from it in many essential ways. The motive for it was the Fenian bombing campaign of 1883–5, which was a real, and criminal, threat. The new Branch was a collection of police officers detached from their divisions to concentrate their energies on that threat, in the same way as they would on any other wave of serious crime. No significant departure from traditional Scotland Yard practices was involved: certainly no departure in the direction of making it into a genuinely political branch. It acted on firm suspicion of particular plots, but did not see it as its task to seek them out by watching men whose political opinions or affiliations might incline them to conspire, which is where the difference lay. This was why it so irritated Jenkinson, who was called in from Dublin by a desperately worried Harcourt a year later to complement the Irish Branch's work, and whose own organisation bore far more resemblance to a proper political police.

The contrast was highlighted a few months after Jenkinson's arrival in England, when Harcourt's initial panic subsided and his attitude towards him cooled as a result. The bad feeling that ensued between them was attributed by Jenkinson to Harcourt's disloyalty, and by others to Jenkinson's empire-building proclivities; but beneath it all there lay important and irreconcilable differences between two contrasting police philosophies. One was the traditional view of Scotland Yard, modified a little to suit the circumstances of the time, but still emphasising the prevention of crime over every other consideration, for which it would sacrifice the conviction of known criminals if it was possible to forestall their plans before they reached the criminal stage. The other put far more emphasis on arrest, conviction and imprisonment as a way to cripple conspiratorial movements long-term, even if that meant allowing conspiracies to develop before going in. The difference was reflected in their choice of methods. Scotland Yard used informants, but not agents; took information where it was volunteered, but did not think it right to employ men full-time to infiltrate criminal organisations from the outside. This was partly a precaution against the obvious danger of *agent provocateuring*, though Jenkinson took it as proof that the police were just not interested in obtaining intelligence. The storm broke when Jenkinson accused Scotland Yard of acting precipitously on intelligence provided by his agents, and decided to hold back information to which the head of the CID reckoned he was entitled. Harcourt took Scotland Yard's part; his successors found themselves embarrassed by Jenkinson's whole position in London, which was highly irregular; and so after a period of discomfort on all sides, the latter was forced to go. The remnants of his organisation were grafted on to the Irish Branch, to form what from then onwards came to be known as the 'Special Branch' of the Metropolitan Police CID.

That left the Special Branch back in the hands of old-fashioned policemen with old-fashioned ways, and the newer methods, which Jenkinson had picked up initially in Ireland, firmly repulsed. The 'Jubilee Plot', which was smothered by the head of the CID shortly afterwards, was the latest in what may have been a whole series of Fenian conspiracies in which Jenkinson's agents had taken crucial, if not leading, parts, which came to an end then. But it was only a temporary respite. Between 1888 and 1893 the leading defenders of the old Scotland Yard ethos against the Jenkinson challenge all left the police, by one route or another, and were replaced by less principled – or differently principled – men. During the course of the 1890s the new methods, including some illegal ones, crept into the Special Branch's armoury, for use this time mainly against anarchists, and for the benefit, or reassurance, of foreign governments. Anarchists and Fenians, for example, were systematically recorded, watched, infiltrated, and *possibly* encouraged to commit indictable crimes; foreign secret police agencies were helped directly; and the brief of the Branch was extended to include not only terrorism, but also unconventional views on sex.

This transformation was more crucial than the original creation of the Scotland Yard Irish Branch, because it was the first stage in a development which was to turn that Branch eventually into a full-scale political one. The explanation for it is a little more complicated than it is for the events of 1883. The change in personnel was obviously important. Much has been made in this book of their Irishness: not to denigrate the Irish people in any way, but only to suggest that it distanced men like Melville and Anderson, and those under them, from the dominant political values of the society they had been called in to protect. It may be that no one else in the Special Branch shared those values either, for other reasons than their nationality. With a few exceptions, like Williamson, detectives of all kinds had a poor reputation in late Victorian Britain, even among their uniformed colleagues. The 1877 de Goncourt turf scandal in particular left Vincent's new CID with a stigma, which is likely to have deterred officers who cared for their own reputations from transferring to it. Another thing deterring them may have been the nature of detective work itself, involving as it did practices and techniques which were still widely regarded as underhand. The result of this was that the CID attracted officers who cared little either for its reputation, or for conventional standards of police morality. The same went for the Special Branch, whose particular line of work would not have been to the taste of every bright young police recruit. Not everyone, for example, is attracted by the twilight world of conspiracy, and those who are are often particular sorts of men. (It would be interesting to know how many early Special Branch men were Masons.) All these things made it likely that the Branch collectively had different concerns and priorities from most people, and most policemen; which they were then able to pursue under the cover of secrecy.

Secrecy was an important factor. It meant, in effect, that the Special Branch was never fully under government control. You can only control what you know. A Home Secretary can issue as stringent 'guidelines' as he likes for the conduct of a Special Branch, but they will not give him control of it if he cannot be sure of what is going on. Of course no minister of state is ever in a position to know at first hand everything that is going on under him; but usually he at least has the means of finding out when his instructions are being contravened. Those means are, firstly, the chain of responsibility emanating from him, and secondly, publicity. Individual officers are stopped or deterred from straying either by their immediate superiors, or by the threat of public exposure in some form. These constraints, however, will not apply in circumstances where superior officers feel a greater responsibility and loyalty to their own departments than to official policy, and are protected from a more general accountability by the confidentiality which surrounds their work.[6] This may have applied to the officers of the early Special Branch. They had their own notions, derived from their backgrounds and experience, about how the Fenian and anarchist menaces should be met. They also had the opportunity to indulge those notions, in the pretty certain knowledge that no one need ever (even today) find out.

That, then, is a possibility: that the Special Branch grew by a sort of internal dynamic of its own, protected by the secrecy which was supposed to be vital for its task. Governments were not responsible for it, except in a negative way: by not doing more to make the Branch more accountable than it was. That of course does not absolve governments entirely, especially if they were vaguely aware of what was going on. It is likely that most were, and were happy not to delve too deep. They delved very shallowly, for example, into the Daly and Walsall cases, where particular malpractices were alleged and the Home Office went no further than to question the men they were alleged against. In these instances the details of those 'enquiries' were kept from Parliament, which was merely told that they had been rigorous and exonerating. Secrecy was as convenient a protection for ministers as for policemen, if they too had ideas of their own about counter-terrorist work. Some of them did, by virtue of their positions. Ordinary people could afford to be blasé about terrorism; government ministers could not. In the first place they were responsible for public safety; in the second place they bore the brunt of foreign complaints. If a public figure were killed in England by Fenians, or abroad by anarchists who had lived in England, then it was the Home and Foreign Secretaries who would be answerable. In these circumstances it required a great deal of liberal courage to rely on the 'grand theorem' to see them through. Harcourt, as we have seen, did not have this sort of liberal courage, or – by another and probably better way of looking at it – naïveté. This is illustrated strikingly by his quarrel with Gladstone over the control of the Metropolitan Police, which all turned on the fact that he no longer trusted either the people (of London) or the future (of Ireland) as Gladstone still clearly did. That was why he gave Jenkinson his head, at least at the beginning, while at the same time keeping his activities out of the public eye.

That was done partly to disguise his hand from the Fenians, and partly because he feared that public knowledge of it would cause a rumpus. That fear may have been exaggerated, or have become less justified as time went by. The philosopher Sissela Bok has said that political policing can never be knowingly accepted by a democratic society, and consequently that when it arises in one it is always through 'duplicity'; but that may be giving a little too much credit to the electorate.[7] Of course Britain in the 1880s and 1890s was not yet a fully democratic society, and some of the means by which the Special Branch's role was extended were undoubtedly duplicitous. It may also be that, with all its extensions, it had still not yet become a political branch in Bok's sense. Nevertheless there is little evidence from Britain's more recent history that public opinion is a notably steadfast barrier against political policing even when it is known about, so long as that policing is directed against what are seen as dangers from outside. 'If MI5 is trying to prevent *anti-British* infiltration into the BBC,' wrote the Conservative MP Sir Anthony Grant to a newspaper at the height of the row over 'political vetting' in August 1985, 'I can only comment that MI5 is making a remarkably poor job of it.'[8] That was how the early Special Branch's targets were also presented, with rather more obvious rationality. It was an internal security organisation, but concerned primarily with an essentially *ex*ternal threat.

That was, broadly speaking, fair. Until 1909, at the earliest, the role of the Special Branch was limited to very tiny, very 'extreme', and in most cases very foreign groups of people, who stood outside nearly every contemporary's liberal pale. It started off with Irish-American Fenians. It then went on to embrace the anarchist community in Britain, whom the police themselves were at pains to emphasise 'consists almost entirely of foreigners'.[9] Later it took on board Russian nihilists, German spies, and Indian and Egyptian nationalists living in London. All of these groups were alien, which meant that they had little bearing on the grand liberal theorem which denied the need for a political police arm in a free society. Dangerous anarchists were the fruits of other national and ideological trees, of a kind it was impossible to conceive ever taking root in Britain's soil. They were not, therefore, Britain's responsibility. They had that in common with most of the fieriest revolutionaries who had lived in Britain since 1848; with this important difference, that the extremes to which their dissent had been pushed now directly threatened every society, be it never so liberal, in a way that Mazzini's and even Marx's never had. This, and their recourse to dynamite, were widely felt to justify measures against them which could never, initially, be contemplated against any native-grown political movement, but without compromising Britain's deepest liberal beliefs. Anarchism stood outside the grand theorem, and so was not bound by its postulates.

That was all very well in respect of anarchists, nihilists and spies, but was maybe not quite so convincing when it came to Irish and colonial nationalists. They, after all, *had* grown on British trees, and were consequently Britain's responsibility. This might be seen to indicate something of a weakness in the grand liberal theorem, though it was one to which Victorian liberals were accustomed to turning a blind eye. The fact was that it did not seem to work abroad. In most of the countries of the world ruled from Britain, which were many, the expansion of her free enterprise system had not – yet – had the same politically liberating effect it had had back home. This dichotomy between their own domestic liberalism and the paternalistic authoritarianism by which they governed most of their colonial subjects was something that troubled fewer Victorians than in strict logic it probably should have done; but they did have an explanation for it, which was that their colonial subjects were not yet mature enough for political liberty. It helped if they were black, which was an immature sort of colour; if not, then Roman Catholicism was an acceptable substitute. This went some way to account for the temporary resistance of certain minorities of Indians and Irish to the benefits of British economic culture, which in its turn provoked into existence Britain's earliest political police agencies, firstly in Ireland and India, and then (on the tail of the Irish) in England itself.

That excuse was valid so long as Ireland and India were considered in a separate category from Britain, which they generally – and conveniently – were. It will not do, of course, if the British state is conceived more inclusively, with Ireland and the colonies (and Britain's commercial empire beyond them) being taken as part and parcel of it; in which case the Special Branch was as much an intrinsic function of that state as France's Third Section was of hers. That, of course, would undermine the grand theorem radically; but it is possible that it was flawed in any case. The idea that free enterprise capitalism was naturally co-extensive with perfect political liberty may always have been an illusion: a dream fostered by extraordinarily fortunate circumstances, and which left out of account the contribution made to Britain's mid-Victorian stability by all kinds of hidden methods of repression and control. It may be that mid-Victorian liberal capitalism was merely *lucky* not to need a political police; but it would have greatly upset a mid-Victorian liberal capitalist to think so. This was why late-Victorian liberal capitalists, too, were anxious that their new political police should as far as possible avoid native British politics; and why the Special Branch, despite its lack of accountability, by and large complied.

For this reason the early Special Branch was far more a creature of the Victorian age, and of its values, than it was a precursor of the present day. The available evidence does not support the notion that it was in any way an intrusive political police agency, except on the foreign fringes of British politics, or that its existence at this time was a serious threat to civil liberties. It was more restrained, more restricted in its field of activity, and far more marginal to the state's concern for security, than are today's Special Branches (and MI5). It may also have been less effective, if Leon Brittan's claim that today's Special Branches have saved 'hundreds of innocent people' is anywhere near the truth;[10] but that is very difficult to say.

At first glance it may look easy. The Special Branch's main function in our period was to prevent political crimes. Between 1883 and 1914 Britain had fewer political crimes than most other European countries: but of course that can be taken to indicate the Branch's redundancy, as well as its success. Crimes that are prevented or deterred are, by their nature, difficult to prove. If there is no tangible evidence of them, then we are thrown back on other resources. Broadly speaking, our view of the Special Branch's effectiveness will depend on our views of four other things. They are: Britain's intrinsic stability at this time; the potency of the threats to it; the general mechanics of subversion; and the trustworthiness of the men charged with countering it.

Some of those men made very large claims for the Special Branch. One was ex-Detective Inspector Herbert T. Fitch, who gave it most of the credit for Britain's pre-war security in the face of the international anarchist and communist menaces. He admitted that there might be other contributory factors, including 'The sound sense of the British working man'; but they, he said, were an insufficient guarantee on their own. In 1917 the Russian working man had probably been no less sensible, but to no avail; for *his* opinions 'were not taken into consideration when the standard of revolt was raised by self-seeking agitators'. In Fitch's eyes that made every society vulnerable.

189

So, in pre-War England, it might have been that solitary outbreaks might have occurred time after time, sponsored but not attended by cowardly anarchists from other lands, and the lives wasted in them would have been those of British workmen, misled by communist tommy-rot . . .

– if it had not been for the strong, silent endeavours of the Branch.[11] That was its achievement. If British society was relatively untroubled before 1914, then it had the Special Branch largely to thank.

That was one version of events. But it rested, as Fitch himself tacitly acknowledged (with all his 'might have beens'), on certain suppositions. No one could be certain that the threat he described was real. Fitch furnished no proof for it; though he insisted that the evidence was there, in the Branch's secret files. That is no longer verifiable, but in any case is unlikely. Perceptions of threats are usually based not on evidence, but on a general cast of mind. Fitch's cast of mind, and perhaps his experience, inclined him towards a view of politics in which conspiracies loomed larger in any situation than they probably did for most of his contemporaries. We have seen how the more liberal-minded among those contemporaries preferred to attribute Britain's stability to her liberal enlightenment. She was safer than other polities from threats of revolution because she provoked them less. That is not something that can be tested empirically. Consequently the value of the early Special Branch in pre-empting revolution in Britain (or anywhere else) must remain in doubt.

We may be on firmer ground with the Branch's more modest claims. One of those was that it stopped bomb plots which never had any hope of subverting society, but were an obvious danger to life and limb. In support of this it could point to the Fenian dynamite campaign, which of course marked a qualified failure for the Irish Branch but was at least evidence of a real threat; and to a number of incidents where Fenians and anarchists were caught red-handed – with dynamite hidden under their coats or buried in their gardens, for example – which were surely conclusive proof of the value and effectiveness of Britain's various counter-terrorist arms. That was indeed how they were presented at the time. The problem with this evidence, however, is the twist that is given to it by suspicions of *agents provocateurs*.

This matter of *agents provocateurs* is tricky, but important, because it cuts right to the heart of the question of the Branch's contribution to late Victorian stability. If the plots it 'foiled' were provoked, then it clearly puts that contribution in doubt. There is no conclusive proof of the participation of *agents provocateurs* in any Fenian or anarchist incident of the 1880s and 1890s, but there is a great deal of circumstantial evidence which seems to point that way. It is strongest in three particular cases: two of them (Daly and the Jubilee Plot) involving Jenkinson and the RIC, and the other (Walsall) the Special Branch. Those three cases have been discussed at length already, together with the clear temptations and opportunities which existed, and were acknowledged by senior police officers, for plain-clothes policemen and agents to turn into *provocateurs*. The cumulative weight of all this evidence is, at the very least, difficult to discount. On balance it seems more likely that *provocateurs* were implicated in some of the dynamite plots of the 1880s and 1890s than that they were not. They may not always have initiated those plots, and where they encouraged them it may not always have been on the specific instructions of the police: but that is beside the point. If they were employed by policemen, if their actions were taken with a view to profiting from that employment, and if those actions were key factors in the initiation or perpetuation of conspiracies, then the existence of those conspiracies was, in effect, the result of the activity of the police. That means they would not have happened without the police; which in turn means that the police cannot be credited in these cases, though it may in others, with protecting London from dynamite plots.

At bottom it comes down to a question of trust, as it always does with agencies which are to some degree unaccountable. The early Special Branch was unaccountable in a double sense: firstly to its con-temporary masters, and secondly (because of the destruction of its records) to posterity. The conditions in which it worked made it easy for it to conceal things from its masters, if it wanted to, and also to conceal things from us. This is where the trust comes in. If you cannot check properly on the activities of a person or a group of people, then you need to know whether they can be relied upon. Are they the sort of people who are likely to keep within the rules of the game without being checked on? On the whole it must be said of the men who made up Britain's early counter-subversive agencies, at all levels, that they probably were not.

We have already seen why. Those agencies were staffed and led by special sorts of men. By and large they were not representative of the bulk of any contemporary British social class. They were notorious amongst the uniformed branches of both the Metropolitan and provincial police forces – though a dash of jealousy may have come in to it here – for lack of probity. Their backgrounds had something to do with it; together with the very nature of the work they were called upon to do. Much of it was difficult to reconcile with any of the dominant values of the society they lived in, except by stretching them. No one, for example, could be both a gentleman, and a *spy*. For all these reasons men like Anderson, despite his sanctimoniousness, and Jenkinson, despite his liberal view of the Irish question, were never fully trusted by their political superiors, for good prima facie reasons, which should warn us, too, against accepting uncritically what they or anyone else working in this area had to say. This might seem harsh, and to detract unfairly from what may possibly have been their considerable services to the safety both of the realm and of innocent individuals within it before the Great War; but it is only realistic, surely, not to give professional dissemblers the benefit of the doubt.

So we cannot say for certain, even after this length of time, how effective Britain's early political police branches were. They may have been unnecessary, incompetent, corrupt and counter-productive, or they may on the other hand have been an essential complement to freedom as a means of ensuring Britain's stability: the concrete surrounding the liberal steel. Probably the truth lies, as they say, somewhere in between. It is a pity that we cannot make a final judgement on this, but it would be wrong to pretend we can. Fortunately it is not essential to an assessment of the Special Branch's broader significance, which can be made on other grounds.

The main significance of the early Special Branch lay in the simple fact that it existed: a highly secretive 'political' police arm in a society which still took great pride in its liberal openness, and until recently had liked to think that it was above such things. We have seen how it came about, with the transformation, under the cloak of secrecy, of an agency formed for one purpose into something a little different; which might be thought to furnish a historical 'lesson' about the tendency of secret and imperfectly accountable bodies to extend their powers, were it not for the fact that in this case those powers do not seem to have been extended as far as they might have been. The early Special Branch probably abused the privilege of its confidentiality by employing improper and illegal methods; but it was nearly always (at least until the 1910s) against targets which would have been widely accepted as legitimate anyway. This suggests that there were still powerful external restraints on its development, which should consequently be regarded more as a reflection of contemporary society, than as a conspiracy against it.

One thing it undoubtedly reflected was the beginning of the end of an age of liberal innocence, of which there is scarcely any trace left today. The idea that liberal capitalism does not need policing politically is not one which is readily associated with modern free marketism, whose aficionados, despite all their talk of Victorian values, show a less than Victorian respect for some of the political freedoms which were once thought to be capitalism's necessary concomitants. They are probably right, from their point of view, to dissociate the two; but it marks a sad fall from the prevalent optimism of liberalism's heyday. That fall started in the 1880s, with widespread social unrest, a menacing international situation, and crisis in Ireland, to all of which – but especially the last two – the emergence of the Special Branch was a partial response. In itself it was not a particularly important response: the Special Branch was never any government's leading weapon against the problems which confronted it. Nevertheless it is significant that no government any longer felt, as all governments had before 1880, that it could do without it; could run the risk of *not* having an agency on hand to deal with political outrages that might be brewing, or – more crucially – with foreign governments' complaints about the outrages that their dissidents in Britain were brewing for them.

This latter function was always its most valuable one from the British government's point of view, and marked another trend, which was Britain's gradual re-entry into the European concert of nations after years of isolationism. This happened because Britain was far more vulnerable diplomatically than she had been in mid-Victorian times, and so could no longer afford the luxury of the superior liberal tone she had used to adopt (at least in public) with foreign governments which chided her for her toleration of political refugees. Anglo-continental co-operation over anarchism, though it was never as formally close as the Continent would have liked, was a sign that Britain's ideological drift away from Europe during the third quarter of the nineteenth century had finally been reversed; to culminate many years later in their complete assimilation under the impact of another international terrorist crisis. Again, these beginnings in the 1890s and 1900s were only very small ones, and the situation then more different from today's than it is like it; but compared with the situation in the previous few decades it marked the start of a revolution, or more strictly a counter-revolution, against the distinctive and anti-European liberalism of Britain's mid-Victorian past.

To effect this counter-revolution Britain called on men from Ireland and India, which was apt, and probably necessary. Things had always been different there. The grand liberal theorem had never seemed to fit Britain's satellite economies very comfortably, though at one time Britons had hoped it might do eventually; with the result that fewer of their governors laboured under the same illusions that had hindered the development of political policing in Britain for so long. When the need for such policing at last came home to her in the 1880s it was found that the human resources the government had to hand in London – solid Englishmen and Scotsmen like Williamson and Littlechild – could not cope with the new ideas and values it involved, which were wholly foreign to the ethos they had been nurtured in. This was why Jenkinson was called in, and then Anderson, Melville, Monro, MacNaghten, Quinn, Thomson and the lesser fry under them; men whose Irish and colonial backgrounds liberated them from that ethos, and allowed them (after Jenkinson's brief Pyrrhic set-back) to nudge the Special Branch into different paths. J. A. Hobson, the anti-imperialist writer, once warned that this sort of thing was likely to be the effect of the liberal/imperialist dichotomy which he discerned more clearly than most of his contemporaries.[12] The empire was striking back. The contradictions always implicit in Britain's situation in the world were coming home to roost. The Special Branch of the Metropolitan Police CID was one of their perches; though they kept very unobtrusive there, and careful not to make it easy for future historians to trace the marks left by their claws.

APPENDIX 1

Leading Personnel

A. Home Secretaries

1880 April	William Vernon Harcourt
1885 June	Richard Assheton Cross
1886 February	Hugh Childers
1886 August	Henry Mathews
1892 August	Herbert Asquith
1895 June	Matthew White Ridley
1900 November	Charles Ritchie
1902 July	Aretas Akers-Douglas
1905 December	Herbert Gladstone
1910 February	Winston Churchill
1911 October	Reginald McKenna (to 1915)

B. Chief Commissioners, Metropolitan Police

1869 January	Edmund Henderson
1886 March	Charles Warren
1888 November	James Monro
1890 June	Edward Bradford
1903 March	Edward Henry (to 1918)

C. Assistant Commissioners i/c cid

1878 April	Howard Vincent
1884 June	James Monro
1888 August	Robert Anderson
1901 May	Edward Henry
1903 March	Melville MacNaghten
1913 June	Basil Thomson (to 1919)

C. Heads of the Special Branch

1883 March	Adolphus Williamson (Special Irish Branch)
1887 January	John Littlechild
1893 April	William Melville
1903 December	Patrick Quinn (to 1918)

D. Assistant Under-Secretaries for Police and Crime

1882 May	Henry Brackenbury
1882 July	Edward Jenkinson (resigned January 1887)

APPENDIX 2

Chronology of Events

1878 April 8: Metropolitan CID founded.

1881 January 14: Salford Barracks bomb.
January 23: 'Fenian Office' set up in Scotland Yard.
March 13: Assassination of Tsar Alexander II.
March 19: Mansion House bomb discovered.
March 26: Metropolitan Police instructed to watch foreign socialists.
March 30: Arrest of Johann Most; trial June 18.
May 16, June 10: Liverpool bombs.
July 2: Assassination of President Garfield.

1882 May 6: Phoenix Park murders in Dublin.
May 25: Brackenbury made Assistant Under-Secretary, Police and
Crime (Dublin).
July: Brackenbury resigns, Jenkinson takes over.

1883 January 20: Fenian bombs in Glasgow.
March 15: Fenian London bombing campaign begins, with
explosions at the Local Government Board and *Times* office.
March 16: Scotland Yard Special Irish Branch set up; Jenkinson
summoned to London.
April 5: Arrest of Gallagher and Whitehead; trial ends June 14.
April 9: Explosive Substances Act passed.
May 12: Gosselin appointed counter-Fenian secret agent in
provinces.
October 30: London Underground Railway bombs.

1884 February 26–7: Fenian bombs in London railway termini.
March 7: Jenkinson arrives in London at Harcourt's request, to co-
ordinate counter-Fenian effort.
April 11: Arrests of Daly and Egan.
May 30: Fenian explosions at Scotland Yard and St James's Square.
December 13: Attempt to blow up London Bridge.

1885 January 2: Gower Street station bomb.
January 24: Bomb explosions at Palace of Westminster, Tower of
London.

1886   February 8: Trafalgar Square riots ('Black Monday').
May 4: Haymarket affray, Chicago.

1887   Mid-January: Jenkinson resigns; 'Special Branch' formed.
June: 'Jubilee Plot' foiled.
November 13: Trafalgar Square riots ('Bloody Sunday').

1889   February 5: 'Le Caron' testifies to Parnell Commission.
August 19: London Dock strike begins.
December 9: Death of Adolphus Williamson.

1892   January 7: Arrest of Walsall anarchists; trial March 30–April 4.
January 13: Police raid on 'Autonomie' Club, London.
March: Ravachol-inspired bomb explosions in Paris.
March 30: Ravachol arrested at Café Véry, Paris.
April 19: Police raid on *Commonweal* offices; arrest of Nicoll and
    Mowbray; trial May 6.
April 25: Café Véry bomb, Paris.
November 16: François hearing, for extradition.

1893   April: William Melville becomes Head of Special Branch.
Sept 5–9: Strike riots in Featherstone and elsewhere.
Nov 27: Liceo Theatre bomb outrage, Barcelona.
December 9: Bomb thrown into French Chamber by Vaillant.

1894   February 12: Café Terminus bomb, Paris.
February 15: Greenwich Park explosion.
February 16: Police raid on 'Autonomie' Club, London.
April 4: Arrest of Meunier in London, later extradited.
April 14 and 22: Polti and Farnara arrested; trial May 4.
June 24: French president Carnot assassinated in Lyons.
June 29: Police raid on *Commonweal* offices; arrest of Cantwell and
    Quinn; trial July 30.
July 6 and 17: Salisbury presents bill to expel aliens for political
    offences.

1895   February 3 to May 26: McIntyre's 'Revelations' in *Reynolds's
    Newspaper*.
April 5: Arrest of Oscar Wilde; trial May.

1896   June 7: Corpus Christi day bomb outrage, Barcelona.
September 12: Arrests of Tynan and Bell; trial of Bell January 20,
    1897.

1897   August 8: Assassination of Spanish Prime Minister, Cañovas del
    Castillo, at Santa Agueda.
December 16: Arrest of Burtsev; trial February 11, 1898.

1898   May: Arrest of Bedborough; trial October 31.
September 10: Assassination of Empress Elizabeth of Austria in
    Geneva.
November 24 to December 21: Rome Anti-Anarchist Conference.

1900   April 4: Prince of Wales shot at in Brussels by Sipido.
July 29: Assassination of King Humbert of Italy in Monza.

1901   September 6: Assassination of President McKinley in Buffalo.

1903   December 1: Patrick Quinn succeeds Melville as Head of Special
    Branch.

1905   January 22: 'Bloody Sunday' in St Petersburg.
August 5: Aliens Act passed; comes into effect January 1, 1906.
September 15: Antonelli trial.

1907   February 13: Suffragists clash with police at House of Commons.
April 25: Start of spy scare in the *Globe*.
December: Edmonds becomes Head of MO5.

1908   October: Unemployed and suffragist demonstrations in London.

1909   January 23: 'Tottenham Outrages': PC Tyler shot by Hefeld and
    Jacob.
March 29: Foreign Espionage sub-committee of Committee of
    Imperial Defence set up.
July 1: Assassination of Sir Curzon Wyllie at Imperial Institute,
    London.
August 23: New 'Secret Service Bureau' (forerunner of MI5 and MI6)
    set up.
September 11: Suffragette section of Special Branch set up.

1910   July 7: Register of Aliens set up.
September 5: Arrest of Siegfried Helm as a spy.
December 16: Houndsditch affair.

1911   January 1: Body of Leon Beron found on Clapham Common.
January 3: Seige of Sidney Street.
August 1: London Dock Strike begins.
August 17: Arrest of Max Schultz as a German spy.
August 18: Official Secrets Act passed.
August 19: Llanelly strike riots.
September 14: Assassination of Russian Prime Minister Stolypin in
    Kiev.

1912   February 26: Miners' Strike begins.
May 20: Arrest of Malatesta; sentenced to deportation, but
    deportation order lifted June 20.
July 23: Graves convicted as a German spy in Edinburgh.
November 12: Assassination of Spanish Prime Minister Canelejas y
    Mendez in Madrid.

1913   January 16: Parrott convicted of spying for Germany.

1914   June 28: Assassination of Archduke Franz Ferdinand of Austria at Sarajevo.
August 5: Aliens Restriction Act passed.

Notes

Books are published in London unless otherwise stated. Official papers: Home Office (HO), Foreign Office (FO), Metropolitan Police (MEPO), War Office (WO), Admiralty (ADM), Treasury (T), Cabinet (CAB), are at the Public Record Office at Kew (PRO). The locations of private collections are given in the Bibliography. The following abbreviations are used for those most commonly cited:

HHCP   Henry Herbert, 4th Earl of *Carnarvon*
RACP   Richard Assheton *Cross*
CWDP   Sir Charles Wentworth *Dilke*
HJGP   Herbert John *Gladstone*
WEGP   William Ewart *Gladstone*
GLGP   Granville Leveson-Gower, 2nd Earl *Granville*
WVHP   Sir William Vernon *Harcourt*
JPSP   John Poyntz, 5th Earl *Spencer*

Preface

1. R. W. Allason, *The Branch. A History of the Metropolitan Police Special Branch 1883–1983* (1983); Bernard Porter, 'The Historiography of the early Special Branch', in *Intelligence and National Security*, vol. I, no. 3. (1986), pp. 389–90.
2. Harold Brust, '*I Guarded Kings*' (n.d.), p. 44.

Chapter 1

1. [Dinah Craik], *Fair France: impressions of a traveller* (1871), p. 193.
2. G. J. Whyte-Melville, *The Interpreter* (1858; new edn., 1870), p. 269.
3. [Henry Wreford], 'Spy Police', *Household Words*, vol. I, no. 26 (21 Sept. 1850), pp. 611–14.
4. Bloomfield to Palmerston, 14 August 1851: FO 64/332.
5. Palmerston to Seymour, 28 October 1851: FO 65/390.
6. Josephine E. Butler, *Government by Police* (1879), pp. 8, 63. On 'functionarism', see Bernard Porter, ' "Bureau and Barrack": Early Victorian Attitudes towards the Cont'nent', *Victorian Studies*, vol. 27, no. 4 (1984), p. 424.
7. *Daily News*, 3 February 1858, p. 4.
8. Ibid., 25 April 1853, p. 5.

9. Quoted in Leon Radzinowicz, *A History of English Criminal Law and its Administration from 1750*, vol. 3, *Cross-currents in the Movement for the Reform of the Police* (1956), p. 347.

10. Quoted in ibid. p. 359.

11. *Report of Home Office Departmental Committee into Metropolitan Police*, 6 May 1868, pp. 14–15; in HO45/10002/A49463, sub. 2.

12. *Report of the Departmental Commission . . . into the State, Discipline, and Organisation of the Detective Force of the Metropolitan Police*, 25 January 1878, pp. 33–4, in HO45/10002/A49463, sub. 2; and Metropolitan Police Orders for 6 July 1878, in MEPO2/136.

13. See Anthea Trodd, 'The Policeman and the Lady: Significant Encounters in mid-Victorian Fiction', *Victorian Studies*, vol. 27, no. 4 (1984), p. 439.

14. Memo by Sir George Grey, December 1845, in HO45/O.S. 1107.

15. Metropolitan Police Orders for 27 November 1851, p. 116, in MEPO7/15.

16. See Bernard Porter, *The Refugee Question in mid-Victorian Politics* (Cambridge, 1979), pp. 153, 189.

17. Wilkie Collins, *The Woman in White* (1860; new edn., 1975), p. 445.

18. See Christopher Andrew, *Secret Service* (1985), ch. 1.

19. Butler, op. cit., p. 16.

20. Anthony Trollope, *He Knew He Was Right* (1869), quoted in Trodd, op. cit., p. 452.

21. Henry A. Blake, 'The Irish Police', in *Nineteenth Century*, vol. 9 (February 1881), p. 391.

22. See George Dilnot, *The Trial of the Detectives* (1928).

23. *Report of the Departmental Commission . . . into . . . the Detective Force*, 1878, pp. 38–54 *passim*, in HO45/10002/A49463, sub. 2.

24. Undated memo, attached to Henderson memorandum of 25 March 1878, in MEPO 2/134.

25. See Police Orders for 6 July 1878, in MEPO 2/136. Seventeen detective sergeants were promoted to inspector, ninety-five constables to sergeant, and others were moved up a class. The 'Central Office' section was reduced from twenty-seven men (one superintendent, six inspectors and twenty sergeants) to twenty-four (one superintendent, twenty-two inspectors and one sergeant).

26. Memorandum by A. F. Williamson, 22 October 1880, in MEPO 2/134.

27. Memorandum by Howard Vincent, October 1880, in ibid.

28. Memorandum by Henderson, 25 March 1878, in ibid.

29. Porter, *Refugee Question*, pp. 151–2.

30. Philip Thurmond Smith, *Policing Victorian London. Political Policing, Public Order, and the London Metropolitan Police* (Westport, Connecticut, 1985), p. 192.

31. Ibid., p. 188.

32. Ibid., p. 193.

33. Felice Orsini tried to assassinate the French emperor with English-made bombs in the Place de l'Opéra on 14 January 1858. Under pressure from the French government one of his accomplices, Simon Bernard, was arrested and tried for conspiracy, but acquitted by a jury which resented French interference. The full story is told in Porter, *Refugee Question*, pp. 152–60, 170–99, 209–10.

34. Señor de Blas to Señor Rances y Villanueva, 9 February 1872, enclosed in Rances to Granville, 24 February; translation printed in *Parliamentary Papers* (PP) (1872) LXX, pp. 718–20.

35. *Hansard*, 3rd series, vol. 210, col. 1184 (12 April 1872).
36. Ibid., vol. 206, col. 1327 (26 May 1871).
37. On British police surveillance of the communards, see P. K. Martinez, 'Paris Communard Refugees in Britain, 1871–1880' (Ph.D. thesis, Sussex University, 1981), pp. 421–8.
38. Police reports of 24 May and 15 June 1872, in HO45/9303/11335.
39. Robert Payne, *Marx* (1968), pp. 426–8.
40. Liddell (Home Office) to Foreign under-secretary, 12 July 1871, in FO64/735.
41. *The Times*, 15 April 1872, p. 11.
42. Martinez, op. cit., p. 427.
43. Henderson memorandum, 15 October 1878; Lushington memo, 15 October 1878; in HO45/9473/A60556.
44. See Gareth Stedman Jones, 'Some Notes on Karl Marx and the English Labour Movement', *History Workshop*, no. 18, Autumn 1984, pp. 124–37.
45. See John Stevenson, *Popular Disturbances in England 1700–1870* (1979), ch. 13; and Donald C. Richter, *Riotous Victorians* (1981), *passim*.
46. *Annual Register*, 1855, 'Chronicle', p. 107.
47. B. R. Mitchell and P. Deane, *Abstract of British Historical Statistics* (Cambridge, 1962), pp. 366, 343.
48. F. C. Mather, *Public Order in the Age of the Chartists* (Manchester, 1959), p. 98.
49. Ibid., p. 100; and see R. D. Storch, 'The Plague of the Blue Locusts. Police Reform and Popular Resistance in Northern England, 1840–57', *International Review of Social History*, vol. 20 (1975); and Victor Bailey (ed.), *Policing and Punishment in Nineteenth Century Britain* (1981).
50. See Richard Johnson, 'Educational Policy and Social Control in Early Victorian England', *Past and Present*, no. 49 (1970).
51. See Edward C. Mack, *Public Schools and British Opinion since 1860* (New York, 1941).
52. See J. R. Stephens, *The Censorship of English Drama 1824–1901* (Cambridge, 1980), chs 3 and 7; and Frank Fowell and Frank Palmer, *Censorship in England* (1913), ch. 8.
53. See Sir Herbert Maxwell, *Life and Times of the Right Honourable William Henry Smith, M.P.* (Edinburgh, 1893), vol. 1, pp. 48–58; E. A. Akers-Douglas, 3rd Viscount Chilston, *W. H. Smith* (1965), ch. 2; and B. Powell, 'Smith the Censor', *Free Review*, vol. 4 no. 5 (January 1896), pp. 337–51.
54. See Harold Perkin, *The Origins of Modern English Society 1780–1880* (1969), esp. ch. 8; Trygve R. Tholfsen, 'The Transition to Democracy in Victorian England', *International Review of Social History*, vol. 6, no. 2 (1961), and *Working-Class Radicalism in Mid-Victorian England* (1976), esp. ch. 7.
55. See Bernard Semmel, *The Governor Eyre Controversy* (1962).
56. See Gladstone in 1871, quoted in Charles Townshend, *Political Violence in Ireland. Government and Resistance since 1848* (Oxford, 1983), p. 63.
57. Ibid., ch. 2; and Blake, op. cit., pp. 385–96.
58. Blake, op. cit., p. 392.
59. Like Head Constable Shea, who was stationed in London, and in touch with Anderson, in 1880: CSO RP 1880/7312 (State Paper Office, Dublin Castle).
60. See 'Henri Le Caron', *Twenty-five Years in the Secret Service. The Recollections of a Spy* (1892; 18th edn., 1895); and J. A. Cole, *Prince of Spies. Henri Le Caron* (1984).

61. Anandswarup Gupta, *The Police in British India 1861–1947* (New Delhi, 1979), pp. 9, 79–80, 201; and see Sir Percival Griffiths, *To Guard My People. The History of the Indian Police* (1971), chs 10 and 25.
62. Notes on 'Secret Service' (1914?), in T1/11689/25138.
63. Butler, op. cit., pp. 23, 36–7.

Chapter 2

1. J. S. Mill, *Principles of Political Economy*, 3rd edn. (1852), Book II, ch. 1, section 3: p. 208 of 1923 edn, ed. W. J. Ashley.
2. See Peter Keating (ed.), *Into Unknown England 1866–1913. Selections from the Social Explorers* (1976).
3. W. Bagehot, *The English Constitution*, 2nd. edn. (1872), p. xvi.
4. See Bernard Porter, *Britain, Europe and the World 1850–1982* (1983), chs 1–2.
5. Ibid., pp. 41–2.
6. *Annual Register*, 1878, 'Chronicle', p. 112.
7. Robert Louis and Fanny van de Grift Stevenson, *The Dynamiter* (1885; Lothian edition, n.d.), p. 172.
8. Donald Mackay, *The Dynamite Ship* (New York, 1888), p. 94.
9. Stevenson, op. cit., p. 173.
10. Harcourt to the Queen, 25 March 1882; copy in Harcourt Papers (WVHP), box 691, f. 35. The Queen for her part greatly objected to the 'insane' verdict on her attacker, on the grounds that 'it will leave her no security for the future if any man who chooses to shoot at her, is thereby proclaimed to be mad'. Ponsonby to Harcourt, 19 April 1882, in ibid., box 2, f. 58.
11. See *Daily Chronicle*, 1 April 1881, p. 4. That this had become the general practice by 1883 is confirmed in a letter from Harcourt to Ponsonby, 21 November 1883: copy in WVHP, box 691, f. 267.
12. See L. P. Curtis, *Anglo-Saxons and Celts* (Bridgeport, Connecticut, 1968); and, on the whole question of Irish terrorism, Charles Townshend, *Political Violence in Ireland* (Oxford, 1983).
13. Harcourt to Gladstone, 28 December 1883; copy in WVHP, box 696, ff. 181–2.
14. See K. R. M. Short, *The Dynamite War* (Dublin, 1979), ch. 2 *et passim*.
15. See ibid., pp. 2–4.
16. Harcourt to Ponsonby, 17 June 1881; copy in WVHP, box 690, f. 214.
17. Short, op. cit., pp. 104–5. There is a full set of papers on these explosions in the Scottish Record Office: AD14/83/26. The same files contain more information on the London bombs than survives at the Public Record Office at Kew.
18. Short, op. cit., pp. 105–6.
19. Harcourt to Gladstone, 4 April 1883: copy in WVHP, box 696, f. 32.
20. Cabinet memoranda by Harcourt, 3 March(?) and 24 April 1883: WVHP, box 97, ff. 22–3 and 83–4.
21. Short, op. cit., pp. 160–2; and HO45/9638/A32915.
22. Queen to Harcourt, 28 November 1883: in WVHP, box 2, f. 228.
23. Short, op. cit., pp. 176–7.
24. Lewis Harcourt's diary, 27 April 1884: WVHP, box 735, f. 45.
25. Short, op. cit., pp. 184–6; and HO144/137/A35842.
26. Short, op. cit., pp. 200–1.

27. Ibid., pp. 205–8.
28. He had been defeated in Parliament when he had attempted to strengthen Britain's conspiracy laws in response to French complaints in the wake of the Orsini affair. See above, pp. 8–9.
29. A full account of this affair is given in Bernard Porter, 'The *Freiheit* Prosecutions, 1881–2', *Historical Journal*, vol. 23, no. 4 (1980).
30. *Radical*, 2 April 1881, p. 4.
31. *Daily News*, 31 March 1881, p. 5.
32. Ibid., 16 March 1883, p. 4.
33. *The Times*, 20 January 1883, p. 9.
34. Ibid., 26 January 1885, p. 9. *The Times* was referring specifically to the Tower of London bomb, which was put there on a Saturday when the Tower was full of tourists.
35. *Daily Telegraph*, 26 May 1881, p. 6 (my italics).
36. *Pall Mall Gazette*, 6 April 1883, p. 1.
37. 'Whether any remedial legislation that is now possible will extirpate Fenianism, nobody can tell. Reform is to be advocated on its own lines, independently of dynamite and assassination': ibid. 16 March 1883, p. 1.
38. *Morning Advertiser*, 26 January 1885, p. 4.
39. *The Times*, 24 November 1883, p. 9.
40. This was a curious affair. The prosecution's case against William Woolf and Edward Bondurand when they were eventually tried at the Old Bailey in January 1884 under the 1883 Explosives Act was that they planned to cause an explosion at the German embassy and plant a false trail to the house of a German immigrant, in order to secure the reward they presumed would be offered. After a six days' trial the jury failed to agree on a verdict, by eleven to one. The newspapers assumed that the eleven were in favour of a conviction, but a letter to *The Times* from the foreman on 22 January 1884 made it clear that the reverse was the case. The eleven decided after ten minutes that they should acquit. But the twelfth man, after hours of argument, kept stating ' "that his mind was prejudiced against the two prisoners . . . in consequence of their being foreigners. We did not want such men in this country." ' This intelligence led to the prosecution's being withdrawn, and the prisoners' release. The case is reported in *The Times*, 24, 30 November and 7, 8, 14, 21 December 1883; 15–19, 21, 28–9 January 1884.
41. Ibid., 24 November 1883, p. 9.
42. *Morning Post*, 15 December 1884, p. 4.
43. *Daily News*, 26 January 1885, p. 5.
44. *Pall Mall Gazette*, 16 March 1883, p. 1.
45. *The Times*, 24 November 1883, p. 9.
46. Ibid., 17 March 1883, p. 11.
47. Ibid., 16 March 1883, p. 9.
48. Ibid., 14 February 1885, p. 9.
49. *Pall Mall Gazette*, 26 January 1885, p. 2.
50. *The Times*, 15 October 1884, p. 9.
51. *Pall Mall Gazette*, 16 March 1883, p. 1.
52. *The Times*, 6 April 1883, p. 9; and cf. 14 February 1885, p. 9.
53. Sir Algernon West, *Recollections 1832 to 1886* (1899), vol. II, p. 194.
54. *Daily Telegraph*, 17 March 1883, p. 4.

55. *The Times*, 24 November 1883, p. 9.
56. *Standard*, 20 April 1883, p. 4.
57. *Pall Mall Gazette*, 26 January 1885, p. 1.
58. *The Times*, 6 April 1883, p. 9.
59. Ibid., 17 March 1883, p. 11.
60. *Saturday Review*, 2 April 1881, pp. 417–18.
61. *Reynolds's Newspaper*, 31 July 1881, p. 5.
62. Trial transcript, p. 53, in HO144/77/A3385.
63. *The Times*, 20 January 1883, p. 9.
64. The attack on Gladstone was made by Northcote in a speech at Exeter on 26 January 1885, reported in the *Pall Mall Gazette*, 27 January, p. 10. *The Times* was especially critical of the United States government (e.g. 29 February 1884, p. 10, and 26 January 1885, p. 9); and of the Irish Parliamentary Party (e.g. 17 March 1883, p. 9; 7 April 1883, p. 7).
65. Most's comment, that he 'might as well be in Russia', is reported in *Reynolds's Newspaper*, 3 July 1881, p. 2. See also, on 'Russification', *Pall Mall Gazette*, 26 January 1885, p. 1.

Chapter 3

1. Gladstone to Spencer, 9 June 1882; quoted in Peter Gordon (ed.), *The Red Earl. The Papers of the Fifth Earl Spencer*, vol. I (Northampton, 1982), p. 206.
2. Spencer to Gladstone, 23 August 1882: Gladstone papers (WEGP), BL Add. MS 44309, f. 110.
3. See Dilke's 'Memoirs' for 31 January 1884, in Dilke papers (CWDP), BL Add. MS 43938, f. 36. Dilke claims that Gladstone absented himself 'in order not to have to report it to the Queen'.
4. See, for example, Gladstone's own minutes for the cabinet of 17 March 1883: Item 5. 'Harcourt described his measures in consequence of the explosion . . .' WEGP 44644, f. 12.
5. Harcourt to Vincent, 23 January 1881; quoted in S. H. Jeyes and F. D. How, *The Life of Sir Howard Vincent* (1912), p. 106.
6. See Home Office Confidential Letter Book for 1871–81, pp. 400–43 *passim*: HO151/1; and HO144/72/A19, which contains, among other things, references to Fenian torpedoes and infernal machines forwarded to Britain from a spy in Philadelphia. One telegram from the British consul there, dated 7 July 1881, carries the warning: 'Interior chambers must not be examined. They are fitted with friction fuse certain to explode.' Such very material evidence must have seemed fairly compelling.
7. S. Gwynn and G. Tuckwell, *The Life of the Rt. Hon. Sir Charles W. Dilke* (1917), vol. 1, p. 364.
8. Harcourt to Granville, 3 July 1881: Papers of Granville Leveson-Gower, 2nd Earl Granville (GLGP), PRO 30/29/130.
9. Harcourt to Queen, 26 March 1881: Royal Archive (RA) H43/97.
10. Seymour to Spencer, 12 July 1882; quoted in Gordon, op. cit., vol. 1, p. 214.
11. Harcourt to Queen, 13 June 1883 (copy): WVHP box 691, f. 209.
12. Dilke's Diary for 19 February 1883: CWDP 43925, f. 47; and Memoirs: 43937 f. 68.

13. 'Memorandum on the Police Authority in the new Municipality of London' by Harcourt, 1 March 1883; copy in CWDP 43923, ff. 37–40.
14. Gladstone to Harcourt, 18 May 1883 (draft): WEGP 44198, f. 76.
15. Dilke's Diary for 17 March 1883: CWDP 43925, f. 53; and Memoirs: 43927, f. 85.
16. E.g. on 9 February 1883: CWDP 43937, f. 50; and on 31 January 1884: CWDP 43925, ff. 80–1 and 43938, ff. 35–7.
17. Dilke's Diary for 31 January 1884: CWDP 43925, f. 81. O'Donovan Rossa was supposed to be the leading Fenian conspirator.
18. Dilke's Memoirs for 17 March 1883: CWDP 43937, ff. 85–6.
19. E.g. ibid., f. 85; Harcourt to Gladstone, 13 April 1883: WEGP 44198, ff. 46–7.
20. Dilke's Memoirs for 9 April 1883: CWDP 43937, f. 97.
21. Ponsonby to Harcourt, 13 June 1881: WVHP box 1, f. 130; and cf. Ponsonby to Harcourt, 24 April 1886: ibid. box 3 ff. 161–4, expressing the Queen's regret that Harcourt is not returning to the Home Office, where, she says, 'you did your work very well'.
22. Harcourt to Gladstone, 18 March 1883: WEGP 44198, f. 15.
23. E.g. the correspondence with the Queen's secretary about the *Freiheit* affair, in the Royal Archive, and in WVHP box 1, beginning with Ponsonby to Gladstone, 20 March 1881: RA H43/70; and about 'That horrid woman, Louise Michel' in January 1883, in WVHP box 2, ff. 140, 144, 154.
24. Ponsonby to Harcourt, 24 April 1886: WVHP box 3, ff. 161–4.
25. E.g. Ponsonby to Harcourt 26 May 1881 – 'she hopes no weak leniency will be shown': WVHP box 1, f. 122; and the Queen to Harcourt, 22 June 1882, where she suggests that Irish Aliens legislation be extended to Britain: ibid. box 2, f. 97.
26. See Bernard Porter, *The Refugee Question in Mid-Victorian Politics* (Cambridge, 1979), ch. 3.
27. Lushington minute attached to Monson to Foreign Secretary, 22 March 1893: HO144/587/B2840C, sub. 21C.
28. See 'aide-memoire' of July 1881 in GLGP PRO 30/29/130; Granville to Wyndham, 21 May 1881: FO65/1109; Wyndham to Granville 6 and 8 June 1881: FO 65/1111.
29. Harcourt to Queen, 28 May 1881: RA H44/55.
30. Harcourt to Queen, 9 April 1881: RA H44/20.
31. Ponsonby to Harcourt, 30 May 1881, copy: RA H44/57.
32. Harcourt to Granville, 3 July 1881: GLGP PRO30/29/130.
33. See Bernard Porter, 'The *Freiheit* Prosecutions, 1881–2', *Historical Journal*, vol. 23, no. 4 (1980), pp. 845–6; Harcourt to G. W. Smalley, 15 February 1885: WVHP box 728, ff. 273–4; and Lushington's submission to the Rome Anti-Anarchist Conference, 1898, in FO45/784, 'Annexe', p. 3, fn. 1.
34. Harcourt to Forster, 24 January 1881: HO144/29/72226.
35. Harcourt to Vincent, 23 January 1881: quoted in Jeyes and How, op. cit., p. 106.
36. Referred to in MEPO3/3070.
37. Vincent, Anderson and Williamson were involved in enquiries into the Liverpool Town Hall bomb in June 1881, documented in HO144/81/A5836. The Irish inspector is mentioned in Harcourt to Henderson, 24 January 1881, in MEPO3/3070. Majendie carried out a survey of his own among provincial chief constables in February 1881: see HO144/73/A72, subs 8 and 14.

38. Harcourt to Queen, 24 February 1881: RA D30/150.
39. See Harcourt to Gladstone, 12 December 1881: WEGP 44196, f. 248; and a printed memorandum on the 'Secret Service', c. 1914, in T1/11689/25138, p. 6. I am grateful to Dr Christopher Andrew for bringing this latter to my attention.
40. Harcourt to Henderson, 24 January 1881: MEPO3/3070.
41. Harcourt to Liddell, 26 March 1881: HO144/77/A3385, sub. 8a.
42. Ibid.
43. Above, p. 7, and see Jeyes and How, op. cit., pp. 53–7.
44. Pearson and Henderson, 5 January 1883: HO144/190/A46472, sub. 1.
45. Their promotion is reported in Metropolitan Police Orders for 6 July 1878, in MEPO 2/136.
46. Harcourt to Granville, 28 June and 21 July 1881: GLGP PRO 30/29/130.
47. Vincent to Harcourt, ?October 1882: WVHP box 100, f. 186.
48. Spencer to Gladstone, 8 May 1882: quoted in Gordon, op. cit., p. 195.
49. Spencer to Gladstone, 6 August 1882: WEGP 44309, f. 89.
50. J. Sandford to Herbert Gladstone, 14 May 1882: H. Gladstone papers (HJGP), BL Add. MS 46049, f. 209.
51. Spencer to Gladstone, 7 May 1882: WEGP 44308, f. 219.
52. Spencer to Gladstone, 7 June 1882: quoted in Gordon, op. cit., p. 205.
53. Spencer to Gladstone, 11 June 1882: WEGP 44309, f. 39.
54. Spencer to Gladstone, 7 May 1882: WEGP 44308, f. 222.
55. Sir Henry Brackenbury, *Some Memoirs of My Spare Time* (Edinburgh, 1909), pp. 263–4.
56. Ibid., pp. 311–12.
57. Ibid., p. 312; and see Spencer to Gladstone, 23 August 1882: WEGP 44309, ff. 110–11.
58. Spencer to Gladstone, 7 June 1882: quoted in Gordon, op. cit., p. 205.
59. Harcourt's doubts, recounted by Gladstone's secretary, are expressed on the back of Harcourt to Gladstone, 15 June 1882: WEGP 44197, f. 63. For the cabinet's sanction, see the telegrams between Spencer and Gladstone, 19 June 1882: WEGP 44309, ff. 43–4; Spencer to Gladstone, 21 June: ibid. f. 46; and Spencer to Trevelyan, 20 June 1882: quoted in Gordon, op. cit., p. 209.
60. For Spencer's reaction to 'the Brackenbury fiasco', see Spencer to Gladstone, 23 August 1882: WEGP 44309, f. 111. On the whole Brackenbury episode, see also K. R. M. Short, *The Dynamite War* (Dublin, 1979), pp. 78–87; Richard Hawkins, 'Government Versus Secret Societies: The Parnell Era', in T. Desmond Williams (ed.), *Secret Societies in Ireland* (Dublin, 1973), pp. 104–6; and Charles Townshend, *Political Violence in Ireland* (Oxford, 1983), pp. 170–1.
61. See F. H. O'Donnell's attack in the House of Commons on 3 August 1882, quoted in Short, op. cit., p. 88.
62. Spencer to Trevelyan, 21 July 1882: quoted in Gordon, op. cit., p. 218; Spencer to Gladstone, 3 August 1882: WEGP 44309, f. 79; and cf. Spencer to Harcourt, 7 March 1884: 'Jenkinson if unskilled in Parliamentary & constitutional usages is very just . . .': WVHP box 43, ff. 67–8.
63. Jenkinson to Spencer, 14 September 1884: Gordon, op. cit., p. 274; Jenkinson to Carnarvon, 26 September 1885: Carnarvon papers (HHCP), PRO30/6/62, item 24. Major Nicholas Gosselin, who came to head the secret service in northern England and Scotland, also had – or developed – Home Rule views: see below, p. 118.

64. See Gladstone to Spencer, 1 December 1882: Gordon, op. cit., p. 227; Harcourt to Queen, 24 January 1883, copy: WVHP box 691, f. 130; Queen to Harcourt, 18 February 1883: ibid., box 2, f. 160; Harcourt to Spencer, 31 March 1883: quoted in Short, op. cit., p. 124.

65. Jenkinson memorandum, 22 March 1883: WVHP box 103, ff. 10–15.

66. Spencer to Gladstone, 30 March 1883: WEGP 44310, f. 53.

67. Jenkinson memorandum, 22 March 1883: WVHP box 103, ff. 10–15.

68. Harcourt to Spencer, 16 March 1883 (copy): ibid., box 42, ff. 30–2.

69. Memorandum by Vincent, initialled by Harcourt, 17 March 1883: ibid., box 101, ff. 5–6.

70. Police Orders for 18 March 1883, in MEPO7/45. The original members were Inspectors Pope and Ahern, Sergeants Jenkins, Melville and Regan, and Constables O'Sullivan, Walsh, McIntyre, Foy, Thorpe, and (unless there's a printing error) two Enrights.

71. See Hawkins, op. cit., p. 109; and below, p. 47.

72. Jenkinson memorandum, 22 March 1883: WVHP box 103, ff. 10–15.

73. Jenkinson to Harcourt, 31 May 1883: ibid., box 103, ff. 73–7.

74. Harcourt to Spencer, 31 March 1883 (copy): ibid., box 42, ff. 45–7. On Warren, see below, pp. 81ff.

75. Jenkinson to Harcourt, 31 May 1883: ibid., box 103, ff. 73–7.

76. Jenkinson to Harcourt, 11 August 1883: ibid., box 103, ff. 108–9.

77. Jenkinson to Harcourt, 19 April 1883: ibid., box 103, ff. 60–2.

78. Jenkinson to Harcourt, 18 May 1883: ibid., box 103, f. 70.

79. Harcourt to Queen, 13 June 1883, copy: ibid., box 691, f. 209.

80. Jenkinson to Harcourt, 4 June 1883: ibid., box 103, ff. 78–9.

81. See Gosselin to Harcourt, 7 January 1884: ibid., box 105, ff. 109–10.

82. Gosselin report, 7 July 1883: ibid., box 103, ff. 96–9; Gosselin to Harcourt, 26 August 1883: ibid., box 105, f. 76.

83. Gosselin to Harcourt, 22 August 1883: ibid., box 105, f. 75.

84. Gosselin to Harcourt, 7 January 1884: ibid., box 105, ff. 109–10.

85. Jenkinson to Harcourt, 4 September 1883: ibid., box 103, ff. 116–18.

86. Gosselin Report, 7 July 1883: ibid., box 103, ff. 96–9.

87. Anderson memorandum, 17 March 1883: ibid., box 105, ff. 25–6; Jenkinson to Harcourt, 31 May 1883: ibid., box 103, ff. 73–7.

88. Jenkinson memorandum, 'Secret', 7 May 1883: ibid., box 103, ff. 67–8; Anderson to Harcourt, 21 May 1883: ibid., box 105, ff. 37–8.

89. Jenkinson to Harcourt, 4 September 1883: ibid., box 103, f. 117.

90. 'Agreement' signed by Thomas Beach, 30 April 1883: HO144/1537, file 5.

91. Anderson to Harcourt, 5 January 1884: WVHP box 105, ff. 51–3.

92. Anderson memorandum, 8 May 1884: ibid., box 105, f. 60; and see Anderson to Harcourt, 11 June 1884: ibid. box 728, ff. 150–1, and Troup memorandum, 8 April 1910: HO144/926/A49,962, sub. 7.

93. See Hansard, 3rd series, vol. 277, cc. 1802–11 and 1841–64 (9 April 1883).

94. See Liddell to under-secretary, War Office, 19 March 1883: HO151/2, p. 264.

95. Harcourt to Queen, 13 June 1883, copy: WVHP box 691, f. 209.

96. See Short, op. cit., pp. 139–40.

97. See, for example, Jenkinson to Harcourt, 10 December 1883: WVHP box 103, f. 137.

98. Jenkinson to Harcourt, 2 March 1884: ibid., box 104, f. 16.

99. Harcourt to Spencer, 10 September 1883 (copy): ibid., box 42, ff. 122–3.
100. Gosselin to Harcourt, 29 January 1884: ibid., box 105, ff. 113–14.
101. Gosselin to Harcourt, 24 January 1884: ibid., box 105, f. 112; and cf. cabinet memorandum by Harcourt, 1 February 1884: ibid., box 98, ff. 47–50.
102. See Liddell to Police Commissioner, 20 June 1884: HO151/2, p. 449.
103. Liddell to Mayor of Windsor, 8 July 1884: HO151/2, p. 459.
104. Lushington to Secretary, Office of Works, 11 August 1886: HO151/3, p. 180.
105. Harcourt to Spencer, 4 March 1884: Gordon, op. cit., p. 266.
106. Spencer to Harcourt, 20 January 1884: WVHP box 43, f. 24.
107. Harcourt to Spencer, 6 March 1884: Spencer Papers (JPSP), Harcourt correspondence, box 2.
108. Spencer to Harcourt, 7 March 1884: WVHP box 43, ff. 67–8.

Chapter 4

1. Jenkinson memorandum, 11 March 1884: HO144/133/A34848B, sub. 1; Police Orders for 10 May 1883, in MEPO7/45; report by Williamson, 12 April 1884: MEPO3/3070; and see K. R. M. Short, *The Dynamite War. Irish-American Bombers in Victorian London* (Dublin, 1979), pp. 178–9.
2. Jenkinson to Cross, 9 December 1885: HO144/133/A34848B, sub. 56.
3. Jenkinson memorandum, 6 March 1884: HO144/721/110757, sub. 2.
4. Spencer to Trevelyan. 7 March 1884: Peter Gordon (ed.), *The Red Earl* (Northampton, 1982), vol. I, p. 266.
5. Harcourt to Liddell, 8 March 1884: HO144/721/110757, sub. 2; and Harcourt to Spencer, 8 March 1884: JPSP, Harcourt corresp., box 2.
6. See the correspondence between Murdoch, Maconachie and the Police Receiver, 8–10 March and 2 May 1884: HO155/115/A25928, subs. 15b, 15c, 15d.
7. Jenkinson to Spencer, 17 December 1884: JPSP, Jenkinson corresp., box 1.
8. Jenkinson to Spencer, 2 June 1884: ibid., loc cit.
9. Jenkinson to Spencer, 3 January 1885: ibid., Jenkinson corresp., box 2.
10. Jenkinson to Spencer, 17 December 1884: ibid., Jenkinson corresp., box 1.
11. Jenkinson to Spencer, 12 April 1884: ibid., loc cit.
12. Jenkinson to Spencer, 14 February 1885: ibid., Jenkinson corresp., box 2.
13. Jenkinson to Spencer, 3 May 1884: ibid., Jenkinson corresp., box 1.
14. Jenkinson to Harcourt, 20 September 1883: WVHP box 103, ff. 125–6.
15. Jenkinson to Spencer, 31 May and 2 June 1884: JPSP, Jenkinson corresp., box 1.
16. Jenkinson to Spencer, 3 June 1884: ibid., loc cit.
17. Harcourt to Queen, 25 June 1884, copy: WVHP box 692, f. 69.
18. Jenkinson to Spencer, 15 December 1884: JPSP, Jenkinson corresp., box 2.
19. Jenkinson to Spencer, 12 December 1884: ibid., loc cit.
20. Jenkinson to Spencer, 15 January 1885: ibid., loc cit.
21. Jenkinson to Spencer, 25 January 1885: Gordon, op. cit., p. 289. Jenkinson's prior warning of the Westminster bomb, dated 26 December 1884, is in WVHP box 104, f. 127.
22. Jenkinson to Spencer, 14 February 1885: JPSP, Jenkinson corresp., box 2.
23. Jenkinson to Spencer, 1 July 1885: ibid., loc cit.

24. Though in January 1885 Monro was the one at fault, for refusing to allow Jenkinson to receive information directly from one of his Special Irish Branch constables, Patrick McIntyre; see police report by McIntyre, 27 January 1885, with memos by Monro and Jenkinson attached; Jenkinson to Harcourt, 30 January 1885, and Monro to Harcourt, 30 January 1885: all in WVHP box 104, ff. 132–7. Monro's complaints against Jenkinson are retailed in Harcourt to Jenkinson, 9 June 1885: ibid., box 728, ff. 291–2; Jenkinson memorandum of 16 June 1885: ibid., box 104, f. 161.

25. Jenkinson to Spencer, 17 December 1884 and 20 June 1885: JPSP, Jenkinson corresp., boxes 1 and 2.

26. Jenkinson to Harcourt, 5 September 1883: WVHP box 103, f. 113.

27. Jenkinson to Harcourt, 25 March 1883: ibid., box 103, ff. 16–18.

28. Jenkinson to Farndale, 11 January 1884 (copy): ibid., box 102, ff. 59–60.

29. Gosselin to Harcourt, 7 August 1883: ibid., box 105, f. 68.

30. Jenkinson to Spencer, 1 July 1885; JPSP, Jenkinson corresp., box 2.

31. Harcourt to Spencer, 16 March 1883 (copy): WVHP box 42, ff. 30–2.

32. Harcourt to Spencer, 16 April 1884: JPSP, Harcourt corresp., box 2; Gosselin to Harcourt, 17 October 1883: WVHP box 104, ff. 84–5.

33. Jenkinson to Spencer, 2 June 1884: JPSP, Jenkinson corresp., box 1.

34. Jenkinson to Spencer, 15 December 1884: ibid., Jenkinson corresp., box 2.

35. Jenkinson to Harcourt, 18 December 1884: WVHP box 104, ff. 95–9; and cf. Jenkinson to Harcourt, 17 September 1884: ibid., box 104, ff. 73–82.

36. Harcourt to Spencer, 25 January 1885: ibid., box 44, f. 52.

37. Jenkinson to Harcourt, 10 January 1885: ibid., box 104, ff. 112–13. In fact Phelan survived the attack on him: see Short, op. cit., p. 204.

38. Harcourt to Spencer, 6 January 1885 (copy): WVHP box 44, f. 24.

39. E.g. Jenkinson to Harcourt, 24 and 25 January 1885: ibid., box 104, ff. 119, 126.

40. Jenkinson to Spencer, 21 May 1885: JPSP, Jenkinson corresp., box 2.

41. Jenkinson to Spencer, 17 June 1885: ibid., loc cit.

42. See below, pp. 82–4.

43. Jenkinson to Spencer, 13 August and 15 December 1884, 14 February and 20 June 1885: JPSP, Jenkinson corresp., boxes 1 and 2.

44. Harcourt to Spencer, 23 June 1885 and 3 November 1887: ibid., Harcourt corresp., boxes 2 and 3.

45. Harcourt to Spencer, 23 June 1885: ibid., Harcourt corresp., box 2; Jenkinson to Spencer, 20 and 25 June 1885: ibid., Jenkinson corresp., box 2.

46. Jenkinson to Spencer, 1 July 1885: ibid., loc cit.

47. Jenkinson to Harcourt, 11 August 1883: WVHP box 103, ff. 108–9.

48. Jenkinson to Harcourt, 17 and 18 June 1883: ibid., box 103, ff. 82–3 and 86–7. Jenkinson's lack of a constitutional sense is indicated by the fact that he assumed that Harcourt could order MacDermott's arrest in Canada.

49. Harcourt to Spencer, 10 September 1883 (copy): ibid., box 42, ff. 122–3.

50. Jenkinson to Spencer, 3 June 1884 and 12 March 1885: JPSP, Jenkinson corresp., boxes 1 and 2.

51. Jenkinson to Harcourt, 12 July 1883: WVHP box 103, ff. 93–4.

52. Jenkinson to Farndale, 11 January 1884 (copy): ibid., box 102, ff. 59–60.

53. Jenkinson to Harcourt, 25 and 29 March 1883: ibid., box 103, ff. 16–25.

54. Gosselin to Harcourt, 7 August 1883: ibid., box 105, f. 68.

55. Jenkinson to Spencer, 15 December 1884: JPSP, Jenkinson corresp., box 2 (my italics).

56. Jenkinson to Spencer, 3 June 1884: ibid., Jenkinson corresp., box 1.

57. See below, p. 75.

58. He wrote voluminously to Carnarvon, but without the same openness, and only for the eight months he was in office. The two Viceroys after him, Aberdeen and Londonderry, do not seem to have bothered much with him.

59. 'I am very glad to let you know that I have at last been able to settle all questions between the Metropolitan Police and Mr. Jenkinson entirely to the satisfaction of both parties.' Cross to Carnarvon, 11 July 1885: HHCP PRO30/6/62, f. 3.

60. Monro to Warren, and Warren to Childers, 27 July 1886: MEPO4/487.

61. Henderson to Home Under-Secretary, 22 April 1884, with Harcourt's minute, 'Sanction': HO144/133/A34848B, sub. 12.

62. 'J.T.H.'(?) to Police Commissioner, 9 August 1884: MEPO3/3070.

63. Below, p. 82.

64. Carnarvon to Hicks Beach, 30 December 1885: HHCP PRO30/6/62, f. 45.

65. Jenkinson to Cross, 2 September 1885: ibid., PRO30/6/62, f. 21.

66. Jenkinson memorandum, 5 August 1885: ibid., PRO30/6/62, f. 5.

67. Cross to Carnarvon, 3 September 1885: ibid., PRO30/6/62, f. 20.

68. Carnarvon to Hicks Beach, 3 January 1886: ibid., PRO30/6/62, f. 49.

69. Hicks Beach to Cross, 27 June 1885: Cross papers (RACP), BL Add. MS 51274, f. 68; and printed memorandum on the 'Secret Service', in T1/11689/25138, p. 6.

70. Hicks Beach to Carnarvon, 2 January 1886: HHCP PRO30/6/62, f. 47.

71. Below, p. 78.

72. Cross to Carnarvon, 4 January 1886: HHCP PRO30/6/62, f. 50.

73. Carnarvon to Cross, 6 January 1886: RACP 51268, ff. 157–8.

74. Salisbury to Carnarvon, 6 January 1886 (wrongly dated 1885): HHCP PRO30/6/62, f. 52.

75. Carnarvon to Salisbury, 7 January 1886: ibid., PRO30/6/62, f. 53.

76. 'While Jenkinson has no doubt by his manner engendered friction, I think he has been shamefully treated, & that the Public will lose a great deal by his withdrawal.' Spencer to Harcourt, 13 December 1886: WVHP box 45, ff. 26–7.

77. 'I am sorry for Jenkinson but he had made himself impossible.' Harcourt to Spencer, 14 December 1886 (copy): ibid., box 710, f. 74.

78. Harcourt to Queen, 7 June 1884, copy: ibid., box 692, f. 30; and cf. Harcourt to Queen, 24 February 1881: '. . . the temper of the English people will not tolerate the conditions which are indispensable to an effective Detective police': RA D30/150.

79. Harcourt's speech at the Annual Festival of the Metropolitan and City Police Orphanage, 25 June 1881, reported in The Times, 27 June, p. 12.

80. Ponsonby to Harcourt, 17 June 1883, copy: WVHP box 691, f. 214.

81. The Times, 27 March 1885, p. 9.

82. Anderson memorandum, 17 March 1883: WVHP box 105, ff. 25–6.

83. Freiheit, 12 August 1882; copy in HO144/77/A3385, sub. 47; and see also, for example, 'Northumbrian', 'A Perverted Police', in Reynolds's Newspaper, 15 May 1881, p. 2.

84. See *Report of the Departmental Commission . . . into . . . the Detective Force of the Metropolitan Police*, 1877, p. 36 *et passim*; copy in HO45/10002/A49463, sub. 2.
85. Jenkinson to Harcourt, 17 September 1884: WVHP box 104, ff. 73–82.
86. David Nicoll, *The Greenwich Mystery* (1897), p. 11.
87. Harold Brust, '*I Guarded Kings*' (n.d.), pp. 88–90.
88. See above, p. 36.
89. In Home Office files, that is, which are still extant.
90. See Carnarvon to Cross, 29 July 1885: RACP 51268, f. 143; and Harcourt to Cross, 22 June 1885: RACP 51274, ff. 44–5.
91. Carnarvon to Cross, 28 June 1885: RACP 51268, f. 135.

Chapter 5

1. See above, pp. 4–6 and 59.
2. Patrick McIntyre, 'Scotland Yard. Its Mysteries and Methods', *Reynolds's Newspaper*, 3 and 10 February 1895, p. 5.
3. Jenkinson to Harcourt, 4 September 1883: WVHP box 103 ff. 116–18.
4. See Carnarvon to Salisbury, 7 January 1886, draft: HHCP PRO30/3/62, f. 53; and Andrew Lansdowne, *A Life's Reminiscences. Scotland Yard* (1893), p. 153.
5. Quoted in Sissela Bok, *Secrets. On the Ethics of Concealment and Revelation* (Oxford, 1984), p. 25.
6. See above, p. 66. It should be emphasised here again that the Home Office may have taken more interest than appears from the surviving documents. Another contrary indication, however, is that when charges of impropriety were made against government agents and the police, the Home Office's internal enquiries were very superficial. See below, pp. 74, 139.
7. Le Caron himself denied it. See his *Twenty-five Years in the Secret Service. The Recollections of a Spy* (1892; 18th edn, 1895), p. 277.
8. John Littlechild, *The Reminiscences of Chief-Inspector Littlechild* (1894), p. 96.
9. G. H. Greenham, *Scotland Yard Experiences* (1904), p. 61.
10. A. Pinkerton to W. E. Gladstone, 8 July 1882: HO144/1537/4.
11. Home Office to John B. Monckton, draft: HO144/145/A38008, sub. 1. The Home Office probably had in mind the Woolf-Bondurand case of November 1883: see above, 204 n. 40.
12. *Reynolds's Newspaper*, 10 February 1895, p. 5.
13. R. Anderson, *The Lighter Side of My Official Life* (1910), p. 99.
14. See above, p. 46; and Harcourt to Gladstone, 16 May 1883: WEGP 44198, ff. 70–1.
15. Le Caron, op. cit., pp. 242, 275.
16. Anderson, op. cit., p. 96.
17. See below, p. 83.
18. K. R. M. Short, *The Dynamite War* (Dublin, 1979), pp. 180–3. The claim that the plot was directed against the House of Commons may have been intended merely to dramatise it. In earlier accounts Daly's target is stated to be Dublin Castle. See Farndale's report of 9 January 1884, and Jenkinson to Farndale, 11 January 1884 (copy): WVHP box 102, ff. 53, 59–60.
19. Taken from Henry Manton, *Turning the Last Stone* (Birmingham, [1895]), pp. 3–6, 9. This is a pamphlet reprinting much of the correspondence on this affair,

'for the purpose of supplying the Mayor, Aldermen, and Councillors of the City of Birmingham with information for their private use'. The only extant copy to my knowledge is in HO144/193/A46664, sub. 58.

20. Ibid., pp. 7–8, 17.
21. E.g. *The Times*, 24 September 1890, p. 4, and Birmingham papers for 23–4 September; *Hansard*, 3rd series, vol. 356, cc. 443–70 and 1141–82; 4th series, vol. 1, cc. 236–97 and 324–69.
22. House of Commons, 27 July 1891: ibid., 3rd series, vol. 356, cc. 457–62.
23. See Home Office minutes on Manton to Matthews, 6 October 1887: HO144/136/A35496C; Farndale to Pemberton, 22 October 1887, and Farndale to Matthews, 13 December 1887: HO144/193/A46664.
24. Gosselin report, 5 November 1887: ibid.
25. See Monro to Matthews, 9 November 1887; Gosselin to Monro, 10 January 1888; and Manton to Matthews, 9 May 1888, all in ibid.; and Manton, op. cit., p. 6.
26. House of Commons, 27 July 1891: *Hansard*, 3rd series, vol. 356, cc. 453 and 451.
27. Harcourt to Spencer, 3 November 1887: JPSP, Harcourt corresp., box 3. In a letter to Jenkinson of the same date he makes it clear that these dismissals were 'in civil cases': copy in WVHP box 216, ff. 54–5.
28. Harcourt to Jenkinson, 3 November 1887: ibid., loc. cit.
29. Jenkinson to Harcourt, 1 November 1887: ibid., box 216, ff. 51–3.
30. See Leon Ò Broin, *The Prime Informer. A Suppressed Scandal* (1971), p. 66.
31. See above, pp. 54–6.
32. Harcourt to Spencer, 3 November 1887: JPSP, Harcourt corresp., box 3. In reply Spencer strongly defended Jenkinson against Harcourt's imputations, which he chose to take personally: 'for . . . he consulted me as freely as he did you after you had him over, and if anyone is to blame for all he did I am'. Spencer to Harcourt, 7 November 1887: WVHP box 45, ff. 59–60.
33. O'Connor in House of Commons, 3 August 1891: *Hansard*, 3rd series, vol. 356, c. 1156.
34. Harcourt to Spencer, 3 November 1887: JPSP, Harcourt corresp., box 3.
35. Harcourt, quoted in Short, op. cit., p. 97.
36. Lushington to Matthews, 1 August 1891: HO144/193/A46664; and see Manton, op. cit., p. 6.
37. For example, in letters to Harcourt from Gosselin, 28 October 1883, and Jenkinson, 18 January 1884, in WVHP boxes 105, f. 93, and 104, ff. 7–9.
38. Lushington to Matthews, 1 August 1891: loc. cit.
39. Manton, op. cit., p. 5.
40. Lushington to Matthews, 1 August 1891: loc. cit.
41. *The Times*, 24 September 1890, p. 4.
42. Short, op. cit., p. 266.
43. Jenkinson to Spencer, 12 April 1884: JPSP, Jenkinson corresp., box 1.
44. E.g. B. Porter, 'The *Freiheit* Prosecutions, 1881–2', *Historical Journal*, vol. 23, no. 4 (1980), pp. 839, 843.
45. *Reynolds's Newspaper*, 3 March 1895, p. 5.
46. See below, p. 136–8.
47. Black was allowed to resign from the Birmingham police after being found to be living in sin with a woman who had married an elderly man for his money and then left him. See Farndale to Matthews, 27 March 1892: HO144/193/A46664.

Irish MPs, sensing a scandal which might have a bearing on the Egan case, raised the matter in the House of Commons in 1892: see *Hansard*, 4th series, vol. 3, cc. 22–4, 345–5, 593; vol. 5, cc. 551–2.
48. Farndale to Pemberton, 22 October 1887: HO144/193/A46664.
49. Short, op. cit., pp. 220–1.
50. See, for example, Anderson, op. cit., p. 55; Robert A. Fuller, *Recollections of a Detective* (1912), p. 51; Harold Brust, '*I Guarded Kings*' (n.d.), p. 44.
51. See below, p. 120.
52. *Reynolds's Newspaper*, 15 May 1881, p. 2.
53. Ibid., 24 April 1884, p. 4.

Chapter 6

1. *Pall Mall Gazette*, 12 February 1886, pp. 1–3; 17 February, p. 1; 19 February, p. 1; 20 February, pp. 1–2; 23 February, p. 3; 6 March, pp. 1–2.
2. Ibid., 27 February 1886, p. 4. Brackenbury was its favourite candidate; 'but he deserted an analogous post in Ireland a few years ago, in a manner which seemed to indicate a want of loyalty and steadfastness of purpose, which for some time threw him completely into the shade of professional displeasure'.
3. Ibid., 13 March 1886, p. 1. Carnarvon compared him to Gordon, in a letter to Cranbrook, 2 September 1885: HHCP PRO30/6/54, f. 59.
4. *Pall Mall Gazette*, 9, 10, 12, 14 and 15 November 1887.
5. See the League's organ, *The Link*, which ran from February to September 1888. The foundation of the League is recounted in no. 1, 4 February 1888, p. 4.
6. Harcourt in House of Commons, 1 March 1888, quoted in Lisa Keller, 'Public Order in Victorian London: The Interaction between the Metropolitan Police, the Government, the Urban Crowd, and the Law' (Ph.D. thesis, Cambridge 1976), p. 280. On this whole question, see ibid., chapters 4 and 5, *passim*.
7. Charles Warren, 'The Police of the Metropolis', *Murray's Magazine*, vol. 4 (1888), p. 589.
8. *Pall Mall Gazette*, 8 October 1888, pp. 1, 3.
9. Monro's first complaint is in a memorandum of 11 November 1887; the quotation from a further letter to Warren of 15 February 1888: HO144/190/A46472B, subs. 2 and 9.
10. Williamson's sick-note, dated 7 February 1888, is in HO144/190/A46472B, sub. 1; Monro's letter to the Home Secretary on the causes of his death, 13 December 1889, is in HO144/190/A46472E, sub. 1.
11. Warren would only support a temporary appointment, for three months while Williamson was away: Warren to Home under-secretary, 15 February 1888, in ibid., sub. 2, and MEPO1/55, p. 119. Monro strongly opposed this, on the grounds that (a) help was needed even with a fit Williamson, and (b) it would take three months to *train* the new man. Monro to Warren, 16 February 1888: HO144/190/A46472B, sub. 9.
12. See Matthews minutes of 17 and 28 March 1888, in ibid., subs. 4 and 6.
13. Monro to Warren, 19 March 1888: ibid., sub. 6.
14. Monro's first letter to the Home Office on this is dated 31 March 1888; the quotation is from a further letter dated 11 April 1888. The letters, or copies, are in ibid., subs. 7 and 9; and in MEPO 1/48, and 1/55 pp. 211–12.

15. Correspondence on this between Warren and Monro, in late April and May, is in HO144/190/A46472B, sub. 9; and in MEPO4/487.
16. Warren to Home under-secretary, 9 May and 7 June 1888: ibid., sub. 9; and Warren, 'The Police of the Metropolis', loc. cit., p. 586.
17. Monro to Home under-secretary, 11 June 1888: ibid., sub. 18.
18. Monro to Home Secretary, 17 August 1888: HO144/190/A46472C, sub. 1.
19. Watkin W. Williams, *The Life of General Sir Charles Warren* (Oxford, 1941), p. 197.
20. Warren, op. cit., pp. 580, 587–90.
21. It was suggested on 10 October 1888 in a despatch from Britain's ambassador in Vienna, Paget, who had it from a plausible informant that Jack the Ripper was a man called Johann Stammer, *alias* Kelly, working for a breakaway section of the 'International Society'. The informant asked for £165 to enable him to travel to London to find the man; Scotland Yard dismissed the tale, but Paget insisted on advancing the money out of his own pocket as 'I believe in his *bona fides* so much' (Paget to Salisbury, 15 October 1888). The informant travelled to Paris, but then demanded another £100, which was refused him (Lushington to Treasury, 20 March 1889). The correspondence is in HO144/212/A48606.
22. Jenkinson memorandum, 28 January 1885: attached at beginning of MEPO1/55; Lushington to Henderson, 4 December 1885: HO151/3 p. 116; Warren to Home under-secretary, 16 December 1887: HO144/208/A48000M, sub. 5.
23. Monro memorandum, 30 October 1886: HO144/133/A34848B, sub. 61; Police Receiver to Home under-secretary, 7 February 1888: HO144/208/A48000M, sub. 9.
24. Monro memorandum, 30 October 1886, and Police Receiver memorandum, 22 December 1886: HO144/133/A34848B, subs. 61 and 62.
25. Above, p. 52.
26. See Stuart Wortley to Treasury, 9 January 1888 (draft), and G. H. Tripp memorandum, 28 July 1888: HO144/208/A48000M, subs. 7 and 23.
27. The earliest reference to Monro as 'Secret Agent' is in Warren to Monro, 4 January 1888: MEPO1/55, p. 99.
28. Troup memorandum, 8 April 1910: HO144/926/A49962, sub. 7.
29. Warren to Home under-secretary, 2 February 1887: HO144/189/A46281, sub. 1; Lushington to Warren, 3 February 1887: HO15/3, p. 248.
30. Lushington memorandum, 12 October 1887: HO144/189/A46281, sub. 3; G. H. Tripp memorandum, 28 July 1888: HO144/208/A48000M, sub. 23.
31. Warren to Home under-secretary, 2 February 1887: HO144/189/A46281, sub. 1; Lushington to Warren, 3 February 1887: HO151/3, p. 248; Murdoch minute attached to Lushington to Warren, 8 November 1888: HO144/189/A46281, sub. 6.
32. E.g. Return signed by Supt. Cutbush, 19 November 1888: HO144/222/A49500M, sub. 3.
33. Jackson (Treasury) to Home under-secretary, 25 February 1888; Tripp memorandum, 28 July 1888; Monro to Home under-secretary, 13 December 1888: HO144/208/A48000M, subs. 5, 12 and 23; Monro to Matthews, 9 November 1887: HO144/193/A46664, sub. 11. There is a list of the personnel of the Special Branch on 19 December 1887, with pay and allowances, in MEPO5/65. It refers to the two 'sections', but does not make it clear which of the four Inspectors was attached to which. The names are: Chief Inspector Littlechild;

Inspectors Pope, Melville, Burke and Quinn; Sergeants McIntyre, Sweeney, Walsh and Nowlan; Constables Gray, Boulter, New, Maguire, Foley, Scott, Kane, McCauley, Craig, Felton, Hunt, Nursey, Haines, Fraser, Eustace, Hemphrey, Read, Beckley, Tyson and McCarthy. For the abolition of the sections, see below, p. 166.

34. See, for example, Lushington memorandum, 12 October 1887; Murdoch minute attached to Lushington to Warren, 8 November 1888: HO144/189/A46281, subs. 3 and 6.

35. Report by E. R. Henry, 7 January 1902: HO45/10254/A36450, sub. 126.

36. Warren to Home under-secretary, 21 April 1888: HO144/212/A48606, sub. 2; Warren to Monro, 14 February 1888, and Warren to Home under-secretary, 9 May 1888: HO144/190/A46472B, sub. 9. At one stage Warren tried to boot the 'Irish Branch' out of Scotland Yard altogether, on the grounds that it was 'really not part of the Police Force'. Warren to Ruggles Brise, 16 May 1888: MEPO1/48.

37. Monro to Warren, 15 February 1888: HO144/190/A46472B, sub. 9.

38. E.g. Matthews to Lushington, 1 April 1888: HO144/212/A48606, sub. 1.

39. See the report in *The Link*, 8 September 1888, p. 3; confirmed by Murdoch's minute on Lushington to Warren, 8 November 1888: HO144/189/A46281, sub. 6.

40. Troup memorandum, 8 April 1910: HO144/926/A49962, sub. 7.

41. See K. R. M. Short, *The Dynamite War* (Dublin, 1979), p. 237.

42. Returns showing the strength of Section B on 19 November 1888, 13 December 1888, and 24 December 1891 are in HO144/222/A49500M, subs. 3 and 5, and in MEPO1/54, p. 82.

43. Hicks Beach to Cross, 27 June 1885: RACP 51274, f. 68; undated Treasury minute in MEPO5/65, sub. 569, f. 3.

44. Warren to Home under-secretary, 20 and 28 April 1888; Murdoch minute, 3 May 1888, on latter; and Dowdall, Irish Office, to Home under-secretary, 12 May 1888: HO144/208/A48000M, subs. 16, 18 and 19.

45. Lushington to Irish under-secretary, 16 December 1890: HO151/5, p. 3.

46. Lushington to Bradford, 15 December 1891: HO151/5, pp. 170–1; Bradford to Home under-secretary, 24 December 1891: MEPO1/54, pp. 79–86; Lushington to Bradford, 31 December 1891: HO151/5, pp. 178–9.

47. 'Henri Le Caron'. *Twenty-five Years in the Secret Service. The Recollections of a Spy* (1895), pp. 281–3.

48. E.g. Ibid., loc. cit.; Robert Anderson, *The Lighter Side of my Official Life* (1910), p. 120; Monro to Warren, 10 February 1888: HO144/211/A48482, sub. 1.

49. Monro to Warren, 10 February 1888: HO144/211/A48482, sub. 1.

50. Minute by H. B. S[impson], 1 March 1888: ibid.

51. E.g. Healy in House of Commons, 14 April 1910, and Macveagh in House of Commons, 21 April 1910: *Hansard*, 5th series, vol. 16, cc. 1398 and 2375.

52. Anderson, op. cit., p. 118.

53. Monro report, 4 November 1887, in Anderson papers: HO144/1538, file 2(b). It is interesting that Monro's report on the same case to Warren on 10 February 1888 (HO144/211/A48482, sub. 1) is not half so revealing as this one.

54. Anderson, op. cit., p. 119. The 'Jubilee Plot' is covered more fully in Short, op. cit., pp. 232–6; and in J. A. Cole, *Prince of Spies. Henri Le Caron* (1984), pp. 146–8.

55. John Sweeney, *At Scotland Yard* (1904), pp. 70–1.
56. Matthews to Lushington, 15 June 1887: HO144/190/A46470B, sub. 5. The other correspondence on this is in the same file, subs. 4–6.
57. Warren to Home under-secretary, 16 December 1887: HO144/208/A48000M, sub. 5.
58. Warren to Home under-secretary, 20 April 1888: ibid., sub. 16; and Lushington to Warren, 13 June 1888; HO151/4, pp. 150–2. See also Monro minute of 27 February 1889: HO45/9687/A48584B, sub. 4.
59. Monro to Majendie, 21 February 1890: MEPO1/55, p. 595; and cf. Monro to Sandars, 14 February 1890: ibid. p. 594.
60. Bradford to Home under-secretary, 24 December 1891: MEPO1/54, pp. 79–86.
61. Below, pp. 102, 138ff.
62. A breakdown of the numbers and locations of the port police on 19 November 1888 is in HO144/222/A49500M, sub. 3.
63. Prowse, London Custom House, to Home under-secretary, 15 January and 22 February 1889; Lushington to Prowse, 7 February and 30 March 1889: HO45/9687/A48584B, subs. 1, 4, 5; and HO151/4, pp. 370–1.
64. Pearson to Home under-secretary, 20 November 1888: HO144/222/A49500M, sub. 3.
65. Warren to Home under-secretary, 9 October 1888: HO144/208/A48000M, sub. 30. The numbers are broken down in detail in a return of 19 November 1888: HO144/222/A49500M, sub. 3.
66. Warren to Home under-secretary, 21 July 1888: ibid., sub. 24.
67. Sweeney, op. cit., pp. 70–2.
68. Monro to Home under-secretary, 17 August 1886: HO144/172/A43793, sub. 7.
69. Monro to Home Office, 17 May 1887: FO65/1210, ff. 175–8.
70. Pemberton and Lushington to Foreign under-secretary, 12 and 14 June 1888: HO151/4, pp. 148–9, 153.
71. Lushington to Foreign under-secretary, 5 August 1890: FO45/658; Foreign under-secretary to Tornielli, 8 August 1890: FO45/656.
72. Leigh Pemberton to Foreign under-secretary, 29 April, enclosing Police report of 27 April 1891: FO45/677.
73. Edwin Mills, Police Receiver, to Home under-secretary, 24 September 1889 (Melville's expenses for guarding the Shah): HO144/225/A50532; Monro to Sandars, 8 July [1889], in Sandars Papers, box 724, f. 15 (again on the Shah); and Foreign under-secretary to Tornielli, 13 July 1891 (on the Prince of Naples's visit): FO45/675.
74. Police reports and other correspondence on this, from 20 September to 27 October 1886, are in HO144/183/A45225, subs. 1–7, and HO151/3, pp. 204–5. Boulter's name is on the Return of Special Branch officers, dated 19 December 1887, in MEPO5/65 (above, fn. 33).
75. Correspondence between Foreign Office, Home Office and Anderson, 14 January to 4 February 1890: HO45/9816/B7734, subs. 1–2.
76. See, for example, HO144/196/A46891.
77. Monro memorandum, 13 October 1887: HO144/205/A47976D, sub. 1.
78. Monro to Bradford, 10 November 1891; and report by Littlechild, 17 December 1891: HO144/209/A48131, subs. 17–19. Monro recounted this in order to plead for Callan's early release. In fact he was not released until January 1893. The permit to allow Littlechild to visit Callan in Chatham prison is the same file, sub. 10.

79. See Redmond in House of Commons, 21 April 1910: *Hansard*, 5th series, vol. 16, cc. 2421–2.
80. See T. W. Moody, '*The Times* versus Parnell and Co., 1887–90', in *Historical Studies*, vol. 6 (Dublin, 1968), pp. 159–67; and Leon Ò Broin, *The Prime Informer* (1971), *passim*.
81. There is a memorandum from Littlechild about the Parnell papers, dated 19 November 1887, among the Anderson papers: HO144/1537, file 8. The government might have saved itself some embarrassment in this affair if it had consulted Jenkinson. He wrote to Harcourt on July 1888 that he was quite sure Parnell had not been implicated in dynamitism: and he was in a position to know. See Jenkinson to Harcourt, 7 July 1888: Harcourt papers, box 216, ff. 82–5.
82. Labouchere first made his charges in Parliament and in his weekly journal, *Truth*, in March 1890. The file on this is HO144/478/X27302.
83. Lushington memorandum, 2 [May] 1890: ibid., sub. 8.
84. There are some rather pathetic letters from Le Caron to Anderson, dated 14 September 1891, 18 November 1893 and 6 February 1894, in Anderson's papers: HO144/1537, file 5. *Reynolds's Newspaper*, 8 April 1894, p. 1, describes him in his latter years perpetually in fear of being poisoned; and reprints a paragraph from the *Admiralty and Horse Guards Gazette* voicing a suspicion that Le Caron's death was fabricated and that 'the famous spy is now on his way to one of the most distant of our colonies'. On 23 June 1895 (p. 1) *Reynolds's* reported an alleged sighting of Le Caron 'in the halfpenny omnibus that plies between the Strand and Waterloo'.
85. Quoted in J. A. Cole, op. cit., p. 173.
86. Quoted in ibid., p. 176.
87. Le Caron, op. cit., p. 269.
88. *Freedom*, March 1889, p. 14.
89. *The Link*, 8 September 1888, p. 3.
90. *Pall Mall Gazette*, 9 October 1888, p. 3.
91. Quoted in Williams, op. cit., p. 196.
92. See above, p. 72; and the Special Branch personnel listed above, p. 215, n. 33, many of which have Irish names. All the emerging prominent Special Branch men – Melville, Sweeney, Quinn, for example – were born in Ireland.
93. William Morris, 'Art and Socialism', in A. L. Morton (ed.), *Political Writings of William Morris* (1984), p. 132.
94. Robert Louis Stevenson, *The Dynamiter* (Lothian edn, n.d.), p. 8.
95. A. Conan Doyle, *The Sign of the Four* (1890).
96. See Richard Lancelot Green, *The Uncollected Sherlock Holmes* (Harmondsworth, 1983), pp. 41ff.
97. McIntyre's, published in *Reynolds's Newspaper* between 3 February and 26 May, 1895.

Chapter 7

1. See, for example, E. E. Williams, *Made in Germany* (1896); William le Queux, *The Great War in England in 1897* (1894); S. Low, 'Should Europe Disarm?', *Nineteenth Century*, vol. 44 (1898), p. 521; W. W. Crane, 'The Year 1899', *Overland Monthly* (San Francisco), 2nd series, vol. 21 (June 1893), pp. 579–89.

2. See H. Giffard-Ruffe, 'A Plea for Posterity', *Westminister Review*, vol. 156 (1901), p. 26.

3. The best known anti-Semitic work of the time is Arnold White, *The Modern Jew* (1899). See Bernard Gainer, *The Alien Invasion* (1972), ch. 5.

4. Articles on 'national degeneracy' and its causes appear in nearly every issue of every monthly political journal around 1900. See Bernard Porter, 'The Edwardians and their Empire', in Donald Read (ed.), *Edwardian England* (1982), *passim*.

5. This concern begins in 1891, and reaches its peak around 1894–6. It can be followed in the confidential Home Office letter-books for the period, HO151/5–7, *passim*; especially HO151/6, p. 248, and HO151/7, p. 259. The Eton expulsion is reported in *Reynolds's Newspaper*, 8 December 1895, p. 6.

6. See William Barry, 'Anarchist Literature', *Quarterly Review*, vol. 178 (1894), pp. 1–30. 'Eroto-mania' was the term Wilde used to describe his 'illness' in two moving petitions he submitted to the Home Office for his release from Reading gaol. The Home Office's reaction to them was that a man who wrote so well clearly could not be suffering as much as he claimed. See HO45/24514/A56887.

7. R. B. Sherard, *The Real Oscar Wilde* (1916), pp. 112–16. Barlas eventually went mad, reportedly as a result of reading the Bible. On hearing of this Wilde said: 'When I think of all the harm that book has done I despair of ever writing anything to equal it.' E. H. Mikhail (ed.), *Oscar Wilde, Interviews and Recollections* (1979), vol. 2, p. 25.

8. The career of the Legitimation League is best traced through its monthly journal, *The Adult* (1897–8). See also below, pp. 144–5.

9. W. H. Lecky, *Democracy and Liberty* (1896), summarised in *Review of Reviews*, vol. 13 (1896), pp. 366–73; and cf. Goldwin Smith, 'The Impending Revolution', *Nineteenth Century*, vol. 35 (1894), pp. 353–66.

10. *Review of Reviews*, vol. 7 (1893), p. 8.

11. Contemporary accounts of these events include Felix Dubois, *The Anarchist Peril* (1894); and Ernest Vizetelly, *The Anarchists* (1911).

12. *Review of Reviews*, vol. 5 (1892), p. 435.

13. Ibid., vol. 9 (1894), p. 8.

14. On foreign anarchists in Britain, see 'Isabel Meredith' [pseudonym of Olivia and Elena Rossetti], *A Girl Among the Anarchists* (1903): William J. Fishman, *East End Jewish Radicals 1875–1914* (1975); and Hermia Oliver, *The International Anarchist Movement in Late Victorian London* (1983).

15. The latest account of the Walsall affair is in Oliver, op. cit., pp. 77–82. The best account of British anarchism generally is John Quail, *The Slow Burning Fuse. The Lost History of the British Anarchists* (1978).

16. Oliver, op. cit., pp. 99–108.

17. Most of the correspondence on this is in HO45/9741/A55680. The ruins of the shelter survived *in situ* until July 1985, when they were removed by Royal Engineers to Chatham Barracks for restoration: Michael Turner, English Heritage, to author, 21 April 1986.

18. Oliver, op. cit., pp. 111–12.

19. See *Reynolds's Newspaper*, 2 December 1894, p. 8, and 23 December 1894, p. 2. The two were arrested, tried, and fined £48 each. It is not recorded whether they won the competition. Other hoax bombs are reported in *Reynolds's Newspaper* for 4 March 1894, p. 3; 1 April 1894, p. 8; 22 April 1894, p. 5; and 18 November 1894, p. 6.

20. See ibid., 9 April 1893, p. 5; 8 September 1895, p. 1; and Anon, 'Dynamite and Dynamiters', in *Strand Magazine*, vol. 7 (1894), p. 120.
21. This is taken from the *Birmingham News*, 13 February 1892; a cutting from which, together with the rest of the documentation on the Cavargna affair, is in HO144/243/A53582C.
22. See *The Times*, 27 April 1897, p. 9; 28 April, p. 12; 29 April, p. 6; and V. D. Majendie's report of 26 May 1897, in MEPO 2/423.
     Other bombs reported in *Reynolds's Newspaper* included one found in Gaer Railway tunnel near Newport, Mon. (23 April 1893, p. 4); a parcel bomb addressed to a provincial theatre which exploded in Islington station (14 January 1894, p. 1); a bomb found against the wall of the Conservative Club in Great Yarmouth (18 April 1894, p. 5); one found in Blackfriars aimed at Cohen's ironworks, whose foreman had given evidence against Polti (5 August 1894, p. 5); a bomb with an anarchist slogan which exploded in a post office in New Cross (19 August 1894, p. 5); two lots of explosives found planted outside a bank in Walsall and a house in West Hartlepool (14 October 1894, p. 4); a bomb, possibly intended for Asquith, which damaged the house of the Hon. Reginald Brett off South Audley Street, Mayfair (11 November 1894, p. 4); two which exploded in the village of East Rainton in Derbyshire (18 November 1894, p. 1); one which blew up near the Corporation Rate Office in Oldham (30 December 1894, p. 6); another which went off in Ealing station, frightening an old cleaner (9 June 1895, p. 8); and a parcel bomb which injured a man in Bath (23 February 1896, p. 8). The Blackfriars and Audley Street bombs are likely to have been placed by anarchists.
23. There were prosecutions directed against the *Commonweal* in May 1892 and July 1894.
24. The Manchester disturbances, on Ardwick Green, were reported in *Reynolds's Newspaper*, 8 October 1893, p. 8, and *Commonweal*, 14 October 1893, p. 1 and 28 October 1893, p. 1. See below, p. 106.
25. E.g. Christopher Davis's trial in Birmingham in January 1893, reported in *Reynolds's Newspaper*, 29 January, p. 5; Henry Conway's at Marlborough Street court in September 1893, in ibid. 1 October, p. 16; and Edward Leggatt's in West Ham, July 1895 and April 1896, in ibid. 7 July 1895, p. 5 and 26 April 1896, p. 2.
26. E.g. Fergus Hume, *The Year of Miracle* (1891); T. Mullett Ellis, *Zalma* (1895); and W. L. Alden, 'The Purple Death', *Cassell's Magazine*, February 1895.
27. *Tit-Bits*, 14 March 1894, p. 404.
28. E.g. George Griffith, *The Angel of the Revolution* (1893); E. Douglas Fawcett, *Hartman the Anarchist* (1893); and George Glendon, *The Emperor of the Air* (1910).
29. J. S. Fletcher, *The Three Days' Terror* (1901). The same author's *The Ransom for London* (1914) also has its villains using chemistry: in this case a 'fatal ether'.
30. W. Holt-White, *The Earthquake* (1906).
31. For foreign invasion stories see I. F. Clarke, *Voices Prophesying War, 1763–1984* (1966). The leading *alien* invasion story is H. G. Wells's *The War of the Worlds* (1898). The main practitioner of the natural disaster story was a writer called Fred M. White. I. F. Clarke's *The Pattern of Expectation* (1979) is a masterly survey of this whole field. The same author's descriptive catalogue of futuristic novels, *Tale of the Future* (1972), has been my main means of entry into the genre.

32. Examples of people turned into anarchists by tsarist tortures are Mazanoff and Radna in George Griffith, op. cit.; Simonoff in Hume Nisbet, *The Great Secret* (1895); and Zara in George Glendon, op. cit. Others are turned into anarchists by having their wives, lovers or daughters seduced by degenerate members of the ruling classes: e.g. Malister in Fergus Hume, op. cit.; Pahlen in J. Mullett Ellis, op. cit. ('"Father, I am not pure"': p. 105); and Poiccart in Edgar Wallace's *The Four Just Men* (1905). For a real-life example, see below, p. 122.
33. T. Mullett Ellis, op. cit., p. 38.
34. George Griffith, op. cit., p. 393.
35. Robert Cromie. *A New Messiah* (1902).
36. E. Douglas Fawcett, op. cit., pp. 180, 209–13.
37. Hume Nisbet, op. cit., p. 65.
38. 'Ivanoff', 'Anarchists: Their Methods and Organisation', *New Review*, vol. 10 (1894), pp. 9–16. See S. Stepniak's riposte to this, 'Nihilism: As It Is', in ibid., vol. 10, pp. 215–22.
39. *Globe*, 30 July 1895, p. 4.
40. 'Ouida' [Marie Louise de la Ramée], 'The Legislation of Fear', *Fortnightly Review*, n.s., vol. 56 (1894), pp. 552–61.
41. S. Stepniak, 'The Dynamite Scares and Anarchy', in *New Review*, vol. 6 (1892), p. 533.
42. Wordsworth Donisthorpe, 'A Defence of Anarchy', *New Review*, vol. 11 (1894), pp. 283–91.
43. *Review of Reviews*, vol. 9 (1894), p. 223.
44. Quoted in M. A. Muller, *Kropotkin* (1976), p. 169.
45. Letter from Reginald Harbinger in *Morning Post*, 19 September 1898: in HO144/545/A55176, sub. 32.
46. Letter from J. Hunter Watts in *The Times*, 22 February 1894, p. 3.
47. Menzies MacDonald, 'Among the Anarchists', in *Good Words*, vol. 35 (1894), pp. 125–9. See also David Watson, 'An Anarchist Meeting in Scotland', in ibid., vol. 35 (1894), pp. 445–7; and Anon., 'Anarchists in London', *Daily News*, 12 August 1897, p. 5.
48. W. J. Sinclair, letter to *Manchester Courier*, 25 October 1893, in HO144/545/A55176, sub. 2.
49. Reported in *Reynolds's Newspaper*, 20 December 1896, p. 6.
50. Charles Malato, 'Some Anarchist Portraits', *Fortnightly Review*, n.s., vol. 56 (1894), p. 319.
51. Quoted by the *Review of Reviews*, vol. 6 (1892), p. 42, from an article in the *Deutsche Revue*.
52. *Review of Reviews*, vol. 9 (1894), p. 8; and vol. 10 (1894), p. 105.
53. William le Queux, *A Secret Service* (1896), p. 6.
54. Watson, op. cit., p. 447.
55. Auberon Herbert, 'The Ethics of Dynamite', *Contemporary Review*, vol. 65 (1894), pp. 667–87.
56. Letter from Reginald Harbinger in *Morning Post*, 19 September 1898: in HO144/545/A55176, sub. 32.
57. *Review of Reviews*, vol. 5 (1892), p. 436; vol. 10 (1894), p. 7.
58. Notable exceptions were H. B. Samuels, 'Bombs!', *Commonweal*, 25 November 1893, p. 3; and G. Lawrence, 'Why I advocate Physical Force to repel the aggressive force of the Governing Class', *Liberty*, March 1894, p. 22.

59. *Liberty*, May 1894, p. 36. The best statement of this point of view is a leading article, 'Anarchism and Homicidal Outrage', *Freedom*, December 1893, p. 81.

60. *Freedom*, August 1894, p. 49.

61. Ibid., August–September 1896, 'Supplement', p. 4.

62. *Torch*, November 1894, front page. The *Alarm*, which ran for just four months in 1896, was particularly insistent on its pacifism. See especially the first issue, 26 July 1896, p. 1.

63. *Commonweal*, 31 March 1894, p. 2.

64. Ibid., loc. cit.

65. E.g. 'Ouida', op. cit., *passim*; and *Review of Reviews*, vol. 10 (1894), pp. 103–4.

66. *Review of Reviews*, vol. 7 (1893), p. 8.

67. Rosebery in House of Lords, 17 July 1894: *Hansard*, 4th series, vol. 27, c. 128.

68. Other calls for legislation against the anarchists were made in the House of Commons on 14 and 27 December 1893: ibid., 4th series, vol. 19, cc. 1369–70 and vol. 20, c. 205; and on 19 February and 28 June 1894: ibid., 4th series, vol. 21, cc. 721–2 and vol. 26, cc. 456–7.

69. Asquith in House of Commons, 14 November 1893: ibid., 4th series, vol. 18, c. 888.

70. Ibid., vol. 18, c. 891.

71. Ibid., vol. 27, c. 142 (17 July 1894) and vol. 26, c. 1052 (6 July 1894).

72. Ibid., vol. 27, c. 129 (17 July 1894).

73. S. Stepniak, 'The Dynamite Scare and Anarchy', *New Review*, vol. 6 (1892), pp. 532–4.

74. *The Times*, 17 February 1894, p. 5.

75. See Bernard Porter, *The Refugee Question, passim*; and 33 & 34 Vict. c. 52, para. 3.

76. *Hansard*, 4th series, vol. 26, cc. 1052, 1056; and cf. Rosebery to Queen, 13 July 1894; 'With regard to the Anarchists, Mr. Asquith assures him that not a single conspiracy against any foreign power or potentate has been hatched in this country': RA A70/55.

77. Goschen to Salisbury, 10 November 1897: Salisbury papers, A/129/30.

78. See, for example, Tornielli to Foreign Office, 13 July 1891: FO45/677; and Memo from M. de Staal, 5 March 1892: FO65/1429, ff. 87–91.

79. Phipps to Salisbury, 16 March 1892, in HO45/10254/X36450, sub. 1; Monson to Rosebery, 22 March 1893, in HO144/587/B2840C, sub. 21c; Del Mazo to Rosebery, 20 November 1893, in FO72/1938; Monson to Rosebery, 20 February 1894, in FO7/1213; Canevaro circular despatch of 29 September 1898, in FO45/791; Russian *pro-memoria* of October 1900, in FO412/67; Foreign Office memorandum of 26 November 1901, in FO83/1970; and Bernstorff to Lansdowne, 28 April 1904, in FO371/78.

80. *Hansard*, 4th series, vol. 26, c. 1055 (6 July 1894).

81. *The Times*, 16 February 1894, p. 9.

82. Rosebery to Wolff, 22 November 1893; in FO72/1923.

83. Sanderson minute, 31 March 1892, attached to 'Col. Majendie's Minute', 23 March 1892: FO27/3102.

84. Salisbury to F. R. St John, 12 October 1898 (copy): HO45/10254/X36450.

85. Salisbury to Sir Philip Currie, 27 October 1898: FO45/981; copies in FO361/364, ff. 30–1, and in HO45/10254/X36450.

86. Foreign Office to Baron Eckhardstein, 3 November 1900: FO83/1970.

87. O'Conor (Constantinople) to Lansdowne, 10 February 1902 (copy): HO144/608/B32482, sub. 16.
88. Undated minute by Lansdowne on Foreign Office memorandum of 26 November 1901: FO83/1970.

Chapter 8

1. There are printed copies, dated March 1899, in HO45/9758/A62185.
2. The proceedings of the Conference, and correspondence with the British representatives, are preserved in HO45/10254/X36450, and in FO45/784. See also Richard Bach Jenson, 'The International Anti-Anarchist Conference of 1898 and the Origins of Interpol', *Journal of Contemporary History*, vol. 16 (1981).
3. The reason for their withdrawal is not stated, but a minute by Lansdowne on a memorandum by Sanderson of 8 December 1901, in FO83/1970, makes it clear that it was perforce.
4. Salisbury to Lushington, 23 November 1898 (draft): Salisbury papers, A/99/87.
5. E.g. Salisbury to Currie, 27 October 1898: FO45/981; Currie to Salisbury, 3 December 1898: printed copy in FO45/784.
6. 'Our colleagues could not fail to recognize the general efficacy of English law to meet the dangers of anarchism . . .': Currie to Salisbury, 22 December 1898: ibid.; and cf. memorandum by Bradford, 28 December 1898: Salisbury papers, A/96/76.
7. Rosebery to del Mazo, 13 December 1893: FO72/1938.
8. *Hansard*, 4th series, vol. 38, c. 1246; and cf. Rosebery to the Queen, 13 July 1894: 'Mr Asquith assures him that . . . our system of police supervision here is much more efficacious than that pursued on the continent.' RA A70/55.
9. Digby to Foreign under-secretary, 10 January 1902: FO83/1970.
10. See E. R. Henry memorandum of 7 January 1902: HO45/10254/A36450; and below, p. 159.
11. *Law Reports, Queen's Bench Division*, 1891 vol. 1, pp. 149–68.
12. *The Times*, 17 November 1892, p. 11.
13. *Law Reports, Queen's Bench Division*, 1894 vol. 2, pp. 415–19; *Law Times*, vol. 71 (1894), pp. 404–6. The Home Office file on the case is HO144/485/X37842.
14. E.g. Barrington (Foreign Office) to Bradford, 5 March 1892: FO65/1430, ff. 94–5; Home Office minute on a reply to the government of Uruguay, on Sanderson to Home under-secretary, 21 January 1897: HO144/545/A55176, sub. 31; and Currie's statement to the Rome Anti-Anarchist Conference, 3 December 1898, printed in FO45/784.
15. E.g. O'Conor, Constantinople, to Lansdowne, 10 February 1902 (copy): HO144/608/B32482, sub. 16. See also Bradford to Barrington, 29 March 1892: 'In fact the attacks on the Russian Govt.' (in Russian emigré journals) 'are characterised by moderation as compared with what is published with impunity in English Papers agst. the Govt. of our own country': FO65/1430.
16. See Alan Kimball, 'The Harassment of Russian Revolutionaries Abroad: The London Trial of Vladimir Burtsev in 1898', *Oxford Slavonic Papers*, vol. 6 (1973). The Home Office files on the case, which Kimball did not see but add very little, are HO144/272/A59222 and A59222B. There is also some valuable material in FO65/1543 and 1544, and in the Salisbury papers, A/129/30–92 *passim*.

17. For references to the Walsall case, see above, p. 219, n. 15; and below, pp. 138–42.
18. See *The Times* reports on their trial, especially 17 April 1894, p. 13; 24 April, p. 13; 3 May, p. 14; 4 May, p. 19. The Home Office file on the case is HO144/259/A55860.
19. The incriminating article is in the *Commonweal*, 9 April 1892, p. 57. A report of Nicoll's trial is in *The Times*, 7 May 1892, p. 14.
20. See ibid., 1 August 1894, p. 3.
21. Brall's trial is reported in *Reynolds's Newspaper*, 3 June 1894, p. 5, and 8 July 1894, p. 4.
22. Minute by Lushington, 13 February 1894: HO45/9861/B13077C, sub. 4.
23. Gosselin to Matthews, 10 March 1892: Sandars papers, box c. 725, ff. 34–5.
24. The Home Office requested the 'gradual' reduction on 15 December 1891: HO151/5, pp. 170–1. On 24 December the Police Commissioner replied that he was anxious about this, but agreed to it 'Having regard . . . to the facilities we possess for strengthening our office at Head quarters upon short notice': MEPO1/54, p. 81. The Home Secretary sanctioned it on 31 December: HO151/5, pp. 178–9. By August 1892 the reduction had been effected: ibid., p. 239.
25. Bradford to Home under-secretary, 29 November 1894: MEPO1/54, p. 256; Cunninghame to Bradford, 1 December 1894: HO151/5, p. 524.
26. The report originated in the *Birmingham Daily Post*, 27 February 1894, and was then taken up by the *Westminster Gazette*, 27 February 1894, p. 5, the *Manchester Courier*, 27 February 1894, p. 5; and the *Police Review*, 9 March 1894, p. 113.
27. Littlechild's resignation and Melville's promotion are reported in *Police Orders* for 10 April and 5 May 1893: MEPO7/55, pp. 264 and 340; in the *Police Review*, 17 April 1893, p. 188, and 26 June, p. 310; and confirmed by Bradford to the Home under-secretary, 19 December 1899: MEPO1/54, pp. 287–9. Melville was transferred from section 'B' to section 'D' in order to take over Littlechild's job; Patrick Quinn switched the other way to fill Melville's post in section 'B'.
28. *Who's Who*, 1914.
29. See *Police Chronicle*, 6 October 1894, p. 6, quoting from an article in the *Dublin County Telegraph*.
30. Ibid.
31. *The Times*, 24 April 1894, p. 13.
32. *Police Chronicle*, 24 February 1894, p. 1, and 6 October 1894, p. 6.
33. *Police Review*, 13 February 1893, p. 73.
34. Arthur Griffiths, *Mysteries of Police and Crime* (1898; 2nd. edn. 1904), vol. 1, pp. 130–1.
35. H. L. Adam, *C.I.D.: Behind the Scenes at Scotland Yard* (1931), p. 167; George Dilnot, *Great Detectives and their Methods* (1929), p. 175.
36. See George Dilnot, *Scotland Yard: Methods and Organisation of the Metropolitan Police* (1915), pp. 250–1; *Police Chronicle*, 6 October 1894, p. 6; and *Freedom*, May 1894, p. 28: 'It is said there is not an Englishman in Melville's gang.' Melville and Sweeney both came from County Kerry; Quinn from 'Castlecarra, Ballyglass': MEPO3/2896. Melville was a Catholic.
37. See the Metropolitan Police's 'General Orders', 1907 edn, p. 1261, para. 52, in MEPO3/1790; and Harold Brust, '*I Guarded Kings*' (n.d.), p. 44. Melville spoke fluent French, and some Italian.
38. Brust, op. cit., p. 44.

39. Herbert T. Fitch, *Traitors Within* (1933), p. 19; Harold Brust, *In Plain Clothes* (1937), p. 64. Conan Doyle is attacked in *Police Review*, 30 January 1893, p. 49.
40. Edwin T. Woodhall, *Crime and the Supernatural* (1935), ch. 8.
41. The earliest published version of the story is by 'Alfred Aylmer' [=Arthur Griffiths], 'The Detective in Real Life', *Windsor Magazine*, vol. 1 (May 1895), pp. 505–6.
42. *Reynolds's Newspaper*, 25 March 1894, p. 1.
43. Anti-Semitism pervades Basil Thomson's *Queer People* (1922), for example, and Herbert Fitch's *Traitors Within*. John Sweeney comes out in favour of alien legislation and the suppression of anarchist doctrine in *At Scotland Yard* (1904), pp. 202, 224, 279 and 346.
44. MEPO3/1760, p. 1261, paras 51–3.
45. Thomson, op. cit., p. 47.
46. Brust, '*I Guarded Kings*', p. 33.
47. Sweeney, op. cit., p. 19.
48. Brust, '*I Guarded Kings*', p. 46.
49. Report by Anderson on 'Henri Talbot', 24 August 1894: HO144/587/B2840C, sub. 42a.
50. Brust, '*I Guarded Kings*', p. 86.
51. Report by Sweeney, counter-signed by Melville, 10 February 1897: FO72/2048.
52. Sweeney, op. cit., pp. 81–2.
53. Lushington to Foreign Office, 5 August 1890: FO45/658; Police report by Melville, counter-signed by Littlechild, 27 April 1891: FO45/677 (both on Malatesta); Bradford to Barrington, 29 March 1892: FO65/1430 (on Burtsev and others); Melville report on Countess Hugo, 2 August 1894: HO144/587/B2840C, sub. 41.
54. Strictly all communications between police forces were supposed to go through normal diplomatic channels, but it was clear that they did not always do so: see, for example, the minute by 'JBS' on Lushington to Foreign Office, 6 June 1892: FO64/1289.
55. Report by E. R. Henry, 7 January 1902: HO45/10254/A36450.
56. Ibid.
57. Report by Anderson, 24 May 1892: HO144/587/B2840C, sub. 8.
58. The history of this dispute can be traced through HO144/587/B2840C and HO144/594/B16627; Home Office confidential letter-books HO151/5 and 6; and various Foreign Office files.
59. Minute by 'CM' (Murdoch), 17 August 1897: HO144/587/B2840C, sub. 92. An example of this procedure is recounted in a report by Quinn on a man called Kaulitz Farlow, 31 March 1902: HO45/10482/X77377, sub. 171.
60. Around 1890 H. Thynne of the Irish Office wrote to Balfour about 'the system now called shadowing, of which (to borrow a term from logicians) the "essential difference" is that the policeman engaged in watching hands his suspect over to another policeman who takes up the duty before the first man can be relieved': Balfour Papers, PRO30/60/7. There is a description of shadowing by Patrick McIntyre in *Reynolds's Newspaper*, 17 February 1895, p. 5.
61. Sweeney, op. cit., p. 35.
62. Ex-Detective Inspector W. H. Thompson, *Guard from the Yard* (1938), p. 33.
63. Fitch, *Traitors Within*, pp. 23–5; *Memoirs of a Royal Detective* (1935), p. 234.

64. See J. G. Littlechild, *Reminiscences* . . . (1894), pp. 76–7; Andrew Lansdowne, *A Life's Reminiscences. Scotland Yard* (1893), pp. 153–4; Brust, *'In Plain Clothes'*, p. 24; George Dilnot, *Great Detectives and Their Methods* (1929), pp. 176–8; Fitch, *Traitors Within*, pp. 24–6, 29, and *Memoirs* . . . , p. 22; Sweeney, op. cit., p. 179.
65. W. C. Hart, *Confessions of an Anarchist* (1906), p. 18.
66. Report by Chief Inspector Swanson, 27 June 1893: HO144/249/A54906.
67. Memorandum by Bradford, 24 May 1902: HO144/545/A55176, sub. 44.
68. Bradford to Home under-secretary, 28 April 1902: HO45/10254/X36450.
69. Sweeney, op. cit., p. 204.
70. Bradford to Home under-secretary, 28 April 1902: HO45/10254/X36450.
71. Dilnot, *Great Detectives and their Methods*, p. 175.
72. See *Reynolds's Newspaper*, 24 April 1892, p. 5, amd 5 August 1894, p. 2; *Commonweal*, 23 April 1892, p. 1, and 25 June 1892, p. 2; *Freedom*, August 1894, p. 56. There is an account of a police raid on an anarchist newspaper, presented as fiction, in 'Isabel Meredith', *A Girl Among the Anarchists* (1903), pp. 294–9.
73. *Reynolds's Newspaper*, 18 February 1894, p. 8.
74. E.g. Fitch, *Memoirs of a Royal Detective*; Brust, *'I Guarded Kings'*; Thompson, *Guard from the Yard*. Sweeney and McIntyre where given the rather less prestigious job of guarding the spy Le Caron from 1888 until his death in 1894: see Sweeney, op. cit., pp. 148–51; *Reynolds's Newspaper*, 12 May 1895, p. 5; J. A. Cole, *Prince of Spies. Henri le Caron* (1984), p. 181.
75. Fitch, *Memoirs* . . . , p. 187.
76. S. T. Felstead (ed.), *Steinhauer: The Kaiser's Master Spy. The Story as Told by Himself* (1930), pp. 310–19.
77. See report by McBrien and Melville, 3 December 1902, with minutes by Henry and others: HO144/683/102620; report by Henry, 9 December 1902: HO144/668/X84164, sub. 7; and memorandum by Henry, 16 March 1903: HO144/545/A55176, sub. 51.
78. Above, pp. 102–3.
79. Edwin T. Woodhall, *Secrets of Scotland Yard* (1936), p. 96, referring to Russian nihilists.
80. See 'Précis of the Case for the Convicts', and the memorandum on it by A. G. E[agleton], 12 September 1895: HO144/242/A53582, sub. 28.
81. Anderson's insistence that Bourdin's bomb was intended for Greenwich Observatory is reported in *Reynolds's Newspaper*, 18 February 1894, p. 8. Asquith, writing to the Queen on 22 February, claimed that the fragments which were found 'point to the conclusion that he was intending to use the bomb . . . for the purpose of injuring the Greenwich Observatory', but did not say how, and then in the very next sentence assured her that 'The character of the explosive was such that it could not have done any serious damage to a building': RA B47/27. In much the same way Daly's bombs in 1884 may have been interpreted in the worst possible light: see above, p. 212, n. 18.
82. Note from French ambassador in Berne enclosed in Waddington to Rosebery, 10 December 1892: FO27/3099. Further correspondence on this is in HO144/485/X37842B, sub. 1.
83. Melville MacNaghten, *Days of My Years* (1914), p. 83.
84. Brust, *'I Guarded Kings'*, p. 46.
85. Fitch, *Traitors Within*, pp. 19, 47.
86. Rosebery in House of Lords, 17 July 1894: *Hansard*, 4th series, vol. 27, c. 127.

87. Brust, '*I Guarded Kings*', p. 23.
88. Bunsen to Grey, 4 August 1906 (copy): HO144/757/118516, sub. 36.
89. Henry to Home Office, 21 August 1906: ibid.
90. Smither to Bunsen, 29 July 1907; Bunsen to Grey, 2 August 1907; memorandum by 'EGD', 2 December 1907: FO371/336.
91. R. J. Johnson, 'The Okhrana Abroad, 1887–1917: A Study in International Police Cooperation' (Ph.D. dissertation, Columbia University, 1970), p. 84.
92. Fitch, *Memoirs . . .* , p. 186.

Chapter 9

1. See, for example, *Freedom*, March 1892, p. 20, March 1894, p. 12, May 1894, p. 28, August 1894, p. 56, and May 1895, pp. 10–11; *Commonweal* 25 June 1892, p. 2, and 2 July 1892, p. 4; *Torch*, February 1895, p. 13. For more detailed references, see Bernard Porter, *The Origins of Britain's Political Police* (Warwick Working Papers in Social History, 1985), pp. 11–12.
2. *Commonweal*, 23 January 1892, p. 13.
3. See, for example, 'The Alleged Anarchist Conspiracy', *Freedom*, May 1892, p. 34; and 'Precis of the Case for the Convicts' [1895], in HO144/242/A53582, sub. 28.
4. *Justice*, 28 April 1894, p. 1.
5. David Nicoll, *The Greenwich Mystery* (1897), *passim*.
6. *Liberty*, March 1894, p. 20.
7. Nicoll, op. cit., p. 16.
8. *Liberty*, September 1894, p. 68.
9. Nicoll, op. cit., p. 11; and see 'Bombs!' in *Commonweal*, 25 November 1893, p. 3.
10. *Freedom*, October 1901, p. 59.
11. *Torch*, February 1895, p. 13.
12. *Liberty*, March 1894, p. 20.
13. *Commonweal*, 28 April 1894, p. 2.
14. *Freedom*, October 1896, p. 104; and cf. *Liberty*, September–October 1896, p. 104.
15. *Commonweal*, October 1888, p. 2.
16. Ibid., August 1887, p. 43.
17. *Reynolds's Newspaper*, 10 January 1892, p. 8; 14 February 1892, p. 3; 20 March 1892, p. 3; 10 April 1892, p. 1; 17 April 1892, p. 6; and (for reports of the case) *passim*.
18. Patrick McIntyre's, published between 3 February and 26 May, and those of 'Tornon' of the 'Secret Service Police', published between 4 August and 1 September.
19. *Reynolds's Newspaper*, 10 November 1895, pp. 1, 6, 8.
20. Ibid., 12 May 1895, p. 1, and 10 November 1895, p. 1.
21. See Bernard Porter, *The Refugee Question* (Cambridge, 1979), pp. 114–16.
22. *Labour World*, 27 September 1890.
23. *Freedom*, February 1897, p. 9. 'Jones' was a police spy who gave evidence against the Fenian Edward Ivory, *alias* Bell, in November 1896.
24. Metropolitan Police memorandum initialled by Anderson, 13 December 1898: HO45/10254/X36450, sub. 77.
25. Confidential 'Observations' by Anderson, 14 January 1899: ibid., sub. 92.

26. E. R. Henry report, 7 January 1902: ibid., sub. 126.
27. In connection with the Walsall case: Anderson to Home under-secretary, 28 April 1892: HO144/242/A53582, sub. 15.
28. Complaints from Irish MPs of being shadowed in 1890 are referred to in the Balfour papers, PRO30/60/7.
29. No one else's names appear both on the 19 March 1887 list of Irish Branch personnel (above, p. 208, n. 70), and on the 21 December 1887 list (above, p. 215, n. 33).
30. Bathurst (Scotland Yard) to Murdoch (Home Office), 17 November 1894: HO45/9977/X50089, sub. 1.
31. *Police Review*, 13 April 1894, p. 173.
32. Minute on cover of HO45/9977/X50089, sub. 1.
33. *Reynolds's Newspaper*, 19 May 1895, p. 5.
34. Ibid., 26 May 1895, p. 3.
35. Report by Alexander D. MacKellar, 1 March 1895: HO45/9977/X50089, sub. 4.
36. There are three versions of this story: one by McIntyre's solicitor, W. H. Morris, to the Home Secretary, 12 February 1895, where he talks of his catching cold as a result of having to stand around naked waiting examination at St Thomas's Hospital: HO45/9977/X50089, sub. 3; the police surgeon's report, 1 March 1895: ibid., sub. 4; and McIntyre's own account, in *Reynolds's Newspaper*, 26 May 1895, p. 3.
37. Bradford to Home under-secretary, 12 December 1894: HO45/9977/X50089, sub. 2.
38. Morris to Home Secretary, 12 February 1895: ibid., sub. 3.
39. Memorandum by A. G. E[agleton], 12 September 1895: HO144/242/A53582, sub. 28.
40. *Police Review*, 1 November 1895, p. 522; and cf. ibid., 11 January, p. 20, and 20 September, pp. 451–2; and *Reynolds's Newspaper*, 15 September 1895, p. 1, and 3 November 1895, p. 1.
41. *Reynolds's Newspaper*, 14 April 1895, p. 4.
42. E.g. minute by (?)H.S., 14 September 1895: HO144/242/A53582, sub. 28.
43. Anderson to Home under-secretary, 28 April 1892: ibid., sub. 15.
44. Minute by Matthews, 2 May 1892, on *idem*; minutes by Lushington, 22 June 1892, and Matthews, 15 July 1892: ibid., sub. 20.
45. The correspondence on this is in ibid., sub. 28.
46. Minute by (?)H.S., 14 September 1895: ibid., sub. 28.
47. *Reynolds's Newspaper*, 14 April 1895, p. 4.
48. See, for example, the reply by Chief Inspector Donald S. Swanson, 27 June 1893, in response to a request for information on this question from the British High Commissioner in Cyprus: HO144/249/A54906.
49. Deakin's statement is summarised in John Quail, *The Slow Burning Fuse* (1978), p. 105. For Coulon's expulsion, see ibid., p. 111.
50. See, for example, his letter published in *Reynolds's Newspaper*, 21 April 1895, p. 5; a report of a libel action initiated by him against McIntyre, in ibid. 28 April 1895, p. 4; and a flysheet beginning 'Anarchy is too true a doctrine . . .', in the British Library (under 'Anarchy' in the catalogue).
51. Anderson to Home under-secretary, 28 April 1892, makes it clear that the Branch knew of the plot from the beginning: HO144/242/A53582, sub. 15.
52. George Dilnot, *Great Detectives and their Methods* (1929), p. 174.

53. E.g. Harcourt to Spencer, 17 August(?) 1888: 'I agree with you as to Anderson's appointment. He was worse than useless & I should think in the U-K it was impossible to find a more unfit man for the place in which [he] has been put – except perhaps the Chief [Warren] under whom he will serve.' JPSP, Harcourt corresp., box 3.
54. Above, p. 71.
55. Lushington to Bradford, 31 December 1891: HO151/5, pp. 178–9.
56. Minute by Sanderson, 31 March 1892, attached to 'Col. Majendie's Minute' of 23 March: FO27/3102.
57. E.g. Dilnot, op. cit., pp. 174–5; and Melville's own boast in *Who's Who* (1914), that he had 'taken an active part in the suppression of Anarchism'.
58. Melville's letter is quoted in a report by Rachkovskii, head of the Foreign branch of the Okhrana, dated 10/12 July 1897, in the Okhrana Archive, Vc-2. I was first alerted to this by Donald Senese's unpublished article '*Le vil Melville*: Evidence from the Okhrana File on the Trial of Vladimir Burtsev', which uses the same source. It is also cited by R. J. Johnson, 'The Okhrana Abroad, 1885–1917: A Study in International Police Cooperation' (Ph.D. dissertation, Columbia University, 1970), pp. 71ff; who however confuses William (here 'G.' for 'Guillaume') Melville with Melville MacNaghton.
59. See, for example, John Sweeney, *At Scotland Yard* (1904), p. 224.
60. Salisbury to Hatzfeldt, 9 August 1900 (draft): FO64/1507. Bradford's objections to the proposed visit, in a letter to the Home under-secretary, 2 August 1900, is in FO64/1512, ff. 76–8; and in HO144/527/X79683, sub. 2. That same file contains refusals to similar requests from Italy, January 1901 (sub. 3), and the Netherlands, February 1901 (sub. 4). On the 1844 case, see F. B. Smith, 'British Post Office Espionage, 1844', *Historical Studies* (Melbourne), vol. 14, no. 54 (1970).
61. Minute by Chalmers, 5 December 1906: HO144/757/118516, sub. 47. There is correspondence about the necessity of acting through diplomatic channels in cases of extradition, in HO144/542/A53204.
62. Donald Senese's translation from the original *Russian* translation: op. cit.
63. See Alan Kimball, 'The Harassment of Russian Revolutionaries Abroad: The London Trial of Vladimir Burtsev in 1898,' *Oxford Slavonic Papers*, vol. 6 (1973).
64. Okhrana Archive (Hoover Institution), Vc, folders 2–3, *passim*.
65. Above, pp. 115.
66. *The Adult*, vol. 2, no. 6 (July 1898), p. 175.
67. Sweeney, op. cit., p. 179.
68. The full indictment is reproduced in Arthur Calder-Marshall, *Havelock Ellis* (1959), pp. 165–6.
69. Accounts of the trial are to be found in all biographies of Havelock Ellis, including the latest by Phyllis Grosskurth, *Havelock Ellis: A Biography* (1980), ch. 13; in Arthur Calder-Marshall, *Lewd, Blasphemous and Obscene* (1972), part 5; and in Havelock Ellis, *My Life* (1940; new edn. 1967). *The Times* reported that the prosecution had promised Bedborough leniency in return for his assurances: 1 November 1898, p. 14.
70. Sweeney, op. cit., pp. 189–90.
71. Sweeney describes his work on a related obscenity case in ibid., pp. 190–7.
72. Sanderson memorandum, 8 December 1901: FO83/1970; Lansdowne to Sir C. Scott, 4 February 1902: printed copy in 'Correspondence respecting the Measures to be taken for the Prevention of Anarchist Crimes', FO412/68, p. 5.

73. Bradford to Home under-secretary, 2 August 1900 (copy): FO64/1512, ff. 76–8.
74. Salisbury to Hatzfeldt, 9 August 1900 (draft): FO64/1507.
75. 'Alfred Aylmer', 'The Detective in Real Life', *Windsor Magazine*, vol. 1 (1895), p. 505; Dilnot, op. cit., p. 175.
76. See, for example, Basil Thomson, *Queer People* (1922); Herbert T. Fitch, *Traitors Within* (1933), and *Memoirs of a Royal Detective* (1935); Harold Brust, *In Plain Clothes* (1937), and *'I Guarded Kings'* (n.d.); and Sweeney, op. cit.
77. *Police Review*, 17 April 1893, p. 188.

Chapter 10

1. Melville's career after 1903 is difficult to trace. He gave evidence at the preliminary hearing of the case of the traitor Parrott in November 1912. The report of his funeral in *The Times*, 6 February 1918, p. 9, describes him as 'recently of the Military Intelligence Department of the War Office'. A Lieut. Curtis Bennett, RN, accompanied his coffin to the graveside. Nicholas Hiley tells me that Bennett was in Admiralty Intelligence, seconded in 1917 to MI5.
2. *The Times*, 10 November 1903, p. 9.
3. 'Standing Orders' for 1 December 1903: MEPO7/65, p. 985. The same volume records some other Special Branch resignations at around the same time: PS Maguire (CID-c) on 11 July; Inspector Sweeney (CID-d) on 7 September; PC Quinn (CID-c) on 5 October; and PS Flood (CID-b) on 9 November.
4. Cunynghame to Henry, 3 December 1903: HO148/7, f. 480.
5. Henry to Home under-secretary, 29 April 1903: HO45/9718/A51540, sub. 5.
6. The file number is HO144/928/A53778. Its subject-matter is referred to in a Home Office Register: HO46/139. I am told that the items relating to Melville's expenses have, in any case, been removed from it: D. J. Blackwood to author, 20 June 1986.
7. Information given me by Nicholas Hiley, and confirmed from Sir James Benjamin Melville's obituary in *The Times*, 2 May 1931, p. 8.
8. MEPO3/2896.
9. See ibid.; D.P., 'A Policeman to Remember. Sir Patrick Quinn, MVO', *Police Journal*, October 1985; and Metropolitan Police Standing Orders, 1 December 1903, p. 985 and 9 December 1903, p. 1001: MEPO7/65.
10. For example, Troup to Henry, 31 May 1910 and 2 August 1913: HO148/16 f. 32, and HO148/20 f. 273.
11. 'D.P.', op. cit.
12. John Sweeney, *At Scotland Yard* (1904); Parmeggiani vs. Sweeney, reported in *The Times*, 26 October 1905, p. 13, 27 October, p. 13, 28 October, p. 3 and 31 October, p. 3; and HO144/606/B31076. Sweeney had accused Parmeggiani of being an anarchist and a 'fence'. The jury decided for him on the first count, and for Parmeggiani – but with the award of only a farthing damages – on the second.
13. W. J. Corbet, 'What Should England Do to be Saved?' *Westminster Review*, vol. 155 (1901), p. 612.
14. See Bernard Porter, 'The Edwardians and their Empire', in Donald Read (ed.), *Edwardian England* (1982).
15. See Herbert T. Fitch, *Traitors Within* (1933), p. 19.

16. Blackwell to Henry, 29 November 1913: HO148/20, f. 693. Franz Ferdinand's visit lasted from 15 to 21 November.

17. On the spy novel, see Julian Symonds, *Bloody Murder. From the Detective Story to the Crime Novel: A History* (1972), ch. 16; David A. Stafford, 'Spies and Gentlemen: the Birth of the British Spy Novel', *Victorian Studies*, vol. 24, no. 4 (1981), and 'Conspiracy and Xenophobia: the Popular Spy Novels of William Le Queux, 1893–1914', *Europe* (Montreal), vol. 4, no. 2 (1981). Stafford also makes the point about the Edwardians' loss of confidence.

18. Christopher Andrew, *Secret Service* (1985), p. 26.

19. David Stafford, 'Spies and Gentlemen', loc. cit., *passim*.

20. Nicholas Hiley, 'The Failure of British Espionage against Germany, 1907–1914', *Historical Journal*, vol. 26 (1983), p. 868, fn. 3.

21. S. T. Felstead (ed.), *Steinhauer: The Kaiser's Master Spy. The Story as Told by Himself* (1930), p. 10.

22. Ibid., p. 53; Charles Lowe, 'About German Spies', *Contemporary Review*, vol. 97 (1910), p. 42; and see David French, 'Spy Fever in Britain, 1900–1915', *Historical Journal*, vol. 21 (1978), p. 363.

23. Basil Thomson, *Queer People* (1922), p. 275.

24. Below, pp. 157 and 178.

25. Most of these augmentations and reductions can be traced through Home Office 'Entry books', HO149/15–22, and HO148/1–5.

26. Quinn to Henry, 7 July 1909; Henry to Troup, 12 July 1909; and Troup to Henry, 12 July 1909: MEPO2/1987.

   The Metropolitan Police files bearing on augmentations of the Special Branch between the mid-1890s and 1909 are incomplete, and many of the relevant Home Office files (e.g. 135053, 159100, 181321 and 303771) have been destroyed. Because of this, estimates of the Branch's strength in this period vary between Allason's fifteen in 1903 (*The Branch*, p. 16), which he claims is taken from 'a PRO document' which he has not had time to trace (Allason to author, 3 August 1984 and 18 September 1985); and the Special Branch's own figure of seventy-four in 1905, which it says is based on 'informed folk-lore' (A/Commander G. L. V. Ison to author, 26 November 1985). If the port police are counted in, Commander Ison's informed folk-lore looks to be slightly nearer the mark than Allason's mysterious 'document'.

27. E. R. Henry to Home Office, 18 May 1904: HO144/757/118516, sub. 2; Chalmers (Home Office) to Foreign Office, 30 May 1904: FO371/78.

28. Henry minute of 22 June 1906: HO144/834/144519, sub. 3.

29. The comment on 'dullness' is found in the issue for January 1905, p. 1, and is typical of others around then. Reports of penury are in *Freedom*, January 1905, p. 1; January–February 1906, p. 41; and August 1906, p. 28.

30. J. Petrikovsky to DPP, 4 July 1902: HO45/10192/B30732C, sub. 361; and see William J. Fishman, *East End Jewish Radicals 1875–1914* (1975).

31. See Home Office Daily Registers for 1905 and 1906, HO46/145 and 148, especially under 'Miscellaneous Criminal: Foreign' and 'Police: Metropolitan'. Most of the files of correspondence have been destroyed, though one or two (e.g. HO144/545/A55176 and HO144/834/114519) survive.

32. Crown Agent, Edinburgh, to Scottish under-secretary, 19 September 1906; Troup to Gascoigne, 20 September 1906; and MacNaghten minute, 20 September 1906: HO144/757/118516, sub. 39.

33. The Home Office file on Sipido's case is HO144/566/A61909.
34. E.g. Currie to Foreign Office, 30 November 1901: FO45/837; MacDonell, cypher telegram, to Foreign Office, 23 April 1902: FO83/1970; Goschen to Grey, 16 September 1907: FO371/196; and HO144/1112/202225, *passim*.
35. The deployment of Special Branch men on royal protection duty abroad can easily be traced through Home Office Registers (HO46/130–181) and Entry Books (HO148/3–22); and in one or two surviving files, such as the one about Princess Ena's marriage to the Spanish king, 1906, in HO45/10332/136042. There is a letter from the Home Office to the Metropolitan Police Receiver on 'special outfits', 21 May 1908, in HO148/13, f. 154.
36. Henry to Home Office, 17 December 1914: registered in HO46/181.
37. The correspondence on this is in HO45/10651/211757. The King and Henry both thought that Henry's previous Indian experience made him the best man for the job. Lord Morley, however, initially opposed the plan on the grounds that the Indian police might take it as a slight.
38. See references to letters from Henry to the Home Office, 22 May 1913, in HO46/175; and 9 January 1914, in HO46/181.
39. See references to letters from Henry to the Home Office, 17 November 1904, in HO46/142 and 14 June 1905, in HO46/145; the letter from Troup to Henry in HO151/9, f. 545; and HO144/1079/193000, *passim*.
40. Cunynghame to [?], 9 April 1907: HO45/10533/150939, sub. 1; Frank Fowell and Frank Palmer, *Censorship in England* (1913), p. 205.
41. HO144/1079/193000.
42. Chalmers minute, 30 August 1906: HO144/757/118516.
43. Bunsen to Grey, 3 January 1907: FO371/364.
44. Cutting from *Daily Mirror*, 31 January 1905, in HO45/10315/125890. At one stage the police contemplated charging the Sausage King with 'a high misdemeanour for doing an act likely to embroil us with a foreign country' (Henry to Home Office, 1 February 1905, in ibid.), but before it came to this he appears to have given way.
45. See *Hansard*, 4th series, vol. 174, cc. 1319–20; correspondence relating to Cremer's question in FO371/323; and E. R. Henry to Gladstone, 9 June 1907, in H. Gladstone Papers, BL Add. MS 46064, f. 196. Two years before this the Foreign Secretary had reduced a ten-page police memorandum on a nihilist conference to a few lines for transmission to the Russians, on the grounds that they 'have their own agent here, watching these people'. Note by T. H. Sanderson on Henry to Sanderson, 10 May 1905, in FO65/1720.
46. R. J. Johnson, 'The Okhrana Abroad, 1885–1917' (Ph.D. dissertation, Columbia University, 1970), p. 207.
47. Ibid., ch. 4; and F. S. Zuckerman, 'The Russian Political Police at Home and Abroad (1880–1917)' (Ph.D. dissertation, New York University, 1973), ch. 8. The British Foreign Office file on this affair is in FO371/322.
48. There is a great deal of correspondence along these lines in the Okhrana Archive (Hoover Institution), VC/2 and 3, and scattered amongst Foreign Office papers. Doubts about rumoured plots appear in a report from Byrne to the Home Office about a Russian revolutionary congress in Notting Hill, 18 August 1908, in FO371/518; and in numerous police reports into the activities of other nationalities of refugee.

49. See McCarthy to Harting, 6 April 1906 and 17 May [1907]; Farce to Harting, 20 May 1907; and Quinn to Krassilnikoff, 11 September 1913, in the Okhrana Archive, vc/2 and 3.

50. Okhrana Archive, vc/2.

51. E. R. Bradford memorandum, 24 May 1902: HO144/545/A55176, sub. 44. On Rubini, see above, p. 126.

52. Chalmers minute, 30 August 1906: HO144/757/118516, sub. 36.

53. Bradford memorandum, 24 May 1902: HO144/545/A55176, sub. 44; Troup to Foreign Office, 10 July 1906, in FO371/136, f. 69; Home Office to Foreign Office (draft), November 1906, in HO144/542/A53204, sub. 18; Foreign Office to Benckendorff, 3 January 1907, in FO371/364.

54. Henry to Home under-secretary, 1 December 1906: HO144/757/118516, sub. 47.

55. Chalmers (Home Office) to Foreign Office, 30 May 1904: FO371/78.

56. Memo by GSHP on Bunsen to Grey, 3 January 1907: FO371/364.

57. See for example Troup to Foreign Office, 26 June 1906: FO371/136.

58. For example, McBrien was sent to Ostend in August 1905 for the Liège Exhibition of 1905 (Henry to Home Office, 18 August 1905, registered in HO46/145); Riley and McNamara went to Madrid for President Loubet's visit in 1905 (Troup to Henry, 25 September and 7 October 1905: HO148/9, ff. 775 and 824); and Bascombe and Powell attended the Brussels Exhibition in 1910 (HO45/10573/176902, sub. 4).

59. The trial is reported in *The Times*, 16 September 1905, p. 12. The Home Office file on the case is HO144/795/131464.

60. There were a few letters of protest in the press; and a 'Defence Fund' for Antonelli netted £28 19s. 11d. (*Freedom*, October 1905, p. 32).

61. Henry to Home Office, 6 May 1905, registered in HO46/145; Chalmers to Henry, 10 May 1905: HO148/9, f. 355.

62. Murdoch to Henry, 26 January 1903: HO148/6, f. 448. Lynch's trial is reported in *The Times*, 20 December 1902, p. 12.

63. See MEP02/632. In November 1911 Scotland Yard expressed concern when the citation for a decoration for Sergeant Hester called him a member of the British 'Secret Police' (*Geheimpolizei*).

64. The police are attacked generally in connection with the Antonelli case in *Freedom*, October 1905, p. 29; and the issue of June 1908 (p. 40) mentions the presence in plain clothes of the 'political section' of the police at a meeting in Hyde Park on 24 May. The Okhrana was attacked in the House of Commons on 20 July 1909 by the Labour MP Will Thorne: see Maxwell's memo of 16 July 1909, in HO45/10400/180714, sub. 23.

65. Harold Brust, '*I Guarded Kings*' [n.d.], pp. 89–90. Lenin was in Britain in April 1902–May 1903; August 1903; and May 1907. I have been able to find no Home Office file on him, and no reference to his real name or to his various aliases in Home Office registers of letters. This suggests that there never was a Home Office file on him, which is likely, and throws doubt on Colin Holmes's suggestion that it was destroyed: Colin Holmes, 'Government files and privileged access', *Social History*, vol. 6 (1981).

Chapter 11

1. The latest of many books on the Tottenham, Houndsditch and Sidney Street affairs are Colin Rogers, *The Battle of Stepney. The Sidney Street Siege: Its Causes and Consequences* (1981); and F. G. Clarke, *Will-o'-the-Wisp. Peter the Painter and the anti-tsarist terrorists in Britain and Australia* (Melbourne, 1983).
2. H. Fletcher Moulton, *The Trial of Stinie Morrison* (1922); Eric Linklater, *The Corpse on Clapham Common* (1971).
3. Linklater, pp. 201–3. There is nothing to confirm this hypothesis in the Okhrana archive.
4. Donald Rumbelow, *The Houndsditch Murders and the Siege of Sidney Street* (1973), p. 119.
5. Gladstone was made aware of the dangers of the Act as originally implemented early in 1906 by a series of parliamentary questions (see *Hansard*, 4th series, vol. 153, cc. 86–7, 88–9, 134–9, 297–8), and by his Home Office staff (e.g. Chalmers to Gladstone, 6 March 1906: HJGP 47993, f. 17). He first announced his relaxation of the rules in the Commons on 12 March 1906: *Hansard*, 4th series, vol. 153, cc. 916–17.
6. Printed versions of Gladstone's and Churchill's bills are in HO45/10403/184435, and in CAB37/105 no. 2.
7. See Owen Seaman to Gladstone, 11 February 1909, and Gladstone to Owen Seaman, 15 February 1909: HJGP 46066, ff. 224, 253–5; and cf. Gladstone in House of Commons, 25 February 1909: *Hansard*, 5th series, vol. 1, cc. 975–85.
8. Names of known Special Branch officers, and communications from Russia, are to be found in the Metropolitan Police file on the case: MEPO3/191; in the main Home Office file, HO144/19780/201678; and in the Okhrana Archive (Hoover Institution), VC-2.
9. Rogers, op. cit., p. 116.
10. Ibid., pp. 76–7.
11. The judge at his trial (for libel) recommended deportation, but the Home Secretary, McKenna, lifted the order on him in June 1912. The history of the case can be traced through *The Times*, 21 May 1912, p. 4 and 10 June 1912, p. 6; Herman Cohen (ed.), *The Criminal Appeal Reports*, vol. 7 (1912), pp. 273–5; and *Hansard*, 5th series, vol. 38, cc. 1931–2, 2012–30; vol. 39, cc. 1834–5.
12. Quinn to Henry, 7 July 1909: MEPO2/1297.
13. Henry to Gladstone, 12, 13 and 14 July 1909: HJGP 46067, ff. 73–5, 77–8, 83–4. In January 1910 this led to the transference of Supt. John Wallinger of the Bombay Police to London to liaise with the Branch: information supplied by Nicholas Hiley.
14. E.g. Fitch's Report on Abd-el-Ghaffar, 14 August 1913: FO371/1639 f. 380.
15. Gladstone to Troup, 9 September 1909: HO144/1043/183461 sub. 1.
16. C. T[roup] to Gladstone, 10 September 1909: HJGP 45993, f. 234.
17. Bruce to Home under-secretary, 15 September 1909: HO144/1043/183461 sub. 1.
18. Troup to Henry, copy, n.d.: HO144/1043/183461 sub. 1; and see the list of police officers giving evidence at Mrs Pankhurst's trial in the summer of 1912, in HO144/1119/203651, sub. 117.
19. MacNaghten to Gladstone, 9 September 1909: HJGP 46067, f. 157. Underlined in the original.
20. HO144/1119/203651, sub. 117.

21. See Elliott to Henry, 18 September 1913, authorising the payment of £5–17–6d from Police funds for a door broken down in the course of the raid: HO148/20, f. 454.
22. Report by Quinn, 29 April 1913: HO144/1254/234646, sub. 43.
23. 'M.W.' to Home Office, 13 May 1910: HO144/1079/193000, sub. 51a.
24. See above, p. 156; and Elliott to Henry, 13 May 1913: HO148/19, f. 934.
25. Quinn to Henry, 7 July 1909: MEPO2/1297.
26. Henry to Home under-secretary, 4 May 1910: MEPO1/54, pp. 349–50.
27. Quinn to Henry, 6 July, and Henry to Home under-secretary, 11 July 1914: MEPO2/1297.
28. Troup to Henry, 12 July 1909: MEPO2/1297.
29. Bruce to Troup, 15 September 1909: HO144/1043/183461, sub. 1; Troup to Henry, 22 September 1909: HO148/15, f. 12; Henry to Troup, 10 April 1913, and Troup to Henry, 16 April 1913: HO45/10932/163556, sub. 63.
30. Police Orders, 24 May 1913: MEPO7/75.
31. Basil Thomson memorandum, 20 November 1914, and Henry to Home Office, 2 December 1914: MEPO2/1643.
32. Aitken(?) to Henry, 14 June 1911: HO148/17, f. 519.
33. Basil Thomson, Queer People [1922], p. 265.
34. The Times, 21 August 1908, p. 9.
35. Charles Lowe, 'About German Spies', Contemporary Review, vol. 97 (1910), p. 50.
36. Lecture on 'The Powers possessed by the Executive in times of emergency and war' (1908), in Edmonds papers (Liddell Hart Centre, King's College, London), IV/4, pp. 2, 19.
37. Nicholas Hiley, 'The Failure of British Counter-Espionage against Germany, 1907–1914', Historical Journal, vol. 28, no. 4 (1985), pp. 844–5.
38. Byrne, Home Office, to Secretary of Army Council, 5 June 1909: HO151/9,f.331.
39. Hiley, op. cit., p. 850.
40. See Churchill's memorandum of 12 April 1911, with the new 'draft clauses', in CAB37/106, no. 50.
41. Report . . . of the Standing Sub-Committee of the Committee of Imperial Defence on the Treatment of Aliens in Time of War, August 1913, p. 3: CAB17/90.
42. Hiley, op. cit., pp. 850 and 853; Troup memorandum, 12 October 1911: HO45/10629/199699, sub. 3.
43. Report . . . on the Treatment of Aliens in Time of War, August 1913, p. 2: CAB17/90. A copy of the form on which details of aliens were to be entered is in HO45/10629/199699, sub. 1.
44. Troup to Foreign under-secretary, 10 March 1913: HO151/9, f. 921.
45. Hiley, op. cit., p. 853; and see below, p. 176.
46. Hansard, 5th series, Lords vol. 9, cc. 641–7; Commons vol. 29, cc. 2251–60. Files of correspondence on the Official Secrets Act are among those not yet released by the Home Office.
47. Printed Cabinet paper on 'Pacifist Propaganda', November 1917: CAB24/4, Paper G173.
48. Home Ports Defence Committee Memorandum, 4 May 1912: ADMI/8264.
49. W. Guy Granet to Churchill, 15 August 1911: Churchill papers, 12/10, f. 76, reproduced in Randolph Churchill, Winston S. Churchill, vol. II Companion vol. 2, pp. 1271–2; printed Cabinet paper on 'Pacifist Propaganda', November 1917, Appendix, p. 3: CAB24/4, Paper G173; and cf. Fitch, Traitors Within (1933), p. 128.

50. Wade (or Brade), War Office, to Home under-secretary, 29 May 1909; minutes by Troup on meetings on the inter-departmental conference on Civil Trouble in the Metropolis in Case of War, July 1909 and 30 January 1913: HO144/1650/179987, subs. 1, 2 and 5; printed paper on 'Suppression of Civil Disturbance in London', enclosed in Cubitt, War Office, to Home Office, 4 March 1915: WO32/5270.

51. F. W. Black memorandum, 21 December 1912; Troup to Admiralty Secretary, 4 June 1913; Kell Memorandum, 1 July 1913: ADM1/8264. In the end the 'force' comprised just two (Scottish) police sergeants.

52. Kell, according to his wife's biography of him, was 'laughingly called the man with the golden tongue': Kell papers, microfilm copy in Imperial War Museum, SVK/1, p. 124.

53. Paper A, 'Notes on the Work of Counter-Espionage', and Paper B, 'Notes on the Work and Methods of Foreign Secret Service Agents', both dated October 1912, in CAB17/90.

54. See W. J. Pringle (Blackpool Police) to Kell, 2 January 1918: HO45/10892/357291, sub. 1.

55. John Bulloch, *MI5* (1963), p. 29.

56. James Edmonds, 'Memoirs': Edmonds Papers, III/5/1.

57. Lecture notes on 'Security Intelligence in War', marked '2nd copy, 1934', in Kell papers (microfilm copy), Imperial War Museum, SVK/2, p. 10.

58. Edmonds papers, VII/3. 'DMI' stands for Director of Military Intelligence.

59. S. T. Felstead (ed.), *Steinhauer: The Kaiser's Master Spy. The Story as Told by Himself* (1930), pp. 64, 70, 74.

60. Edwin T. Woodhall, *Spies of the Great War* (1932), pp. 8–11.

61. Ibid., p. 8.

62. Home under-secretary to chief constables (draft), 6 August 1914: HO45/10629/199699, sub. 7.

63. Lord Chancellor in House of Lords, 25 November 1914: *Hansard* 5th series, Lords, vol. 18, c. 145.

64. Hiley, op. cit., p. 859.

65. Basil Thomson memo., 20 November 1914, and Blackwell to Henry, 23 December 1914: MEPO2/1643; Henry to Home under-secretary, 2 December 1914: HO45/11888/258207, sub. 95.

66. Hiley, op. cit., p. 860.

67. 'Memoirs', in Edmonds papers: III/5/3–4.

68. Henry memorandum, 2 March 1915: MEPO3/243.

69. William Le Queux, *German Spies in England. An Exposure* (February 1915), p. 55.

70. Ibid., p. 11; and William Le Queux, *Spies of the Kaiser. Plotting the Downfall of England* (1909), p. 1.

71. *Report . . . of a Sub-Committee of the Committee of Imperial Defence to Consider the Question of Foreign Espionage . . .* (July 1909), Appendix 1: copy in CAB16/8.

72. Report by Supt. [?Illegible], 2 July 1911: MEPO2/1467.

73. Edmonds' 'Memoirs', in Edmonds papers, III/7, p. 23; and pencilled memorandum by Edmonds, 20 August 1911: ibid., VII/5.

74. Macready, 'Diary of Events', 12 November 1910: HO144/1551/199768, sub. 43; and memorandum, 5 January 1911: HO144/1553/199768, sub. 207a.

75. Moylan report, 23 November 1910: HO144/1552/199768, sub. 121.

76. Moylan report, 18 November 1910: HO144/1551/199768, sub. 78.

77. Moylan report, 23 November 1910: ibid., sub. 121. Two Metropolitan CID men were sent in the middle of November, but to investigate the theft of some dynamite, and not for purposes of intelligence: Moylance to Troup, 14 November 1910, and Moylan memorandum, 15 November 1910: HO144/1551/199768, sub. 63a.
78. Macready, 'Diary', 14 November 1910: ibid., sub. 51.
79. Freeth Memorandum, 13 February 1911: HO144/1553/199768, sub. 276.
80. Macready to Churchill, 19 November 1910: HO144/1551/199768, sub. 96.
81. Lindsay to Churchill, 23 November 1910: HO144/1552/199768, sub. 111.
82. Byrne to War Office, 5 January 1911 (draft): ibid., sub. 197a.
83. Macready, 'Diary', 17 December 1910: ibid., sub. 187.
84. Macready, 'Diary', 18 and 23 December 1910: ibid., subs. 189 and 198.
85. Macready, 'Memorandum' of 5 January 1911: HO144/1553/199768, sub. 207a.
86. Thomson to Home under-secretary, 15 October 1913, and minute by Troup, 23 October 1913: HO45/10625/198406, sub. 3.
87. J. Bond to Churchill, 1 October 1910; Henry to Home under-secretary, 15 October and 2 November 1910; and note by Troup, 5 November 1910: idem., subs. 1–2.
88. H. Gladstone to Postmaster General, 2 July 1909: HO151/9, f. 334b.
89. Above, p. 168.
90. Walkley, GPO, to Home Office, 30 March 1912: HO144/1194/220196, sub. 306.
91. Herbert Fitch, *op. cit.*, p. 109.
92. W. H. Thompson, *Guard from the Yard* (1938), p. 25.
93. See the books by Brust, Fitch, W. H. Thompson and Woodhall cited in the bibliography; and Bernard Porter, 'The Historiography of the Early Special Branch', *Intelligence and National Security*, vol. 1 (1986).
94. Basil Thomson, *The Scene Changes* (1939), p. 10.
95. Basil Thomson, *The Diversions of a Prime Minister* (Edinburgh, 1894), p. 160. He also reorganised the Tonga police: ibid., pp. 115–16.
96. Basil Thomson, *Queer People*, p. 263.
97. Thomson, *The Scene Changes*, p. 226.
98. Thomson to Home under-secretary, 10 July 1914: HO45/24665/253239, sub. 6.
99. See, for example, the evidence accumulated against the Pethick-Lawrences and Mrs Pankhurst late in 1911, in HO144/1119/203651, *passim*.
100. House of Commons, 28 April 1911: *Hansard*, 5th series, vol. 25, c. 2145.
101. Henry to Troup, 11 April 1913: HO144/1254/234646, sub. 30.
102. Gladstone to Campbell-Bannerman, n.d.: Campbell-Bannerman Papers, BL, Add. MS. 41217, ff. 302–3.
103. House of Commons, 21 April 1910: *Hansard*, 5th series, vol. 16, c. 2407.
104. Ibid., c. 2354.
105. Ibid., c. 2358.
106. Troup to War Office, 10 March 1915: WO32/5270; and HO144/1650/179987, sub. 15.
107. Nicholas Hiley, 'Counter-Espionage and Security in Great Britain during the First World War', *English Historical Review*, vol. 101 (1986), *passim*.
108. Nicholas Hiley, 'British Internal Security in Wartime: The Rise and Fall of P.M.S.2, 1915–1917', *Intelligence and National Security*, vol. 1 (1986).
109. Hiley, ' "Not Necessarily a Crime": The Development of British Counter-Espionage during the First World War', paper read to the British-American

Colloquium on 20th Century Intelligence, London, September 1984, pp. 16–17; and 'Counter-Espionage and Security . . .' *passim*.

Conclusion

1. *House of Commons. Fourth Report from the Home Affairs Committee, Session 1984–5. Special Branch* (1985), p. 96.
2. E.g. Rupert Allason, *The Branch* (1983), p. 166; and Christopher Dobson and Ronald Payne, 'The political arm of the police', *Police Review*, 6 May 1983, p. 856, which gives the Metropolitan Special Branch a strength of 550.
3. *Fourth Report from the Home Affairs Committee*, pp. xi, xiii.
4. Examples are given in ibid., *passim*.
5. Neal Ascherson, 'Law and order in the market-place', *Observer*, 26 May 1985.
6. On this subject see Sissela Bok, *Secrets. On the Ethics of Concealment and Revelation* (Oxford, 1984), ch. 17.
7. Ibid., p. 265.
8. *Observer*, 28 August 1985; italics added.
9. E. R. Henry report of 7 January 1902: HO45/10254/X36450, sub. 126.
10. Quoted in *Daily Telegraph*, 31 January 1985.
11. Herbert T. Fitch, *Traitors Within* (1933), p. 47.
12. J. A. Hobson, *Imperialism: A Study* (1902), part 2, ch. 1.

Select Bibliography

Place of publication for books and journals is London unless otherwise stated.

1. Manuscript Sources

(a) Official
Admiralty papers, Public Record Office
Cabinet papers, PRO
Foreign Office papers, PRO
Home Office papers, PRO
Metropolitan Police papers, PRO
Treasury papers, PRO
War Office papers, PRO
Administrative Archives, Scottish Record Office
Irish Chief Secretary's Office, Registered Papers, Dublin Castle.

(b) Private
Asquith papers, Bodleian Library, Oxford
Balfour papers, British Library and PRO
Hicks Beach papers, Gloucestershire Record Office
Campbell-Bannerman papers, BL
Carnarvon papers, PRO
Childers papers, Royal Commonwealth Institute
Chilston papers, Kent Archives Office, Maidstone
Churchill papers, Churchill College, Cambridge
R. A. Cross papers, BL
C. W. Dilke papers, BL
Edmonds Papers, Liddell Hart Centre, King's College, London
Herbert Gladstone papers, BL
W. E. Gladstone papers, BL
Granville papers, PRO
W. V. Harcourt papers, Bodleian Library, Oxford
Vernon Kell papers, Imperial War Museum (microfilm copy)
McKenna papers, Churchill College, Cambridge
Okhrana archive, Hoover Institution
Royal Archive, Windsor Castle
Salisbury papers, Hatfield House
John Satterfield Sandars papers, Bodleian Library, Oxford
W. H. Smith papers, Strand House, New Fetter Lane, London
Spencer papers, BL

239

2. Contemporary Periodicals

In addition to mainstream daily and weekly newspapers, the following have been consulted extensively:

Adult
Alarm
Annual Register
Commonweal
Freedom
Freiheit
Illustrated Police News
Illustrated Police Budget
Justice
Liberty
The Link
Police Chronicle
Police Guardian
Police Review
Radical
Review of Reviews
Reynolds's Newspaper
Torch and *Torch of Anarchy*
Truth

3. Contemporary Books and Articles

Anon., 'Dynamite and Dynamiters', *Strand Magazine*, vol. 7 (1894).
'Alfred Aylmer', 'The Detective in Real Life', *Windsor Magazine*, vol. 1 (1895).
William Barry, 'Anarchist Literature', *Quarterly Review*, vol. 178 (1894).
Henry A. Blake, 'The Irish Police', *Nineteenth Century*, vol. 9 (1881).
Josephine Butler, *Government by Police* (1879).
Felix Dubois, *The Anarchist Peril* (1894).
Arthur Griffiths, *Mysteries of Police and Crime* (1898).
Hansard's Parliamentary Debates, 4th and 5th series.
W. C. Hart, *Confessions of an Anarchist* (1906).
'Ivanoff', 'Anarchists: Their Methods and Organisation', *New Review*, vol. 10 (1894).
Law Reports, Queen's Bench Division, passim.
Henry Manton, *Turning the Last Stone* (Birmingham, 1895).
'Isabel Meredith', *A Girl Among the Anarchists* (1903).
David Nicoll, *The Greenwich Mystery* (1897).
Ernest Vizetelly, *The Anarchists* (1911).
Charles Warren, 'The Police of the Metropolis', *Murray's Magazine*, vol. 4 (1888).
[Henry Wreford], 'Spy Police', *Households Words*, vol. 1 (1850).

4. Memoirs

Robert Anderson, *The Lighter Side of My Official Life* (1910).
Henry Brackenbury, *Some Memoirs of My Spare Time* (Edinburgh, 1909).

Harold Brust, '*I Guarded Kings*' (n.d.).
—— —— *In Plain Clothes. Further Memoirs of a Political Police Officer* (1937).
S. T. Felstead (ed.), *Steinhauer: the Kaiser's Master Spy. The Story as Told by Himself* (1930).
—— —— *In Search of Sensation. Being Thirty Years of a London Journalist's Life* (1945).
Herbert T. Fitch, *Traitors Within* (1933).
—— —— *Memoirs of a Royal Detective* (1935).
Robert A. Fuller, *Recollections of a Detective* (1912).
G. H. Greenham, *Scotland Yard Experiences* (1904).
Andrew Lansdowne, *A Life's Reminiscences. Scotland Yard* (1893).
'Henri Le Caron', *Twenty-five years in the Secret Service. The Recollections of a Spy* (1892).
John Littlechild, *The Reminiscences of Chief-Inspector Littlechild* (1894).
Patrick McIntyre, 'Scotland Yard. Its Mysteries and Methods', *Reynolds's Newspaper*, February–May 1895.
Melville Macnaghten, *Days of My Years* (1914).
Ernest Nicholls, *Crime within the Square Mile* (1935).
Percy Savage, *Savage of Scotland Yard* (1934).
John Sweeney, *At Scotland Yard* (1904).
W. H. Thompson, *Guard from the Yard* (1938).
Basil Thomson, *Queer People* [1922].
—— —— *The Scene Changes* (1939).
'Tornon', 'The Fenian Movement', *Reynolds's Newspaper*, August–September 1895.
W.H.-H. Waters, '*Secret and Confidential.*' *The Experiences of a Military Attaché* (1926).
Edwin T. Woodhall, *Detective and Secret Service Days* (n.d.).
—— —— *Spies of the Great War. Adventures with the Allied Secret Service* (1932).
—— —— *Secrets of Scotland Yard* (1936).

5. Secondary Works

H. L. Adam, *C.I.D.: Behind the Scenes at Scotland Yard* (1931).
R. W. Allason. *The Branch. A History of the Metropolitan Police Special Branch 1883–1983* (1983).
Christopher Andrew, *Secret Service. The Making of the British Intelligence Community* (1985).
Victor Bailey (ed.), *Policing and Punishment in Nineteenth Century Britain* (1981).
John Clement Bird, 'Control of Enemy Alien Civilians in Great Britain 1914–1918', (unpublished Ph.D. thesis, London University, 1981).
Sissela Bok, *Secrets. On the Ethics of Concealment and Revelation* (Oxford, 1984).
Séamus Breathnach, *The Irish Police: From earliest times to the present day* (Dublin, 1974).
Tony Bunyan, *The History and Practice of the Political Police in Britain* (1976).
Randolph Churchill, *Winston S. Churchill*, vol. II: *Young Statesman 1901–1914* (1967).
F. G. Clarke, *Will-o'-the-wisp. Peter the Painter and the Anti-tsarist Terrorists in Britain and Australia* (Melbourne, 1983).
I. F. Clarke, *Tales of the Future* (1972).
Belton Cobb, *Murdered on Duty. A Chronicle of the Killing of Policemen* (1961).
J. A. Cole, *Prince of Spies. Henri le Caron* (1984).
Richard Deacon, *A History of British Secret Service* (1969).

241

George Dilnot, *Scotland Yard: Methods and Organisation of the Metropolitan Police* (1915).
—— —— *The Trial of the Detectives* (1928).
—— —— *Great Detectives and their Methods* (1929).
Christopher Dobson and Ronald Payne, 'The political arm of the police', *Police Review*, 6 May 1983.
S. T. Felstead, *German Spies at Bay* (1920).
Thomas G. Fergusson, *British Military Intelligence, 1870–1914. The Development of a Modern Intelligence Organization* (1984).
William J. Fishman, *East End Jewish Radicals 1875–1914* (1975).
David French, 'Spy Fever in Britain, 1900–1915', *Historical Journal*, vol. 21 (1978).
Peter Gordon (ed.), *The Red Earl. The Papers of the Fifth Earl Spencer*, vol. 1 (Northampton, 1982).
Percival Griffiths, *To Guard My People. The History of the Indian Police* (1971).
Anandswarup Gupta, *The Police in British India 1861–1947* (New Delhi, 1979).
Richard Hawkins, 'Government versus Secret Societies: The Parnell Era', in T. Desmond Williams (ed.), *Secret Societies in Ireland* (Dublin, 1973).
Nicholas Hiley, 'The Failure of British Espionage against Germany, 1907–1914', *Historical Journal*, vol. 26 (1983).
—— —— 'The Failure of British Counter-Espionage against Germany, 1907–1914', *Historical Journal*, vol. 28 (1985).
—— —— 'Counter-Espionage and Security in Great Britain during the First World War', *English Historical Review*, vol. 101 (1986).
—— —— 'British Internal Security in Wartime: The Rise and Fall of P.M.S. 2, 1915–1917', in *Intelligence and National Security*, vol. 1 (1986).
Barry Hollingsworth, 'The Society of Friends of Russian Freedom: English Liberals and Russian Socialists, 1890–1917', *Oxford Slavonic Papers*, n.s. vol. 3 (1970).
House of Commons. Fourth Report from the Home Affairs Committee, Session 1984–5. Special Branch (1985).
R. B. Jensen, 'The International Anti-Anarchist Conference of 1898 and the Origins of Interpol', *Journal of Contemporary History*, vol. 16 (1981).
S. H. Jeyes and F. D. How, *The Life of Sir Howard Vincent* (1912).
R. J. Johnson, 'The Okhrana Abroad, 1887–1917: A Study in International Police Cooperation' (unpublished Ph.D. dissertation, Columbia University, 1970).
Lisa Keller, 'Public Order in Victorian London: the Interaction between the Metropolitan Police, the Government, the Urban Crowd, and the Law' (Ph.D. thesis, Cambridge University, 1976).
Walter Kendall, *The Revolutionary Movement in Britain 1900–21* (1969).
Alan Kimball, 'The Harassment of Russian Revolutionaries Abroad: The London Trial of Vladimir Burtsev in 1898', *Oxford Slavonic Papers*, vol. 6 (1973).
Eric Linklater, *The Corpse on Clapham Common* (1971).
P. K. Martinez, 'Paris Communard Refugees in Britain, 1871–1880' (unpublished Ph.D. thesis, Sussex University, 1981).
F. C. Mather, *Public Order in the Age of the Chartists* (Manchester, 1959).
T. W. Moody, '*The Times* versus Parnell and Co., 1887–90', *Historical Studies*, vol. 6 (Dublin, 1968).
H. Fletcher Moulton, *The Trial of Stinie Morrison* (1922).
A. P. Moore-Anderson, *Sir Robert Anderson, KCB, LLD, A Tribute and Memoir* (1919).
M. A. Muller, *Kropotkin* (Chicago, 1976).
Bernard Newman, *Spies in Britain* (1964).

Leon Ò Broin, *The Prime Informer. A Suppressed Scandal* (1971).

Hermia Oliver, *The International Anarchist Movement in Late Victorian London* (1983).

D.P., 'A Policeman to Remember, Sir Patrick Quinn, MVO.', *Police Journal*, October 1985.

Bernard Porter, *The Refugee Question in mid-Victorian Politics* (Cambridge, 1979).

—— —— 'The *Freiheit* prosecutions, 1881–1882', *Historical Journal*, vol. 23 (1980).

—— —— 'The British Government and Political Refugees, *c.* 1880–1914', in John Slatter (ed.), *From the Other Shore. Russian Political Emigrants in Britain, 1880–1917* (1984).

—— —— 'The Origins of Britain's Political Police': *Warwick Working Papers in Social History*, no. 3 (1985).

—— —— 'The Historiography of the early Special Branch', *Intelligence and National Security*, vol. 1 (1986).

Margaret Prothero, *The History of the Criminal Investigation Department at Scotland Yard from Earliest Times until Today* (1931).

John Quail, *The Slow Burning Fuse. The Lost History of the British Anarchists* (1978).

Colin Rogers, *The Battle of Stepney. The Sidney Street Siege: Its Causes and Consequences* (1981).

Donald Rumbelow, *The Houndsditch Murders and the Siege of Sidney Street* (1973).

David Saunders, 'Aliens in Britain and the Empire during the First World War', unpublished paper.

K. R. M. Short, *The Dynamite War. Irish-American Bombers in Victorian London* (1979).

F. B. Smith, 'British Post Office Espionage, 1844', *Historical Studies*, vol. 14 (Melbourne, 1970).

Philip Thurmond Smith, *Policing Victorian London. Political Policing, Public Order, and the London Metropolitan Police* (Westport, Connecticut, 1985).

David A. Stafford, 'Spies and Gentlemen: The Birth of the British Spy Novel', *Victorian Studies*, vol. 24 (1981).

—— —— 'Conspiracy and Xenophobia: the Popular Spy Novels of William le Queux, 1893–1914', *Europe* (Montreal), vol. 4 (1981).

R. D. Storch, 'The Plague of Blue Locusts. Police Reform and Popular Resistance in Northern England, 1840–57' in *International Review of Social History*, vol. 20 (1975).

Julian Symonds, *Bloody Murder. From the Detective Story to the Crime Novel: A History* (1972).

Basil Thomson, *The Story of Scotland Yard* (1935).

Charles Townshend, *Political Violence in Ireland. Government and Resistance since 1848* (Oxford, 1983).

Anthea Trodd, 'The Policeman and the Lady: Significant Encounters in mid-Victorian Fiction', *Victorian Studies*, vol. 27 (1984).

Watkin W. Williams, *The Life of General Sir Charles Warren* (Oxford, 1941).

F. S. Zuckerman, 'The Russian Political Police at Home and Abroad (1880–1917)', (Ph.D. dissertation, New York University, 1973).

Index

Aberdeen, 156
accountability, 69, 144, 146, 181, 186, 189, 191
Acton, 1st Baron, 69
Admiralty, 169
Adult, The, 144–5
agents provocateurs, 66, 68–71, 73–7, 88–9, 130–4, 138–42, 149, 162, 178, 180, 184, 190–1
air, conquest of, 103–4
Akers-Douglas, Aretas, 195
Alarm, The, 222n
alarmism, 131, 172
Albert Memorial, 91
Albion colliery disaster (1894), 107
Aldersgate station, 103
Alexander II, Tsar, assassinated (1881), 24, 29, 40, 196
Alexander III, Tsar, 101
Alfonso, King of Spain, 165
aliens, problems of, 167, 171, 180; *see also* immigration
aliens legislation: Britain's lack of before 1905, 110, 122; 1894 bill, 108–11, 114, 197; 1905 Act, 157, 162, 198, 234n; 1909 bill, 162; 1911 bill, 162, 168, 178; 1914 Act, 198
aliens register, 168, 170, 179–80, 198
Allason, Rupert, xi
Allen, Grant, 100
alliances, military, 22–3
American, North, 17, 44, 57; *see also* United States of America
American Irish: *see* Fenians
anarchism: definitions and explanations of, 101, 105–7, 109–110, 116, 127–8, 187–8, 221n; fictional accounts of, 103–5; 'literary', 100; association with

violence, 100–1, 105–9, 114, 155, 163; on continent, 39, 101–2, 155; in Britain, 39–40, 66, 79, 86, 91–2, 101–18, 121–33, 154–63, 184–7; native British, 102–3, 107–8, 110, 116–17, 127; press, 65–6, 103, 107–8, 123, 125, 130–3, 154–5; proposals to outlaw, 111, 116, 142
anarchist press: *see Alarm; Commonweal; Freedom; Freiheit; Liberty; Torch*
Anderson, Robert: background, 72, 185, 194; early secret service role, 8, 17, 78, 194; and Fenian bombing campaign (1881–5), 41, 45–6, 65, 75, 206n; removed (1884), 47–8; brought back by Monro (1887), 85; as head of CID (1888–1901), 87, 121–2, 135–7, 139, 141, 144, 146, 148, 192, 195, 229n; methods, 70–1, 135–6; distaste for secret work, 72; and *Times* articles attacking Parnell, 94–5; 'revelations' (1909), 88–9, 178–9
Angiolillo, 101
Annual Register, 12
anti-anarchist conference: *see* Rome anti-anarchist conference
anti-semitism, 120, 162
Antonelli, Adolfo, 160, 198
Antwerp, Metropolitan Police at, 50
Armenians, 155
arms smuggling, 158
Army, 13, 15, 17, 23, 167, 169–70, 179–80; *see also* military
Asquith, Herbert Henry, 109, 115, 117, 195
assassination, advocacy of, 27, 29–30, 39, 116; *see also* names of assassination victims